Parsley

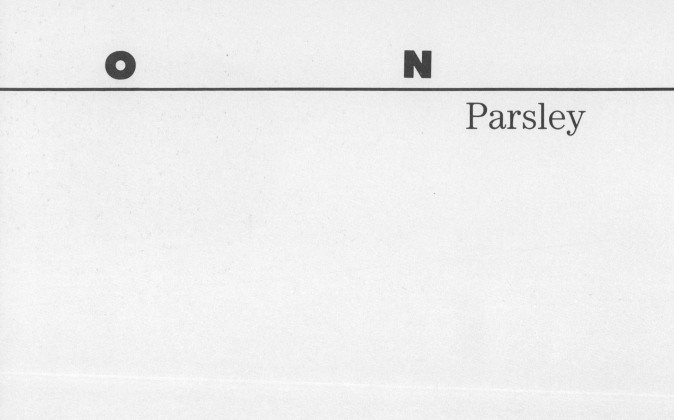

BEAUTIFUL

FOOD

PRESENTED

BY

THE

JUNIOR

LEAGUE

OF

KANSAS

CITY,

MISSOURI

TABLE OF CONTENTS

Additional copies of BEYOND PARSLEY
may be obtained by writing:

BEYOND PARSLEY
4651 Roanoke Parkway
Kansas City, Missouri 64112

First Edition First Printing August, 1984

Second Edition First Printing October 1984

Second Edition Second Printing April 1985

Second Edition Third Printing October 1985

Second Edition Fourth Printing March 1986

Second Edition Fifth Printing September 1986

Second Edition Sixth Printing January 1988

Second Edition Seventh Printing April 1990

Copyright © 1984

The Junior League of Kansas City, Missouri,
Inc.

Kansas City, Missouri

ISBN 0-9607076-1-1

Printed in the United States of America

The purpose of the Junior League is
exclusively educational and charitable and
is to promote voluntarism, to develop the
potential of its members for voluntary
participation in community affairs and to
demonstrate the effectiveness of trained
volunteers.

The profit realized by the Junior League of
Kansas City, Missouri, Inc., from the sale of
Beyond Parsley will be used for projects it
sponsors in the community.

THE COMMITTEE

Chairman **Karen Winfrey Craft**

Co-chairman **Jane Egender Bruening**

Editor **Jean Elmburg Helmers**

Food Consultant **Linda Zey Davis**

Design Chairmen **Lizbeth Henson Barelli**

Helen Jones Lea

Editorial Assistant **Margaret Weatherly Hall**

Marketing Chairman **Jo Stewart Riley**

Recipe Chairman **Mary Reiff Hunkeler**

Testing Coordinators **Elizabeth Westbrooke Haw**

Judi Spicer Knight

Design **Kroh/Hunter Design**

Photography **Glen Wans**

Food Design **Annemarie Hunter**

Art Direction **Mary Lou Kroh**

Food Styling **Vicki Johnson**

"Garnish with a sprig of parsley."

In the past, cooks were satisfied with this directive, and parsley became the herb that launched a thousand disposals. Today, more creative and appealing options are available. We would like to introduce some of them to you.

When you look beyond parsley, you will find that both your grocer's racks and your own garden are full of intriguing possibilities. We like the idea of edible but unusual garnishes. Have you considered using violets or nasturtiums? Experiment with lesser known herbs . . . lovage, chervil, cilantro. Even the major supermarkets are introducing new fruits and vegetables daily, so finding starfruit or yellow tomatoes should not be difficult.

Today's cooks look for menu ideas that are simple and easy to prepare. But simple should not be equated with dull. By varying food textures and experimenting with color, you can change a plain meal into a work of art. Sometimes, just by bringing out a long-forgotten or unused serving piece you can effect this transformation.

We see each meal as a celebration of food. Even a simple family dinner can be made special by a few minutes of extra attention. After all, food is a traditional expression of thoughtfulness and caring, and who deserves this more than your family? Treat them as your most important guests.

We feel that by using the freshest ingredients available you can improve the flavor of any recipe and at the same time control salt content and food additives. Each region of the country has its own specialties which are available fresh and in season. In the Midwest, we can look forward to bountiful crops of black walnuts, sweet peaches and crisp apples. We anticipate a largesse of country ham, prime beef and even the humble catfish. Our hickory forests supply us with wood for succulent barbeques. Our hot, humid summer nights and even hotter days are perfect for ripening luscious tomatoes and sweet corn. Discover the fresh and seasonal specialties of your area.

The recipes in this book have been tested and re-tested. Presentation ideas, serving suggestions and menus have been worked out by a group of our most creative hostesses and further refined by others. We have tried to be innovative in our recipe selection while at the same time reflecting our bias toward American cooking. In several instances, familiar recipes have been revised to incorporate contemporary food trends.

Our presentation ideas and suggestions are just that; they are not marching orders. We are reminded of the woman, who upon reading a recipe suggested for a post-opera supper protested, "But I don't GO to the opera!" Be flexible and adapt our ideas to your lifestyle. By careful selection of fresh ingredients and close attention to the visual and taste appeal of each meal, we can all extend our vision BEYOND Parsley.

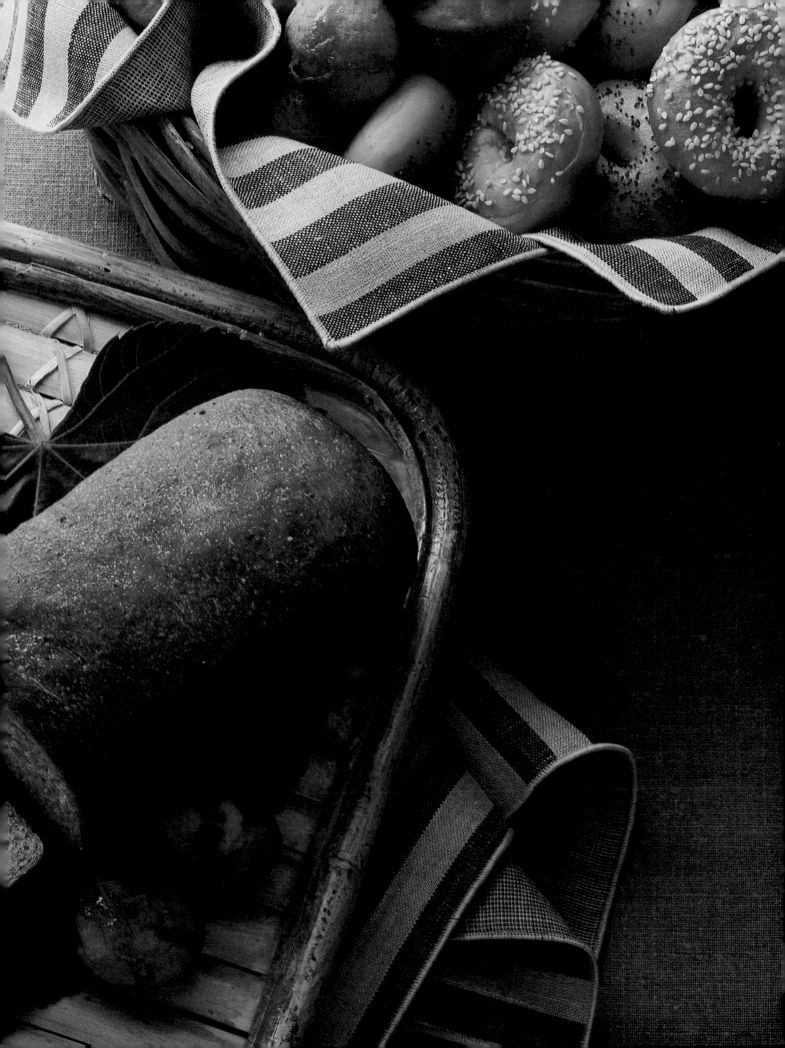

PHOTOGRAPHS

 A parsley sprig denotes a recipe which stands on its own within another recipe.

Whenever a recipe title appears in italics, it refers to a recipe which can be found elsewhere in the book. Consult the index for page number.

Tortilla Crisps

4 12-inch flour tortillas

1/2 cup oil

1/2 cup butter

1/4 pound Monterey Jack cheese, grated

1/4 pound Cheddar cheese, grated

Green chilies, chopped

Scallions, chopped

Chili powder

Optional toppings

Pepperoni slices

Red and green peppers

Pimiento

Ripe olives

Scallions

Cut tortillas in triangles and soak in melted butter and oil for about 30 minutes. Place on rimmed cookie sheets and bake at 400 degrees for about 10 minutes or until crisp and bubbly. Watch carefully. Remove from oven, sprinkle with cheeses and bake again, until cheese melts. Decorate immediately with green chilies and scallions. Add a dash of chili powder.

To recreate the Tortilla Crisps in our photograph, use scissors or aspic cutters to fashion shapes from cheese and pepperoni slices. Arrange on crisps, return to oven briefly to toast the pepperoni and cheese and add additional shapes cut from peppers, pimientos, olives or scallions.

Artichokes in Batter with Hot Mustard Sauce

1 14-ounce can artichoke hearts, drained and patted dry

1/2 cup flour

1/4 teaspoon baking powder

Dash of salt and pepper

1 egg

1/4 cup milk

1 tablespoon lemon juice

Mustard Sauce

2-3 tablespoons dry mustard

3 tablespoons sugar

3 tablespoons vinegar

1 egg

1 teaspoon butter

Cut each artichoke heart into 4-6 pieces. Sift flour and baking powder. Add rest of batter ingredients and beat until smooth. Coat artichoke pieces with batter and deep fry in hot oil (about 375 degrees) until golden brown on all sides. Remove with slotted spoon and drain on paper towel. Serve immediately with mustard sauce. (If desired, artichokes can be held in foil in warm oven for 1 hour.)

To make Mustard Sauce, mix dry mustard and sugar. Add vinegar, then egg. Heat over low heat until thick, stirring constantly. Mixture will be lumpy. Remove from heat and add butter. Cool, then strain. May be refrigerated and kept several weeks.

Black Caviar Mousse with Cucumbers Vinaigrette

Mousse

9	ounces black caviar
1/4	cup chopped parsley
1 1/2	tablespoons grated onion
1	teaspoon grated lemon zest
2	cups sour cream
2	tablespoons unflavored gelatin
1/4	cup water
1	cup heavy cream, lightly whipped
	Pepper to taste

Cucumbers Vinaigrette

3	medium cucumbers, scored, thinly sliced and halved
4	tablespoons tarragon vinegar
1	tablespoon best-quality olive oil
	Salt and pepper to taste
1/4-1/3	cup heavy cream

Combine first four ingredients. Add sour cream. Dissolve gelatin in water over low heat and add to caviar mixture. Fold in whipped cream. Add pepper. Pour into an oiled 3 1/2-cup mold or ring mold and chill at least 2-3 hours. Unmold onto serving platter.

Note: **When unmolding, place hot towels on top of mold to loosen from pan. This mixture softens easily and may melt too much if dipped in hot water.**

To make Cucumbers Vinaigrette, combine all ingredients and chill 2 hours.

Spread mousse on crackers and top with cucumbers.

For an impressive presentation, circle mousse with thin slices of lemon and cucumber, alternating colors. Serve cucumbers vinaigrette from a footed dish in the center of the mold.

Black-Eyed Susans

1	cup unsalted butter, room temperature
1	pound sharp Cheddar cheese, grated
2	cups all-purpose flour
	Salt to taste
	Cayenne pepper to taste
1	pound pitted dates, halved lengthwise
	Sugar

Blend butter and cheese together. Mix with flour, salt and cayenne pepper to form dough. Chill. Roll out thinly and cut into small rounds with biscuit cutter. Place date half on one side of dough round; fold remaining dough over. Pinch edges together like a turnover. Bake on non-stick cookie sheet at 250-300 degrees for 30 minutes. Roll in sugar while hot. Serve warm.

A family recipe from the South . . . sweet succulent dates encased in flaky cheese pastry.

Baked Brie with Pecans

1	pound wheel Brie cheese
1/3	cup pecans
1/4	cup butter
1/4	cup minced parsley

Place Brie in an oven-proof dish. Toast pecans in butter and stir in parsley. Heat cheese at 300 degree for 8-10 minutes or until just warm. Top with pecan mixture. Serve immediately with unsalted crackers or sliced French bread.

There are many variations to this lovely appetizer: top with fresh herbs, toasted poppy seeds, toasted walnuts or currants soaked in sweet red wine.

Glazed Brie

1	pound wheel Brie cheese, rind removed
1	cup chopped pecans
2	cups brown sugar
2	tablespoons good Cognac

Place Brie on a pie plate or oven-proof serving plate. Cover top of the Brie with the pecans. Pat brown sugar over the top and drizz with Cognac. Heat at 300 degrees for 8-10 minutes or until Brie melts. Serve immediately with unsalted crackers.

Brie Crisps

Use your leftover Brie to make these lovely wafers.

4	ounces Brie cheese, rind removed, room temperature
1/2	cup butter, room temperature
2/3	cup flour
2	generous dashes cayenne pepper or to taste
1/8	teaspoon salt
	Paprika

Combine cheese and butter (may use food processor) and mix until creamy. Add remaining ingredients and blend until dough almost forms a ball in food processor. Shape into a roll 2 inches round and wrap tightly in plastic wrap. Refrigerate overnight. Slice rolls into 1/4-inch pieces, place 2 inches apart on cookie sheet and bake at 400 degrees for 10-12 minutes or until edges are brown. Cool on rack. Sprinkle with paprika and serve.

Great with a glass of sherry!

arpaccio

Beef tenderloin, about 3 ounces per person, with all fat and silver skin removed

Carpaccio Dressing

2	egg yolks
1	tablespoon Dijon mustard
1	teaspoon salt
1-2	cloves garlic (about 1 tablespoon)
	Dash Worcestershire sauce
1/2	teaspoon freshly ground pepper.
1/2	cup freshly grated Parmesan cheese
1	cup best-quality olive oil (or 1/2 cup oil and 1/2 cup olive oil)
1/4	cup tarragon vinegar

Spiced Herb Sauce

1/2	onion, cut in chunks
1	clove garlic
2	egg yolks
3/4	cup best-quality olive oil
1/4	cup chopped Italian parsley
1/4	cup chopped fresh basil
1	tablespoon chopped fresh oregano
1/4	teaspoon cayenne pepper
1	teaspoon salt
1/3	cup white wine herb vinegar, such as tarragon

Partially freeze tenderloin and slice meat paper thin (or have butcher do this). Place slices on waxed paper and refreeze until ready to serve, but no longer than 1 day.

To make dressing, use a food processor with steel blade and combine egg yolks, mustard, seasonings and cheese until well blended. With machine running, add oil in a slow, steady stream until emulsified. Add vinegar and blend. Chill dressing for at least 2 hours before serving.

2 cups

As an alternative dressing for Carpaccio, try Spiced Herb Sauce.

To make Spiced Herb Sauce, mince onion and garlic in food processor, using steel blade. Add egg yolks and process to blend. With machine running, add oil slowly until emulsified. Add herbs and seasonings; blend. Add vinegar and blend. Leave at room temperature to develop flavor.

Note: **This is similar to steak tartare in that the meat is not cooked.**

Your guests will know to expect an extraordinary evening when you begin with this magnificent first course. To serve, spread a platter or individual serving plates with enough dressing to coat the plate 1/8-inch thick. Arrange tenderloin on top of dressing, overlapping slices slightly. Serve with toasted French bread and additional Parmesan cheese.

Blue Cheese Mousse

1	tablespoon unflavored gelatin
1/4	cup water
12	ounces sour cream with chives
1	8-ounce package cream cheese, room temperature
1	cup small curd cottage cheese
1	package Good Seasons cheese-garlic salad dressing mix
4	ounces blue cheese, crumbled

Soften gelatin in water over low heat. Combine sour cream and cream cheese. Add cottage cheese and salad dressing mix. Stir in blue cheese. Add gelatin and mix well. Pour into oiled, 4-cup mold. Refrigerate overnight. Unmold prior to serving.

Serve with pita bread triangles that have been split, buttered and toasted at 325 degrees for 10 minutes or until brown.

Surround with black Greek olives.

Savory Cheese Cake

1/3	cup fine bread crumbs
1/4	cup grated Parmesan cheese
3 1/2	8-ounce packages cream cheese
4	large eggs
1/2	cup heavy cream
1/2	pound bacon
1	medium onion, finely chopped
1/2	pound blue cheese, crumbled (Roquefort, Stilton, gorgonzola)
	Salt and freshly ground pepper to taste
	2-3 drops Tabasco sauce

Sprinkle bread crumbs and Parmesan cheese in a buttered, water-tight 8-inch round springform pan. Set aside.

Combine cream cheese, eggs and cream in mixer. Sauté bacon until crisp; drain and chop finely. Reserve 1 tablespoon drippings and sauté onion until clear. Add onion, bacon, blue cheese, salt, pepper and Tabasco to cream cheese mixture. Pour into prepared pan. Set pan inside a larger one; pour boiling water 2 inches deep into larger pan. Bake 1 hour and 40 minutes at 300 degrees. Turn off oven and let "cake" set for 1 hour. Remove pan from water and cool 2 hours.

50 servings

Search no further for something special to serve a crowd. Savory Cheese Cake is stunning on a dark platter adorned with leafy greens. Serve with an assortment of crackers.

Freezes well; recipe can be halved.

Cossack Cheese

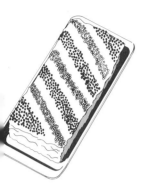

1	tablespoon unflavored gelatin
1/4	cup warm water
1	tablespoon lemon juice
1	tablespoon vodka
1	8-ounce package cream cheese, room temperature
1/4	cup mayonnaise
1/4	cup sour cream
1 1/2	teaspoons paprika
1	teaspoon salt
1/4	teaspoon white pepper
1/4	teaspoon onion powder
1/8	teaspoon dill weed
3-4	ounces caviar, red or black

Dissolve gelatin in water. Add lemon juice and vodka. Set aside. Mix all other ingredients, except caviar. Add gelatin mixture. Fold in caviar. Pour into an oiled, 2-cup loaf pan and chill. Unmold and serve with light wafers. (Can be mixed in food processor, but fold in caviar by hand.)

Arrange alternating rows of red and black caviar diagonally on the top. Tuck fresh basil around the loaf.

Monterey Jack Wafers

1	pound Monterey Jack cheese

Cut cheese into 1/4-inch slices, then into circles or squares approximately 1 1/2 inches in diameter. On a non-stick cookie sheet, space at least 3 inches apart. (This is important as they spread while baking.) Bake 10 minutes at 400 degrees. Do not overbake. Remove immediately and allow to cool. Store wafers in airtight cookie tin.

Note: **This recipe works only with Monterey Jack cheese.**

Makes 36-48 wafers

Light and lacy and couldn't be easier. Fabulous with cocktails, soups and salads.

French Herb Cheese

1	clove garlic
1	tablespoon parsley
1	8-ounce package cream cheese, room temperature
1/4	cup butter, room temperature
1/8	teaspoon salt
1/8	teaspoon pepper
	Dash Tabasco sauce

Mince garlic clove in food processor with steel blade by tossing into feed tube with machine running. Add parsley and chop. Add all other ingredients and blend until smooth. Refrigerate.

Delicious with unsalted crackers, *Mir Bagels* or lahvosh.

Stuffed Miniature Beets

1	8 1/4-ounce can small beets
	French Herb Cheese
	Parsley for garnish

Drain beets well. Scoop out center with melon ball cutter and fill with French Herb Cheese. Top with a sprig of parsley. (Do not fill until ready to serve or beets will "bleed."

Herb Cheese Stuffed Mushrooms

3	ounces *French Herb Cheese*
1/4	cup grated Parmesan cheese
1	pint large mushrooms, cleaned and stems removed
2	tablespoons butter

Cream the two cheeses together and fill mushroom caps. Melt butter and pour over mushrooms. Bake at 450 degrees for 15 minutes.

Kohlbrussel
Stuffed Brussels Sprouts

30	small fresh Brussels sprouts
	French Herb Cheese

Cook Brussels sprouts in boiling salted water, covered, for about 5 minutes until a brilliant green. Rinse under cold water. Cut each sprout about three-fourths through the center with small knife and stuff with French Herb Cheese. Sprinkle sprouts with salt and let stand at room temperature for 30 minutes before serving.

Arrange with *Stuffed Miniature Beets* on a bed of alfalfa sprouts for a colorful holiday appetizer.

Mexican "Caviar"

2	4-ounce cans chopped ripe olives, well drained
2	4-ounce cans chopped green chilies, well drained
2	tomatoes, peeled, seeded, chopped and drained
8	scallions, chopped
2	cloves garlic, minced
2	teaspoons best-quality olive oil
2	teaspoons red wine vinegar
1	teaspoon pepper
	Dash of seasoned salt

Combine ingredients, making sure that olives, chilies and tomatoes are thoroughly drained. Do not use a food processor. Chill overnight. Mixture may need to be drained again through a slotted spoon before serving.

Irresistible with Margaritas! Use as a dip in a festive pottery bowl next to a basket of tortilla chips.

Shrimp Pâté

1½	pounds shrimp, cooked, peeled and deveined
1	small onion, minced
½	cup butter, melted
⅓	cup mayonnaise
1	tablespoon fresh lemon juice

Cucumber-Dill Sauce

1	large cucumber, peeled, seeded and chopped
⅔	cup *Crème Fraîche*
⅔	cup sour cream
⅔	cup mayonnaise
2	tablespoons lemon juice
	Salt and pepper to taste
¼	cup chopped fresh dill
	Dash of cayenne pepper

Chop shrimp coarsely and combine with onion, butter, mayonnaise and lemon juice. Press firmly into a 4-cup mold. Refrigerate several hours or overnight. Unmold and serve with Cucumber-Dill Sauce.

To make Cucumber-Dill Sauce, place cucumbers in a colander, salt lightly and let drain 20-30 minutes. Blot cucumbers between layers of paper towels to remove remaining liquid. Combine other ingredients thoroughly. Add cucumbers, season and refrigerate.

Capitalize on fresh dill and cucumbers when they are in season to create this refreshing sauce. Pour it over the unmolded pâté or serve it separately. Braid long stems of chives and encircle pâté.

Curried Spinach-Apple Spread

2	10-ounce packages frozen chopped spinach, thawed and squeezed dry
1	cup mayonnaise
	Curry powder to taste
1	large unpeeled apple, finely diced by hand
3/4	cup chutney
3/4	cup peanuts, chopped

Combine spinach with mayonnaise and curry. Add apple, chutney and peanuts. Mix well and refrigerate. (Do not mix in food processor.)

Serve with wheat wafers, lahvosh or crudités.

Snow Peas with Lemon-Anchovy Dipping Sauce

1 1/4	pounds fresh snow peas or 2 pounds young, sugar snap peas (blanched, if desired)
Sauce	
2	egg yolks
3-4	tablespoons Dijon mustard
1	2-ounce can anchovies, undrained
	Juice of 1 lemon
1	shallot, chopped
1	cup vegetable oil
1/4	cup sour cream
	Salt and pepper to taste
1	tablespoon capers, rinsed and drained

String peas and crisp in ice water. Drain well.

Combine egg yolks, mustard, anchovies, lemon juice and shallot food processor and mix until foam and pale. With processor running, add oil until absorbed. Pour into a bowl and stir in sour cream by hand. Season to taste. Gently fold in capers. Cover and refrigerate. Garnish with additional capers.

Arrange peas in a sunburst pattern on flat basket or platter. Place bowl of sauce in center.

Lovely and refreshing! The anchovies add interest but don't overwhelm. T serving this dip in a hollowed artichoke with other vegetables. Endive, English cucumber, blanched asparagus and blanched green beans are nice choices.

Saganaki

Flaming Greek Cheese

1	pound Kasseri cheese or any firm white goat cheese, room temperature
3	tablespoons butter, melted
3	tablespoons brandy
	Juice of half a lemon

Cut cheese into 3 pieces and place a 12-inch oven-proof serving dish. Pour butter over cheese and broil 6-8 inches from the heat until chee is golden. Pour brandy over chees and flame. Extinguish flame by squeezing lemon juice over the to Serve at once on toasted pita brea

ried Walnuts

8	cups water
4	cups English walnut halves
1/2	cup sugar
	Cooking oil
	Salt

Bring water to a boil in large kettle; add nuts and boil 1 minute. Remove nuts, drain and rinse with very hot water. Drain again. While still hot, place nuts in a separate bowl, stir in sugar and toss until melted.

Heat oil (1-inch deep) to 360 degrees. Add 2 cups of nuts at a time and fry 3-4 minutes or until golden brown. Drain in sieve. Spread in a single layer and sprinkle with salt. Cover tightly and store at room temperature up to 3 days or freeze indefinitely.

Delicious any time, but particularly tantalizing after dinner with a glass of port.

hrimp Wrapped n Snow Peas

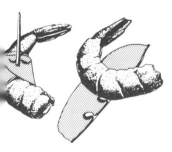

2 1/2	pounds medium shrimp, cooked, peeled and deveined (about 50)
1	pound snow peas, strings removed.

Marinade

1/4	cup fresh parsley
1 1/2	cups best-quality olive oil
1/4	cup sherry vinegar
1 1/2	tablespoons Dijon mustard
1	tablespoon fresh lemon juice
2	teaspoons salt
2	tablespoons fresh or 2 teaspoons dried rosemary (or dill)
1/2	teaspoon sugar
	Freshly ground pepper to taste
1	clove garlic, crushed
2	tablespoons chopped shallots

Mince parsley in food processor for 10 seconds, using steel blade. Add remaining ingredients and process for 5 seconds to mix. Transfer marinade to a 4-quart bowl and set aside.

While shrimp are still warm, cut in half lengthwise. Add to marinade and toss to coat evenly. Cover and refrigerate at least 6 hours or overnight.

Blanch snow peas in 2 quarts boiling salted water for 30 seconds. Drain and run under cold water to cool completely. Drain again and pat dry. Split snow peas in half lengthwise.

Wrap a snow pea half around a shrimp half horizontally and secure with a toothpick. Refrigerate.

Makes 100

Colorful and tempting. Secure shrimp with 10-inch bamboo skewers into an inverted pineapple half and place on a basket tray lined with palm fronds.

Stuffed Artichokes

4	artichokes, cleaned and trimmed
2	quarts water
2-3	tablespoons salt
1	bay leaf
1	tablespoon vinegar
1 1/2	cups butter, divided
2	large cloves garlic, minced
1/2-3/4	cup Italian bread crumbs
1/2	teaspoon Italian seasoning
1/2	teaspoon lemon juice
1/2	cup grated Parmesan cheese, divided

Place artichokes in a large pot with water, salt, bay leaf and vinegar. Simmer 30 minutes or until bottom is tender when pierced with a fork. Remove and invert to drain. Cool. Remove center leaves and scrape out choke with a spoon.

Melt 3/4 cup butter and add garlic, bread crumbs, seasoning and lemon juice. Cool. Stir in 1/4 cup Parmesan cheese. Stuff center of artichokes with filling and place in baking dish. Melt remaining butter and pour over artichokes. Cover with double foil. Bake at 350 degrees for 20 minutes. Sprinkle with remaining Parmesan.

4 servings

For a first course, add sautéed shrimp to the bread crumb mixture.

Cotie's Mushroom Sandwiches

20	slices thinly sliced white bread
2	tablespoons grated onion
1/4	cup butter
3/4	pound mushrooms, finely chopped
2	tablespoons flour
1/2	teaspoon Tabasco sauce
1	teaspoon salt
1/8	teaspoon pepper
1/2	cup half and half
	Butter and vegetable oil for frying

Cut each slice of bread with a biscuit cutter into four 1 3/4-inch rounds. Sauté onion in butter. Add mushrooms. Sauté until all moisture is cooked out of mushrooms. Add flour; stir until thick. Add Tabasco, salt, pepper and half and half. Cook until thick.

Spread 1 teaspoon mushroom mixture on each bread round. Top with another bread round to make sandwich. Repeat procedure until 40 sandwiches are made. Fry sandwiches in equal portions butter and oil until brown and crisp, about 1 minute for each side. Drain thoroughly. Keep warm, uncovered in a 300-degree oven.

Makes 40 sandwiches

At long last . . . the secret is out. Now you can create the popular petite sandwiches served for years at Junior League functions. Take the time to prepare plenty; they freeze beautifully.

Prosciutto and Cheese Torta

12 ounces cream cheese, softened

1/4 cup freshly grated Parmesan cheese

1 1/2 teaspoons minced garlic

1 1/2 teaspoons dried basil

1/2 teaspoon salt

1/4 teaspoon pepper

1 teaspoon oil (for pan)

4 slices provolone cheese, 1/8-inch thick

1/2 cup pine nuts or almonds, lightly toasted

12 slices mozzarella cheese, 1/4-inch thick

4 thin slices prosciutto

Cream together cream cheese, Parmesan cheese and seasonings. Refrigerate for 12 hours. Prepare 3-cup loaf pan by oiling it, then lining it with plastic wrap which has also been brushed with oil, using 1 teaspoon oil in all.

Bring cream cheese mixture to room temperature and set 1/4-1/2 cup aside. Cut 2 slices provolone cheese to fit bottom layer of pan; spread 1/4 cup cream cheese mixture over provolone, then arrange 1/4 cup nuts in rows on cream cheese. (Push down lightly so they will stick.) Spread 2 tablespoons cream cheese mixture carefully over nuts (use icing knife if possible). Trim half the mozzarella cheese to fit pan in a single layer. Cover with 2 tablespoons cream cheese mixture. Layer with 2 slices prosciutto, trimmed to fit in a single layer, and spread with 2 more tablespoons cream cheese mixture. Repeat layers, ending with prosciutto.

Cover with plastic wrap and refrigerate loaf at least 12 hours. Before serving, bring remaining cream cheese mixture to room temperature. Remove loaf from pan and ice with remaining cream cheese. Slice thinly and serve on light crackers.

Satisfy your creative urges by fashioning "flowers" from purple-hued eggplant peel to embellish the top.

Torta Primavera

12-14 crepes

1	pound fresh spinach, washed, dried and chopped
2	tablespoons butter, melted
1	clove garlic, minced
	Salt and pepper to taste
1/4	cup mayonnaise
1	8-ounce package cream cheese, room temperature

Filling Suggestions

6	ounces provolone or mozzarella cheese, sliced paper thin
6	ounces Genoa salami, sliced paper thin
6	ounces prosciutto or baked ham, sliced paper thin
6	ounces smoked turkey, sliced paper thin
3	hard-cooked eggs, sliced thin

Make crepes ahead and refrigerate or freeze.

Sauté spinach in butter and garlic. Season with salt and pepper. Set aside to cool. Reserve to use as a filling. In separate bowl, blend mayonnaise and cream cheese together until smooth. (A food processor facilitates this procedure; use steel blade.) Reserve as a spread for each crepe.

To assemble Torta: Spread each crepe with a thin layer of cream cheese mixture (or use mayonnaise alone, if you prefer). Top the first crepe with reserved spinach filling. (Build edges up more than the center.) Continue to layer crepes, using suggested fillings and pressing down as you go. Ice the top layer with cream cheese mixture. Garnish with carrot strips or curls, dill sprigs, cherry tomatoes, olives or whatever you choose.

This can be made a day ahead, as it takes time to assemble. Refrigerate; slice with an electric or serrated knife, pie fashion.

16 servings as first course
8 servings as main course

By all means, use your imagination and try other filling ingredients — experiment with fried bacon, scallions, smoked salmon, cooked chicken, crab or shredded romaine.

Cheddar Carousel

1	pound sharp Cheddar cheese, grated
3/4	cup mayonnaise
1	medium onion, finely chopped
1	clove garlic, pressed
1/2	teaspoon Tabasco sauce
1	cup strawberry preserves
1	cup chopped pecans

Combine all ingredients except strawberry preserves and mix well. Put in ring mold. Chill thoroughly. (Mixture will form together when chilled.) Unmold and fill center with preserves.

Unusual? Undoubtedly. Delicious? Definitely. This surprising combination calls for crackers or small pumpernickel bread slices.

Pesto Torta

2 8-ounce packages cream cheese, room temperature

1 pound unsalted butter, room temperature

Pesto Sauce

1/4 cup pine nuts

2 cloves garlic

1 cup fresh spinach, tightly packed

1 cup fresh basil, tightly packed

1/2 cup fresh parsley

1/2 teaspoon salt or less

1/2 cup best-quality olive oil

3/4 cup freshly grated Parmesan cheese

3 tablespoons butter, room temperature

Beat cream chese and butter until blended smoothly.

To make Pesto Sauce, roast pine nuts for 10 minutes at 325 degrees. (Watch carefully to prevent burning.) In a food processor with steel blade, purée nuts, garlic, spinach, basil, parsley and salt. Add olive oil and blend. Add cheese and butter and pulse briefly. Do not overblend.

Cut an 18-inch square of cheesecloth; moisten with water, wring dry and smoothly line a 6-cup plain or charlotte mold (or clean flowerpot!) with the cheesecloth; drape excess over rim of mold. With a rubber spatula, make an even layer with one-sixth of the cheese in the bottom of the mold. Cover with one-fifth of the pesto sauce, extending it evenly to the sides of the mold. Repeat until mold is filled, finishing with cheese. (In wider molds, use fewer layers.) Fold ends of cheesecloth over torta and press lightly to compact. Chill several hours or overnight. Invert onto a serving dish and gently pull out of mold. Remove cheesecloth. Present torta with crackers.

To store: Remove cheesecloth, wrap air-tight with plastic wrap and refrigerate up to 5 days. Can be frozen.

It's superb! Add a layer of sun-dried tomatoes, if desired. Decorate top of torta with sun-dried tomatoes cut in fan shapes. Serve with assorted crackers.

An appetizer that commands attention! Double the Pesto Sauce recipe and freeze half for later use. It's fantastic spooned over cooked vegetables and hot pasta; blended into mayonnaise, spread on French bread or used as a zesty addition to soup.

Phyllo

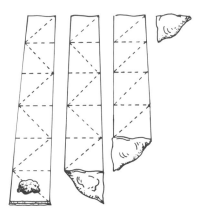

1	package frozen phyllo dough
1½	cups melted butter per package of phyllo

Defrost phyllo according to package directions. Before unrolling, cut crosswise into four 3-inch-wide pieces. Unroll each piece. While working, keep unused dough covered with a damp cloth until ready to use.

Take one strip of dough and brush with melted butter. Place a teaspoon of prepared filling on one end of pastry strip and fold corner in the form of a triangle. Continue folding, flag fashion, until desired size is reached. Proceed this way until all filling and phyllo are used. Place triangles on a buttered cookie sheet or baking pan and proceed according to filling instructions.

Unbaked phyllo freezes beautifully. Place buttered and filled phyllo triangles, unwrapped, on cookie sheet and freeze. When solid, wrap in plastic and then with foil. Do not allow to thaw before baking as texture will become soggy.

Crab Filling for Phyllo

4	scallions, finely chopped
12-16	ounces crab meat
¼	cup butter
2	tablespoons flour
8	ounces cream cheese, room temperature
½	teaspoon dry mustard
2	teaspoons lemon juice
½	teaspoon Worcestershire sauce
1	teaspoon horseradish
4-5	drops Tabasco sauce
6	tablespoons cocktail sauce
2	egg yolks
	Parmesan cheese for topping

Sauté scallions in butter. Add crab. Sprinkle lightly with flour. Cook 2 minutes. Combine remaining ingredients, except egg yolks, and stir into crab mixture. Cook until thick. Add egg yolks and stir well.

Fill and fold phyllo as directed. Spread filled triangles with melted butter and top with Parmesan cheese. Bake at 375 degrees for 12-15 minutes.

Keep filled phyllo triangles in your freezer for an impressive last-minute hors d' oeuvres. Assemble them on large flat basket with fresh flowers clipped from your garden.

Greek Cheese Filling for Phyllo

4	eggs, slightly beaten
1	pound feta cheese
1	pound ricotta cheese, crumbled
4	ounces Swiss cheese, grated
1/2	cup butter, room temperature
	Parmesan cheese for topping

Blend eggs and cheeses together, then add butter. Stir well. Follow directions for phyllo preparation.

Spread filled triangles generously with melted butter and top with grated Parmesan cheese. Bake at 375 degrees for 12-15 minutes.

Note: **The cheese and butter in this filling may cause phyllo to be greasy; drain on paper towels before serving, if necessary.**

Salsa Cruda

2	cups canned Italian tomatoes, drained and chopped
2	tablespoons red wine vinegar
1/2	cup finely chopped onion
1-2	fresh or canned serrano chilies, finely chopped
1	tablespoon (or more) chopped fresh coriander or parsley
	Salt and pepper to taste

Combine all ingredients and refrigerate.

Zesty and versatile, Salsa Cruda is nice as a dipping sauce with corn chips and toasted tortillas.

Chutney-Chicken Spread

8	ounces cooked chicken, cut in 1-inch pieces
1	8-ounce package cream cheese, room temperature
2	tablespoons chutney
1	teaspoon curry powder
2	tablespoons grated onion or sliced scallions
1/4	cup mayonnaise
	Dash pepper
1/4	cup slivered almonds, toasted

Process chicken in food processor for 5 seconds, using steel blade. Add cream cheese, chutney, curry, onions, mayonnaise and pepper; process for 5-10 seconds until well blended. Place in au gratin dish, sprinkle with almonds and bake at 350 degrees for 15 minutes.

Serve with large corn chips.

S O U P S

Curried Pumpkin Soup

1	large onion, sliced
3/4	cup sliced scallions, white part only
1/4	cup butter
1	16-ounce can pumpkin
4	cups chicken broth
1	bay leaf
1/2	teaspoon sugar
1/2	teaspoon curry powder
1/8	teaspoon nutmeg
	Several parsley sprigs
2	cups half and half
	Salt and freshly ground pepper to taste

Sauté onions and scallions in butter until golden brown. Stir in pumpkin, broth, bay leaf, sugar, curry powder, nutmeg and parsley. Bring to a simmer and continue simmering, uncovered, for 15 minutes, stirring occasionally. Transfer soup to food processor in batches and purée. Return to pan; add half and half, salt and pepper. Simmer 5 to 10 minutes.

6 servings

Paint streaks of sour cream or swirl a teaspoon of heavy cream carefully on the surface. Top with chopped chives or a sprinkling of toasted pumpkin seeds.

Chilled Sorrel Soup

Chive blossoms or pansies add a springtime touch to this lovely soup.

1	bunch leeks, well cleaned and sliced into rounds
3	tablespoons butter
1	large baking potato, peeled and chopped
5	cups chicken broth, divided
1/2	cup torn sorrel leaves
1	cup heavy cream, whipped
1/2	teaspoon lemon juice
	Minced sorrel for garnish

Sauté leeks in butter until limp. Add potatoes and cook without browning. Add 2 1/2 cups broth; cover and simmer on low heat 10-15 minutes. Purée in food processor with sorrel leaves. Add remaining broth. Refrigerate. Before serving, mix in whipped cream and lemon juice and top with minced sorrel. Soup will keep several days in refrigerator.

4 servings

Sorrel, also known as sour grass, grows easily in your garden. This soup is a nice complement to any dinner featuring chicken or fish.

Curried Spinach Soup

2	bunches scallions, chopped
1	large potato, peeled and thinly sliced
7	tablespoons butter, divided
3/4	pound fresh spinach, stemmed, or 2 10-ounce packages frozen spinach, thawed
1/2	teaspoon lemon juice
5	tablespoons flour
1	tablespoon curry powder or to taste
1	quart chicken broth
2	egg yolks, lightly beaten
1/2	cup heavy cream

Sauté scallions and potatoes in 3 tablespoons butter until scallions are soft. Add spinach, cover and steam until potatoes are cooked and spinach is limp. Add lemon juice and purée in food processor. In a large saucepan, melt 4 tablespoons butter, stir in flour and curry powder and cook for 2 minutes over medium heat. Add chicken broth and spinach purée and bring to a boil to thicken. Heat egg yolks and cream. Pour 1 cup of the hot soup into the egg mixture and then return mixture to remaining soup. Cook over low heat for several minutes, but do not allow soup to boil. Serve hot or cold. If serving chilled, you may need to thin soup with a little milk.

6-8 servings

Garnish with thinly sliced tomatoes and chopped chives and serve with *English Muffins Melba Style.*

French Watercress Soup

1	large onion, chopped
1	clove garlic, minced
1/3	cup butter
3	tablespoons best-quality olive oil
1	large potato (1/2 pound), peeled and thinly sliced
	Salt and pepper to taste
1 1/4	cups water
1 1/2	bunches watercress, divided
1 1/4	cups milk
1 1/4	cups chicken broth
2/3	cup half and half
2	egg yolks

Sauté onion and garlic in butter and olive oil. Add potato, salt, pepper and water. Simmer until potato is tender. Put aside 1/4 bunch watercress for garnish, then chop remaining watercress and add to potatoes. Stir in milk and chicken broth. Simmer 15 minutes. Purée mixture in food processor and return to pan. Combine cream and egg yolks and add to soup. Heat slowly until soup thickens. Do not boil. Garnish with watercress sprigs. May be served hot or cold.

6 servings

A light, welcome preliminary to any dinner party. Use your most delicate soup bowls or soup cups.

This may be made a day or two in advance.

Spinach Soup Provolone

1	10-ounce package frozen chopped spinach, thawed but not drained
1/4	cup finely chopped onion
1/4	cup butter
4	tablespoons flour
4	cups milk
1 1/2	teaspoons salt or to taste
1/2-3/4	cup grated provolone cheese
	Crumbled bacon

Purée spinach in food processor. Sauté onion in butter. Add flour, stirring constantly for 2 minutes, and then add milk to make a thin white sauce. Add puréed spinach and salt. Heat thoroughly. Serve topped with a generous sprinkling of grated cheese and crumbled bacon.

6 servings

Spinach soup with a difference — the provolone is essential. For a smashing buffet presentation, serve soup in a large hollowed Hubbard or banana squash.

Cream of Zucchini and Almond Soup

1	onion, minced
3	tablespoons butter
3	zucchini, peeled and thinly sliced
1/2	cup slivered almonds
4	cups chicken broth
1/2	cup ground blanched almonds
3/4	cup heavy cream
1	tablespoon brown sugar
1	tablespoon amaretto
1/4	teaspoon cinnamon
1/2	teaspoon freshly grated nutmeg

Sauté onion in butter until soft. Add zucchini and slivered almonds and cook for about 5 minutes until zucchini is tender-crisp. Add chicken broth and simmer until liquid is reduced by one-third (about 25 minutes). Add ground almonds and simmer 10 more minutes. Over low heat, stir in cream, brown sugar, amaretto, cinnamon and nutmeg. Garnish with zucchini zest or toasted almonds, if desired.

6-8 servings

Perfect at a luncheon or as an unusual first course, this pale, slightly crunchy soup has a delightful flavor.

For a luncheon menu, try this soup with *Bibb and Endive Salad* and *Old-Fashioned Honey Wheat Bread*.

Fresh Asparagus Soup

2	pounds fresh asparagus, peeled and cut into pieces
3	cups chicken broth
2	shallots, finely chopped
1/4	cup butter
5	tablespoons flour
3	cups half and half
1	teaspoon curry powder or to taste
	Salt and pepper to taste
1-2	tablespoons sherry

Place asparagus in large saucepan with broth and shallots and cook until asparagus is tender. (Remove 6-8 asparagus tips and set aside for garnish.) Pour into food processor and blend until smooth. (May have to strain if asparagus is pithy.) Melt butter, add flour and cook for 3 minutes, stirring constantly. Add asparagus purée and half and half. Stir until blended. Add seasonings and sherry and simmer 15 minutes. Garnish with asparagus tips.

6-8 servings

For a lovely addition, cut croutons in a favorite shape; sauté in butter and bake until crisp. Spread with a thin layer of tomato purée and float on top of soup.

Artichoke Sausage Soup

12	ounces Italian sausage
2	14-ounce cans artichoke hearts, drained, or 2 9-ounce packages frozen artichoke hearts, thawed
3	14-ounce cans Italian plum tomatoes
1	package onion soup mix
3-4	cups water
1/2	teaspoon Italian seasoning
1/2	teaspoon oregano
1/2	teaspoon basil

Crumble sausage into pieces in a soup pot; brown and drain off fat. Cut artichoke hearts and tomatoes into bite-sized pieces and add to sausage. Add remaining ingredients and heat through.

8 servings

A comforting country soup that makes a meal with a freshly baked loaf of *Old World Peasant Bread*.

Can be made several days in advance.

Avocado-Cucumber Soup

2¹/₂	cups plain yogurt
2	cups half and half
	Salt and white pepper to taste
1¹/₂	avocados, finely diced
3	cucumbers, peeled, seeded and finely diced
1	tablespoon grated onion
1	cup cold chicken broth

Condiments

	Fresh chives, finely chopped
	Bacon, crisp and crumbled
	Almonds, toasted and chopped
	Tomato, peeled, seeded and chopped

Combine yogurt, cream, salt and pepper. Add avocados, cucumbers, onion and chicken broth. Chill overnight. Serve very cold with condiments sprinkled on top.

8 servings

Serve this summertime cooler in clear soup cups nestled in cracked ice. Try it as a first course or as a luncheon entrée.

Iced Tomato-Lime Soup

1	large onion, chopped
2	tablespoons chopped shallots
1	tablespoon butter
6	large tomatoes, peeled, seeded and chopped
³/₄	cup chicken broth
1	tablespoon tomato paste
1	tablespoon minced fresh thyme
¹/₂	teaspoon sugar or to taste
	Salt and freshly ground pepper to taste
³/₄	cup heavy cream
¹/₃	cup sour cream
	Juice of 1 large lime (about 4 tablespoons)
	Dash of Tabasco sauce

Sauté onion and shallots in butter, covered, until soft but not browned. Add tomatoes, chicken broth, tomato paste, thyme, sugar, salt and pepper. Cover and simmer 20 minutes over medium heat. Remove from heat; cool. Transfer mixture to food processor. Add cream, sour cream, lime juice and Tabasco; purée until smooth. Cover and place in freezer for 2 hours. Adjust seasonings if necessary and serve garnished with lime slices.

6 servings

To retain the unique slushy nature of this soup, serve it in clear glass bowl over crushed ice. Swirl the top of each bowl with *Pesto Sauce* and place a sprig of fresh basil on the ice.

Walk in the Woods Soup

1	ounce dried cèpes, morels or chanterelles
1/3	cup white wine
1/4	cup unsalted butter
1	cup finely chopped onion
3/4	pound fresh mushrooms, thinly sliced
	Salt and freshly ground pepper to taste
2	cups chicken broth
1	cup heavy cream

Croutes (optional)

3/4	pound Pepperidge Farm puff pastry sheets
1	egg, lightly beaten with a little water and salt

Rinse dried mushrooms in cold water and soak them in wine for 1 hour, stirring occasionally. Melt butter in soup pot and sauté onions until tender. Add fresh mushrooms; season and cook, uncovered, over low heat for 15 minutes. Transfer dried mushrooms to pot, saving wine. Let wine settle, then pour carefully into pot, leaving sediment behind. Add chicken broth and bring to boil. Reduce heat, cover and simmer for 45 minutes or until dried mushrooms are very tender. Strain soup. Purée solids plus 1 cup liquid in food processor. Return broth purée to pot and heat. Add cream until soup is the desired consistency. Garnish with a thin slice of fresh mushroom and serve.

4 servings

For your most distinguished guests, we suggest serving this soup with puff pastry:

Mushroom Soup en Croute

Chill soup thoroughly. Fill four 16-ounce Charlotte molds half full with chilled soup.

Roll pastry into a rectangle 1/4 inch thick. Cut circles 1 inch larger than the molds. Heavily paint a 1-inch rim around outside of molds with egg glaze. Tightly fit pastry caps over molds and press edges to seal. Be certain the caps are taut and do not sag. Paint caps with egg glaze and chill for at least 3 hours. Paint again with glaze. Bake in a 425-degree oven for 20 minutes or until a glorious golden brown.

Dried mushrooms are available at most specialty food shops and definitely make an appreciable difference in this sumptuous soup.

Essence of Summer Soup

1	pound leeks, well cleaned and cut into 1-inch slices*
1/2	cup coarsely chopped celery (including leaves)
2	tablespoons butter
3	tablespoons lemon juice
1	cup fresh or frozen peas*
1	cup finely shredded spinach or Swiss chard*
1	cup finely shredded lettuce
5	cups chicken broth
2	cups half and half
	Salt and pepper to taste
1	tablespoon minced fresh mint leaves
1	tablespoon minced fresh parsley
	*Reserve about 24 1/4-inch rings of leeks and small amount of shredded spinach and peas for garnish

Sauté leeks and celery in butter and lemon juice until leeks are tender, about 15 minutes, stirring occasionally. Stir in peas, spinach, lettuce and broth and bring to a boil. Reduce heat and simmer until all vegetables are tender, about 10 minutes. Cool. Add half and half and purée in batches in food processor. Season with salt and pepper. Refrigerate several hours or overnight. Stir in mint and parsley just before serving and garnish with reserved leek rings, spinach and peas.

8 servings

A delightful blend of flavors. Pretty served in chilled flat glass bowls. Float fresh spring peas around the rim.

Strawberry-Peach Soup

Fresh and sweet!

1	quart fresh strawberries
1	large ripe peach
1/2	cup unsweetened pineapple juice
2	cups chicken broth
1/2	cup sour cream or *Crème Fraîche*
3	tablespoons chopped almonds, toasted

Purée strawberries and peach in food processor with pineapple juice Combine with chicken broth. Chill for several hours. Garnish each serving with a dollop of sour cream or *Créme Fraîche* and some toasted almonds.

8-10 servings

We love this on a picnic. Bring the chilled soup in a thermos and add the sour cream and almonds when you serve. Or, for an elegant summer first course, serve in chilled glass bowls with rims dipped in finely chopped mint.

Cold Cherry Soup

3	cups cold water
1	cup sugar
1	cinnamon stick
4	cups pitted fresh tart cherries or frozen unsweetened
1	tablespoon arrowroot
1/2	cup heavy cream
1/2	cup dry red wine

Combine water, sugar and cinnamon stick and bring to a boil. Add cherries and simmer, partially covered, over low heat for 30 minutes. Remove cinnamon. Mix arrowroot with 2 tablespoons cherry mixture to make a paste. Return to soup, stirring constantly. Bring to a boil, then reduce heat and simmer until soup thickens slightly, about 30 minutes. Chill. Before serving, stir in cream and wine.

8-10 servings

If you have not tasted a fruit soup, give this one a try. Serve it in oversized wine goblets, topped with a dollop of sour cream and a cinnamon stick. Those who already love fruit soups will be thrilled with this version. A delightful choice for a brunch or a meeting.

Hot and Sour Soup

4	dried black Oriental mushrooms
1/4	pound ham, slivered
1/2	cup slivered bamboo shoots
1	tablespoon soy sauce
4	cups chicken broth
	Salt and freshly ground white pepper to taste
1	cup thinly sliced tofu
3	tablespoons red wine vinegar
2	tablespoons cornstarch mixed with 3 tablespoons cold water
1	egg, slightly beaten
1	teaspoon sesame oil
1	scallion, including top, cut into 2-inch diagonal slices

Soften mushrooms in warm water. Drain; remove and discard stems. Slice caps and combine in a large saucepan with ham, bamboo shoots, soy sauce and broth. Bring to a boil; reduce heat and simmer 3 minutes. Season to taste. Add tofu and vinegar and bring to boil again. Add dissolved cornstarch and cook, stirring constantly, until soup is slightly thickened. While stirring gently, slowly add egg. Remove from heat and add oil. Ladle into bowls and garnish with chopped scallions.

4 servings

A superb Oriental soup with more flavor and substance than an egg-drop soup. Serve in lotus bowls.

Cioppino a la Marti

We include with pleasure this grand prize winner from the 1984 Kansas City Gourmet Gala.

Tomato-Wine Sauce (may be prepared in advance)

1/4	cup olive oil
2	tablespoons butter
1	medium onion, chopped
1	leek, white part only, well cleaned and finely sliced
1	large shallot, finely chopped
1	green pepper, chopped
2	cloves garlic, finely chopped
20	fresh mushrooms, sliced
1	ounce dried cèpes, soaked briefly in 1/3 cup water and chopped; reserve liquid (cèpes are optional)
1/2	cup fresh lemon juice
	Grated zest of 1 lemon
1	teaspoon oregano
1	tablespoon fresh basil
1	bay leaf, crumbled
	Salt and pepper to taste
1	1-pound, 12-ounce can Italian plum tomatoes
1	6-ounce can tomato paste
2	cups white wine

Seafood (prepare day of serving)

1/2	onion, sliced
1	carrot, sliced
2	stalks celery with leaves, coarsely chopped
	Sprigs of parsley
	Oil
	Bouquet garni of bay leaf, 3 white peppercorns, crushed, and thyme
2	pounds fresh fish (sea bass, r⸱ snapper or halibut)
1	cup white wine
2	cups water
1	pound medium shrimp, shelle⸱ and deveined; reserve shells
1/2	pound crab legs (about 2)
1/2	pound scallops, rinsed
1	pound clams or cockles, scrubbed well (optional)

In a heavy saucepan, heat olive oi⸱ and butter. Add onions, leeks, shallots, green pepper, garlic, mushrooms and cèpes. Simmer 5 minutes. Add lemon juice, zest, spices, tomatoes and tomato past⸱ Gradually add wine and reserved mushroom liquid if cèpes were us⸱ Stirring well to blend, bring mixtu⸱ to a boil; reduce heat, partially cover and simmer at least 1/2 hou⸱ then cover and simmer another 1/⸱ hour. Longer simmering produce⸱ richer sauce.

To prepare seafood, sauté vegetables and parsley in a bit of oil; add the bouquet garni. Lay fi⸱ on this vegetable bed and add wi⸱ and water. Cover fish with a piec⸱ of buttered waxed paper, cover p⸱ and simmer gently until fish is just cooked (opaque and flaky). Let c⸱ in liquid. Remove fish and reserv⸱ return any fish bones to liquid. A⸱ shrimp shells and simmer another 10-15 minutes. Strain and reserv⸱ this fish broth. Cook shrimp in broth; add crab legs, scallops, reserved fish and clams or cockle⸱ available, and heat 5 minutes.

Combine seafood and broth with Tomato-Wine Sauce. Heat gently⸱ Garnish with cilantro (Chinese parsley) or parsley and lemon sli⸱

10-12 servings

Artichoke and Mushroom Soup

2	tablespoons finely chopped onion
3/4	cup thinly sliced mushrooms
3	tablespoons butter
2	tablespoons flour
1 1/2	cups chicken broth
2 1/2	cups half and half
1	16-ounce can artichoke hearts, drained and diced
	Salt, cayenne pepper, and Beau Monde seasoning to taste

Sauté onion and mushrooms in butter for 5 minutes. Stir in flour and cook slowly for 2 minutes. Slowly add broth and half and half. Stir with whisk over low heat to thicken. Stir in artichokes and seasonings.

4-6 servings

Artichokes and mushrooms — a renowned merger! Perfect with a *French Market Sandwich,* crudités and homemade relish.

Ladle into bowls and garnish with finely chopped scallions or thinly sliced mushrooms.

Sunrise Soup

1	onion, coarsely chopped
1	large potato, peeled and coarsely chopped
1	large leek with 2 inches of green, coarsely chopped
2	tablespoons butter
3	cups chicken broth
3	sprigs fresh parsley
	Salt and pepper to taste
2	cucumbers, peeled, seeded and chopped
5	ounces spinach, blanched and chopped
1/2	cup sour cream
1	tablespoon mayonnaise
1	teaspoon horseradish
	Juice of 2 lemons
	Dash Tabasco sauce
1	avocado, diced

Over low heat, sauté onion, potato and leek in butter, covered, about 5 minutes. Add chicken broth, parsley, salt and pepper and bring to a boil. Reduce heat and simmer 20 minutes. Cool and purée in food processor until smooth. Chill thoroughly. Add remaining ingredients except avocado and purée until smooth. Chill. Taste and adjust seasonings. Just before serving, stir avocado into the soup.

4 servings

An unusual blend of cucumber and spinach, with horseradish and avocado adding special interest. Try it for a brunch or summer picnic.

For color, garnish with thin slivers of red bell pepper, a spinach leaf or sliced avocado.

Italian Sausage Soup

1½	pounds Italian sausage, medium spice, broken into bite-sized pieces
2	cloves garlic, minced
2	onions, chopped
2	pounds tomatoes, peeled and cored, or 2 1-pound cans Italian plum tomatoes
1½	cups dry red wine
5	cups beef broth
½	teaspoon dried basil
½	teaspoon dried oregano
3	tablespoons chopped fresh parsley
1	medium green pepper, seeded and chopped
2	medium zucchini, sliced ¼-inch thick
2	cups *Spinach Pasta* noodles
	Salt and pepper to taste
½	cup grated Parmesan cheese

In heavy stock pot, cook sausage over medium heat until lightly browned. Remove with slotted spoon to a paper towel to drain. Reserve. Drain all but 3 tablespoons of fat from the pot. Add garlic and onions and sauté for 2-3 minutes, stirring constantly. Add tomatoes, stirring to break them apart. Add wine, broth, basil and oregano and simmer, uncovered, for 30 minutes. Skim excess fat from top of soup. Add parsley, green pepper, zucchini noodles, salt, pepper and reserved sausage. Simmer, covered, 25 minutes. Serve in deep soup bowls, passing the Parmesan separately.

10 servings

Allow the flavor of this hearty soup to deepen by preparing a day in advance, saving the final 25 minute simmering until just prior to serving. With a fresh green salad and crusty bread, Italian Sausage Soup makes satisfying meal.

Pine Nut Soup

¼	cup plus 1 tablespoon pine nuts
3	tablespoons butter
1	small onion, chopped
3	tablespoons flour
⅛	teaspoon nutmeg
2½-3	cups chicken broth
1	10-ounce package frozen chopped spinach, thawed and drained
2	cups milk

Sauté pine nuts in butter until golden. Remove with slotted spoon and blot with paper towels. Chop in food processor. Add onion to butter remaining in pan and sauté until tender. Add flour and nutmeg and stir over low heat 3 minutes. Blend 3 tablespoons nuts. Add broth and bring to a boil. Add spinach and milk. Reduce heat and simmer 5 minutes. Sprinkle with remaining nuts and serve.

6-8 servings

This is a subtle, intriguing soup that we suggest you serve as a first course on a brisk fall night.

Mexican Seafood Soup

1	quart milk
5	medium potatoes, peeled and cooked
3	tablespoons butter
1¼	cups grated Monterey Jack cheese, divided
1	cup sour cream
1	teaspoon chili powder
	Seasoned salt and pepper to taste
1	cup minced clams and juice
2-3	cups cooked shrimp
1	tablespoon chopped pimiento
¼	cup sherry
¼	cup minced scallions

Blend milk and potatoes in food processor in batches, making sure not to overprocess. Put in a large pot, add butter and bring to a simmer. Add 1 cup of cheese and stir until melted. Return small amount of soup to processor and blend with sour cream. Return to soup pot; add chili powder, salt, pepper, clams, shrimp and pimientos and simmer for 5 minutes. Add sherry. Sprinkle with scallions and remaining cheese. Serve immediately.

6-8 servings

A hearty soup with wonderful Mexican flavor — most definitely a meal in itself.

May be made ahead successfully if the seafood is added just before serving.

Sopa Caliente

2	tablespoons oil
2	tomatoes, peeled, seeded and diced
1	green pepper, sliced
1	4-ounce can chopped green chilies
1	10-ounce can Ro-tel tomatoes and green chilies
1½	cups chicken broth
1	cup evaporated milk
¼	pound Monterey Jack cheese, grated
	Salt to taste
	Sour cream
	Toasted sunflower seeds (optional)

Heat oil; add tomatoes and green pepper and cook until soft. Add chilies, tomatoes and green chilies and chicken broth. Simmer 10 minutes. Stir in milk, cheese and salt, making sure the soup does not boil. Serve as soon as cheese melts. Top with sour cream, more chopped green chilies and toasted sunflower seeds.

4 servings

Lovers of Mexican food — beware. This lusty, spicy soup is addicting.

Serve in earthenware bowls and pass flour tortillas, buttered, rolled and warmed.

Gazpacho Blanca

3	medium cucumbers, peeled, seeded and coarsely chopped
3	cups chicken broth
3	cups sour cream or 2 cups sour cream and 1 cup yogurt
3	tablespoons white vinegar
2	teaspoons salt or to taste
2	cloves garlic, crushed

Condiments

4	medium tomatoes, peeled, seeded and chopped
3/4	cup chopped almonds, toasted
1/2	cup sliced scallions
1/4	cup chopped fresh parsley

Whirl cucumber chunks in a food processor a very short time with a little chicken broth. Pour into mixing bowl; add remaining broth, sour cream, vinegar, salt and garlic. Stir just enough to mix. Chill thoroughly, at least 2-3 hours. Before serving, stir again. Pour into chilled bowls. Sprinkle condiments on top.

8 servings

Here's a wonderfully refreshing summer soup. A nice variation of the traditional Spanish 'liquid salad'.

Sopa de Pollo

The lightness whispers "Japanese", but the flavor shouts "Mexican"!

1 1/2	pounds chicken breasts
3	quarts chicken broth
1 1/2	teaspoons salt or to taste
1/2	cup chopped onion
1	clove garlic, crushed
2	tablespoons oil
1	medium tomato, peeled, seeded and finely chopped
1 or 2	canned Jalapeno peppers
2	medium avocados, peeled and thinly sliced
12	radishes, trimmed and thinly sliced
3	scallions with tops, thinly sliced
1	cup garbanzo beans
8	ounces Monterey Jack cheese, diced into 1/4-inch cubes
3	limes, quartered

Cook chicken breasts in broth and salt until tender, about 20 minutes. Reserve broth. Remove and discard skin and bones from chicken and cut meat into 3/8-inch strips. You should have about 2 cups.

Sauté onion and garlic in oil until onion is softened but not browned. Add tomato and cook, uncovered, stirring frequently, until mixture is reduced and somewhat dry, about 5 minutes. Remove from heat. Purée Jalapeno peppers in food processor with 1/2 cup chicken broth. Add Jalapenos and tomato mixture to reserved chicken broth; simmer over low heat 15 minutes. Divide chicken strips, avocados, radishes, scallions, garbanzos and cheese evenly among 12 warmed soup bowls. Ladle hot chicken broth into bowls and serve immediately with lime wedges on the side.

12 servings

Choose Mexican pottery bowls for casual entertaining or flat soup bowls for a more formal event.

Sopa de Tortilla

1/2	green pepper, minced
3	ribs celery, minced
1	medium onion, minced
1	Jalapeno pepper, minced
2	cloves garlic, minced
2	tablespoons oil
1	14 1/2-ounce can tomatoes
5	ounces Ro-tel tomatoes and green chilies (1/2 can)
1 1/2	cups beef broth
3 1/2	cups chicken broth
1	10 3/4-ounce can tomato soup
2	cups water
1	teaspoon ground cumin
1	teaspoon chili powder
1	teaspoon salt or to taste
1/2	teaspoon lemon pepper seasoning
2	teaspoons Worcestershire sauce
6	corn tortillas, cut in 1-inch squares
1/2	cup grated Cheddar or Monterey Jack cheese

Sauté the first 5 ingredients in oil in a large kettle until soft but not brown. Add remaining ingredients, except tortillas and cheese, and simmer for 50 minutes. Add tortillas and cook 10 minutes. Pour into mugs and sprinkle with cheese.

6-8 servings

Ladle soup into bowls and let your guests help themselves to chopped tomatoes, chopped ripe olives, chopped scallions, sour cream, cheese or toasted tortilla triangles.

Garden Zucchini Soup

...ine first course, whatever the ...son.

2-2 1/2	pounds zucchini, thinly sliced
4	tablespoons chopped shallots
1/4	cup butter
2	teaspoons curry powder
	Salt to taste
1	cup half and half
3	cups chicken broth

Sauté zucchini and shallots in butter for 10 minutes. Add curry powder, salt, half and half and chicken broth. Bring to a boil and simmer 15 minutes. Purée in food processor.

8 servings

Serve hot, garnished with zucchini zest. On a scorching summer day, serve thoroughly chilled with a swirl of sour cream on top and a sprinkling of zucchini zest.

Soup of the Sea

1/4 cup butter

2 tablespoons chopped carrots

2 tablespoons chopped celery

2 tablespoons chopped parsley

2 pounds raw shrimp, shelled and deveined

3 tablespoons warm brandy

1/4 cup flour

2 cups hot chicken broth

1 cup hot clam juice

1 bay leaf

1/2 teaspoon thyme

1 tablespoon lemon juice

1 large tomato, peeled and chopped

1 cup half and half

1/2 cup heavy cream

2 egg yolks

Tabasco sauce

Worcestershire sauce

Salt and pepper to taste

Dill sprigs

Melt butter in skillet and sauté carrots, celery and parsley with shrimp for 8 minutes. Flame with brandy, shake skillet and, when flame is extinguished, remove shrimp and reserve. Set aside 3 or 4 shrimp for garnish and chop the rest into bite-sized pieces.

Transfer carrot mixture to large pan. Add flour and cook until smooth and bubbly. Add broth and clam juice, whisking until smooth. Stir in bay leaf, thyme, lemon juice and tomato. Cover and simmer 30 minutes. Discard bay leaf, purée mixture in food processor and return to pan. Slowly add half and half, stirring.

Combine heavy cream and egg yolks. Add a small amount of hot soup to egg mixture and then return slowly to the soup. Add chopped shrimp, dash of Tabasco, Worcestershire sauce, salt and pepper. Heat thoroughly but do not allow to boil. Garnish each serving with a shrimp, cut in half lengthwise, and a sprig of fresh dill.

6-8 servings

Splendid before a formal dinner, as it is not thick. Be sure to use fresh shrimp.

White Chili

1	pound large white beans
6	cups chicken broth
2	cloves garlic, minced
2	medium onions, chopped (divided)
1	tablespoon oil
2	4-ounce cans chopped green chilies
2	teaspoons ground cumin
1½	teaspoons dried oregano
¼	teaspoon ground cloves
¼	teaspoon cayenne pepper
4	cups diced cooked chicken breasts
3	cups grated Monterey Jack cheese

Combine beans, chicken broth, garlic and half of the onions in a large soup pot and bring to a boil. Reduce heat and simmer until beans are very soft, 3 hours or more. Add more chicken broth, if necessary. In a skillet, sauté remaining onions in oil until tender. Add chilies and seasonings and mix thoroughly. Add to bean mixture. Add chicken and continue to simmer 1 hour. Serve topped with grated cheese.

8-10 servings

For a buffet, serve *White Chili* with some or all of the following condiments: chopped tomatoes, chopped parsley, chopped ripe olives, guacamole, chopped scallions, sour cream, crumbled tortilla chips or *Salsa Cruda*.

Provide warm squares of *Hearty Corn Bread*.

Corn and Crab Meat Bisque

Here's just the soup for the big copper soup pot that's collecting dust in your cupboard.

¼	cup chopped onion
¼	cup butter
2	tablespoons flour
¼	teaspoon curry powder
4	cups fresh or frozen corn (uncooked)
4	cups milk
1	cup heavy cream
	Salt and pepper to taste
1	pound crab meat
	Crumbled bacon

Sauté onion in butter. Add flour and curry powder and cook 2 minutes. Chop corn in food processor, add to onion mixture and cook 5 minutes. Add milk, cream, salt and pepper and bring to boil. Stir in crab meat. Serve hot, topped with crumbled bacon.

10-12 servings

To complete the supper menu, serve *Missouri Spring Salad with Walnuts* and *Maple Oatmeal Bread*. For an inexpensive family meal, omit the crab meat and top with a sprinkling of popcorn.

Adobe Eggs

6	hard-cooked eggs, shelled
1	cup canned beet juice
1	cup cider vinegar
1	clove garlic, crushed
1/2	bay leaf
1/4	teaspoon ground allspice
1	teaspoon salt
	Freshly ground black pepper

Put eggs in a quart jar. Combine remaining ingredients and pour over eggs. Cover, cool and refrigerate overnight or at least 8 hours.

These versatile eggs are equally at home surrounding an Easter ham or as an inspired addition to a summer outing. To keep them from slipping off the platter, cut a thin lengthwise slice off each egg.

Chop leftover eggs and add to chicken salads.

Sugared Bacon

1	pound bacon, room temperature (regular bacon, not thick sliced)
1 1/4	cups brown sugar
1	tablespoon cinnamon, optional

Cut each slice of bacon in half, crosswise. Mix sugar and cinnamon together and thoroughly coat each slice of bacon. Twist slices (or leave flat) and place on rack in a broiler pan or jellyroll pan in a 350-degree oven. Bake until bacon is crisp and sugar is bubbly, 15-20 minutes. Watch closely as the sugar burns quickly. Cool on foil. Serve at room temperature. These may be made hours ahead and left at room temperature.

16 servings

The tantalizing aroma of bacon, brown sugar and cinnamon is irresistible. These morsels are fine for either a buffet brunch or a cocktail party.

Fresh Peach Cup

4	fresh peaches, peeled and cut into bite-sized pieces (or 1 package frozen peaches)
1/2	cup super-fine sugar
1/2	cup brandy
2	bottles Rhine wine
1	quart club soda, chilled

Combine peaches, sugar, brandy and wine, making certain that sugar is dissolved. Chill 2-3 hours. When ready to serve, add club soda. (Peaches may be left in bite-sized pieces or puréed.)

Approximately 16 servings

A refreshing brunch punch!

Orange-Lemon Refresher

1	small can frozen orange juice
1/2	small can frozen lemonade
12	ounces milk (2 small orange juice cans)
1/2	teaspoon vanilla
1/2	teaspoon lemon extract
1	tablespoon sugar
1	egg
	Ice cubes

Put all ingredients into a blender and fill container with ice cubes. Blend until "slushy".

6 servings

Serve this frothy beverage in chilled wine glasses with a slice of lemon or orange on the rim and fresh mint for aroma and color.

Strawberries Devonshire

1	3-ounce package cream cheese, room temperature
2	tablespoons sugar
	Dash of salt
1	cup heavy cream, divided
	Fresh whole strawberries, stems on

In a small bowl, combine cream cheese, sugar, salt and 2 tablespoons heavy cream. Beat until fluffy. Whip remaining cream. Fold into cream cheese mixture. Place in small serving bowl, surrounded by fresh strawberries.

Makes 1 3/4 cups

For morning coffees or afternoon teas, this creamy dip is right for spring entertaining. It is a splendid choice for dessert as well.

Cranberry Tea

1	pound fresh cranberries
2	quarts water
6	sticks cinnamon
4	whole cloves
	Grated zest of 1 orange
1	12-ounce can frozen orange juice
3	cans water
1	6-ounce can frozen lemonade
1 1/2	cups sugar

Combine cranberries, water, cinnamon, cloves and orange zest; boil until berries pop. Strain liquid into large pitcher or container. Add orange juice, water, lemonade and sugar. Stir until sugar dissolves. Serve hot or cold.

Float thin slices of orange peel in bowl or cup when serving.

12-15 servings

Enjoy the welcoming aroma of this tart punch when it is served hot during the winter months for holiday gatherings or after-skating parties. It is an equally delicious cold repast for brunches and teas.

73

Crème Fraîche

1	cup cream
2	tablespoons buttermilk

Heat cream and buttermilk until just warm. Pour into glass jar and cover with plastic wrap. Set aside 24-36 hours, at room temperature, until almost as thick as sour cream. Refrigerate in a tightly sealed jar. will keep for 2-3 weeks.

True Crème Fraîche is the naturally thick cream of France. Our version a reasonable facsimile. It has a nut-like, slightly sour taste and can b used in soups and sauces.

The delicious simplicity of a bowl of berries topped with crème fraîche w add flair to an al fresco brunch.

Hot Browns

½	cup butter
½	cup flour
3	cups milk
1	teaspoon salt
2	egg yolks, beaten
6	slices cooked turkey breast
3	English muffins, split and toasted
½	cup grated Cheddar cheese
6	tomato slices
6	tablespoons butter
2	tablespoons brown sugar
6	slices bacon, fried crisp
½	cup sliced mushrooms, sautéed in 1 tablespoon butter and 1 tablespoon lemon juice

Melt butter in saucepan and stir in flour. Cook 2 minutes. Add milk gradually, stirring over medium hea until thickened. Season. Add some of the sauce to beaten egg yolks, then return mixture to saucepan. Heat through and keep warm.

Arrange turkey on muffins. Top ea muffin with sauce, Cheddar cheese 1 slice tomato, 1 tablespoon butter and a sprinkling of brown sugar. (May be prepared ahead to this point and refrigerated.) Before serving, broil 3-5 minutes or until lightly brown. Garnish with bacon and warm sautéed mushrooms.

6 servings

A do-ahead brunch or luncheon ide from the Brown Hotel in Louisville, Kentucky.

Bombay Eggs

Eggs

12	hard-cooked eggs, shelled
1/2	cup mayonnaise
1	tablespoon curry powder or to taste
1	tablespoon soy sauce
1	tablespoon minced scallions
1	tablespoon minced parsley
1	teaspoon Dijon mustard
	Cayenne pepper to taste

Sauce

1/4	cup chopped onion
1/4	cup peeled, cored and chopped apple
1/4	cup unsalted butter
2 1/2	tablespoons flour
1	tablespoon curry powder or to taste
1	cup chicken broth
1	cup heavy cream
	Lemon juice to taste
	Salt and white pepper to taste

Halve eggs lengthwise and remove yolks, reserving the whites. Press yolks through a sieve into a bowl and add remaining ingredients, mixing well. Spoon yolk mixture into reserved egg white halves, mounding it slightly and re-forming the eggs by pressing the halves together. Chill overnight, covered.

To make sauce, cook onion and apple in butter over moderate heat for about 5 minutes or until onion is clear. Add flour and curry powder; continue cooking and stirring 3 minutes. Stirring with a wire whisk, add broth in a stream, bringing the mixture to a boil and simmering for 20 minutes. Add cream, bring to a boil and cook over moderate heat, stirring, for 15 minutes or until slightly thickened. Add lemon juice, salt and white pepper.

Arrange eggs in a buttered baking dish. Cover with sauce and bake at 350 degrees for 10-15 minutes or until sauce is just bubbling.

Serve with rice and chutney.

6 servings

Curried dishes are always enhanced by offering condiments with them. Additional possibilities include chopped scallions, white raisins, currants, coconut, peanuts or cashews.

Orange Upside Down French Toast

1/4	cup butter
1/3	cup sugar
1/4	teaspoon cinnamon
1	teaspoon grated orange zest
4	eggs, slightly beaten
2/3	cup fresh orange juice
8	slices firm white bread

Melt butter in 10 x 15-inch jelly roll pan. Combine sugar, cinnamon and orange rind. Sprinkle mixture on top of the melted butter. In a separate bowl, mix eggs and juice; dip bread, soaking well. Arrange bread on top of the butter-sugar mixture. Bake at 325 degrees for 20 minutes or until done, watching carefully. Lift out and flip over onto plate.

Sour Cream Eggs

1 cup sour cream or *Crème Fraîche*

8 eggs

2 tablespoons butter

Chopped fresh chives

Chopped fresh parsley

Spread sour cream into a small buttered baking dish. Make 8 dents in the sour cream and carefully break an egg into each dent. Dot with butter and sprinkle with chives and parsley. Bake at 375 degrees for about 15 minutes, making certain that egg whites are set. Scoop egg and sauce onto each plate.

8 servings

Bring new style to this dish by preparing eggs in individual ramekins. Rest each ramekin on a folded pastel napkin. Serve with *Sherried Tomatoes* and *Maple Oatmeal Bread*, toasted.

Spinach and Cheese Tart

9-inch pie crust or 6 individual shells, partially baked

Custard

2 cups heavy cream

5 eggs

1/2 cup grated Parmesan cheese

1/4 teaspoon thyme

1/2 teaspoon Tabasco sauce

1/4 teaspoon nutmeg

1/8 teaspoon cayenne pepper

1 teaspoon salt

Filling

3 cups fresh spinach, stemmed, chopped and cooked

6 ounces Gruyère cheese, grated

2 tablespoons chopped fresh basil

1 tablespoon chopped fresh oregano

Combine Custard ingredients, mixing well.

Combine Filling ingredients and place in bottom of pie shell. Gently pour in custard. Bake at 300 degrees for 40-50 minutes for large shell, 20 minutes for tart shells.

6 servings

Use fresh basil or shredded fresh spinach as garnishment to accentuate the flavors and add a dash of color. Both custard and filling may be made a day ahead.

Mexican Cheese Soufflé

5 4-ounce cans whole green chilies

1 pound sharp Cheddar cheese, sliced

1 pound Monterey Jack cheese, sliced

4 eggs, separated

3 tablespoons flour

1 13-ounce can evaporated milk

Dash of salt and pepper

Wash, flatten and remove seeds from chilies. Place half the chilies in the bottom of a 9x13-inch casserole. Cover chilies with Cheddar cheese slices. Add remaining half of chilies and cover with Monterey Jack slices. Beat egg yolks, flour and milk. Add salt and pepper. Beat egg whites until stiff and fold into egg yolk mixture. Pour over chilies and cheese layers. Bake at 325 degrees for 45 minutes to 1 hour or until top is brown.

8 servings

A festive Mexican brunch is always popular. Serve this mildly spicy soufflé with Spanish hot sausages (chorizos), fresh fruit with lime slices, hot *Tortilla Crisps* and assorted Mexican breads. Ole!

Tempting also as a side dish with steak.

Italian Cheese Pie

3/4 cup shredded Swiss cheese

3/4 cup shredded mozzarella cheese

1/2 cup finely chopped pepperoni

1 1/2 tablespoons diced scallions

1 9-inch unbaked pastry shell

3 eggs, beaten

1 cup half and half

3/4 teaspoon fresh oregano or 1/4 teaspoon dried

Combine cheeses, pepperoni and scallions. Sprinkle in pastry shell. Combine eggs, half and half and oregano and beat with an electric mixer. Pour into pastry shell. Bake at 350 degrees for 45 minutes. Allow to stand 10 minutes before cutting.

6 servings

This quiche has a distinctively Italian flavor. You might like to emphasize this by using more oregano. Julienne slices of cheese and pepperoni make an appropriate garnish.

Zucchini Frittata

1½	cups chopped onion
2-3	tablespoons butter or best-quality olive oil
½	pound zucchini, peeled and shredded
12	eggs, beaten
2	tablespoons fresh basil or 2 teaspoons dried
2	teaspoons salt
	Cracked pepper to taste
3	tablespoons dry bread crumbs
2	cloves garlic, minced (optional)
2	tomatoes, peeled and sliced
1	cup grated Cheddar cheese
½	cup grated Parmesan cheese

Sauté onion in butter or oil; add zucchini and cook about 2 minutes. To beaten eggs, add basil, salt and pepper. Fold in onion-zucchini mixture, bread crumbs and garlic, if desired. Pour into buttered quiche dish. Arrange tomatoes on top and sprinkle with Cheddar and Parmesan cheese. Bake at 350 degrees for 20-25 minutes or until set.

6 servings as an entrée
12 servings as a first course

A frittata is an Italian omelet in which the filling is usually combined with the eggs before cooking.

This peasant dish, studded with zucchini, red tomatoes and two cheeses, is equally adaptable as a brunch, luncheon or first course choice. Can also be served cold.

Broccoli and Ham Wrap-Around

1	pound fresh broccoli or 2 packages frozen broccoli spears
16	slices ham
3	cups cubed French or Italian bread
1½	cups white wine
¾	pound Swiss cheese, shredded
3	tablespoons flour
2	tablespoons Dijon mustard
½	clove garlic, crushed

Cook broccoli in boiling salted water until tender-crisp; drain. Wrap a ham slice around each spear and arrange in a shallow 3-quart casserole. Toast bread cubes in 350-degree oven for 10 minutes and sprinkle around sides of casserole. Heat wine in heavy saucepan until hot. Do not boil. Mix cheese and flour together and add to the wine, ½ cup at a time. Stir with wooden spoon until cheese melts. Add mustard and garlic. Drizzle sauce over entire surface of casserole. Bake at 350 degrees for 40 minutes or until heated throughout and bread cubes are golden brown.

8 servings

When the casserole has finished baking, arrange blanched broccoli florets around the perimeter of the casserole and serve with *Summer Fruit in Cassis*.

hilled Broccoli Iousse

1/4	cup butter
4	tablespoons flour
1 1/2	cups warmed milk
1/2	cup warmed cream
1	envelope unflavored gelatin, dissolved over low heat in 1/4 cup water
1	teaspoon salt or to taste
1/2	teaspoon pepper or to taste
1/8	teaspoon nutmeg
1	teaspoon Dijon mustard
1	tablespoon lemon juice
1	bunch broccoli, cooked until tender-crisp and drained

In a saucepan, melt butter and stir in flour. Cook 2 minutes. Add milk and cream, stirring to make a smooth sauce. Add dissolved gelatin, salt, pepper, nutmeg, mustard and lemon juice. Purée broccoli in food processor. Stir purée into sauce and taste for seasoning. Pour into oiled 2-quart mold. Chill overnight. To unmold, rub outside of mold with a hot towel and invert onto serving plate.

6 servings

A sublime first course with smoked salmon . . . or a tempting addition to a cheese and charcuterie buffet. Could be made in individual ramekins and served with a drizzling of hollandaise or *Two Mustard Sauce.* A touch of carrot purée would add color.

ustard Mousse

1/2	cup sugar
2	tablespoons dry mustard
1	tablespoon unflavored gelatin
3/4	teaspoon ground turmeric
1	teaspoon celery salt
4	large eggs, room temperature
1	cup water
1/2	cup white wine vinegar or cider vinegar
1	cup heavy cream, whipped until it holds a soft shape; do not overbeat

In top of a double boiler, combine dry ingredients. Stir to break up mustard lumps. Beat in eggs with wire whisk until thoroughly combined, then add water and vinegar. Place pan over boiling water on low heat; whisk constantly until gelatin dissolves and mixture thickens slightly. Be careful it does not curdle.

Transfer mixture to a bowl and chill until it mounds slightly when dropped from spoon. (If it gets too firm, liquefy over warm water).

Fold cream into mustard mixture and pour into greased 5-6-cup ring mold. Chill several hours until set.

16 servings

For a buffet, surround mousse with thinly sliced *Summer Baked Ham* or smoked turkey. Tuck fresh flowers, parsley and lemon roses in appropriate places to complete the picture.

Artichoke-Olive Timbale

2 14-ounce cans artichoke hearts, drained

1/3 cup heavy cream

1 small onion, minced

2 scallions, chopped

Butter

1/2 cup pitted ripe olives

1 tablespoon chopped fresh parsley

1 cup dry bread crumbs, preferably light wheat, soaked in 1/3 cup milk

5 eggs, beaten

Salt and pepper to taste

Parmesan Sauce

2 tablespoons butter

2 tablespoons flour

1 cup milk

1 rounded tablespoon freshly grated Parmesan cheese

Salt to taste

Tarragon Sauce

2 tablespoons butter

2 tablespoons flour

1 cup chicken broth

1 tablespoon tarragon

2 teaspoons parsley

Salt to taste

2 tablespoons heavy cream

Generously butter a ring mold, charlotte mold, individual timbales or custard cups. (If using a charlotte mold, cut waxed paper to fit bottom and place buttered side up.) Refrigerate mold.

In food processor, purée artichokes with cream. Sauté onions and scallions in butter until soft but not brown and add to purée. Add olives and parsley and process only slightly, so that pieces of olive remain. Stir in bread crumbs.

In mixing bowl, combine eggs and artichoke mixture. Season with salt and pepper. Pour into mold and place in a pan of hot water so that water covers one-third of the mold. Bake at 375 degrees for 45-50 minutes for large mold or 25-30 minutes for small molds or until timbale draws away from the sides and an inserted knife comes out clean. Invert onto serving platter. Serve with Parmesan Sauce, Tarragon Sauce or your favorite hollandaise.

6 servings

This timbale is compatible with either ham or grilled fish. Add a fruit compote and *Almond-Glazed Poppy Seed Bread* for a brunch menu.

To make Parmesan Sauce, melt butter in a saucepan over low heat and blend in flour. Cook 2 minutes. Gradually add milk, stirring constantly until sauce is thickened. Add Parmesan and salt and remove from heat.

To make Tarragon Sauce, melt butter in a saucepan. Add flour and cook over low heat until mixture is lightly browned. Slowly add broth, blending well. Cook over medium heat until thickened. Add seasonings. When slightly cooled, add cream and blend.

Sausage Ring

2 pounds hot pork sausage

1 1/2 cups Ritz cracker crumbs

2 eggs

2 8-ounce packages cream cheese, room temperature

Using a mixer, combine sausage, cracker crumbs and eggs. Press into a tube cake pan, ring mold or long loaf pan. Bake 40 to 50 minutes at 325 degrees, occasionally draining off grease. After baking, drain again and unmold.

Using cream cheese as a "frosting", ice the Sausage Ring and serve hot.

10-12 servings

Lavishly surround sausage with Italian, curly and Chinese (cilantro) parsley. Place crossed pimiento strips on the creamed cheese.

Far from the usual, Sausage Ring can be the meat portion in your brunch menu, a hearty appetizer when served with crackers or an addition to your post-football game buffet.

Sundown Farm Cake with Hard Sauce

1 pound mild sausage

2 cups brown sugar

1 cup raisins

1 cup nuts (optional)

1 cup strong coffee

1 teaspoon baking soda

1 teaspoon nutmeg

1 teaspoon cinnamon

2 1/2 cups flour

Hard Sauce

1 cup butter, room temperature

1 cup confectioners sugar

1/4 cup brandy, rum or sherry

Freshly grated nutmeg to taste

Mix sausage and brown sugar together and add remaining ingredients to form a stiff batter. Turn batter into a bundt or tube pan. Bake at 300 degrees for 1 1/2-2 hours. When cake leaves the sides of the pan, it is done. Cut in thin slices and serve with Hard Sauce.

To make Hard Sauce, cream butter and sugar. Add brandy, a few drops at a time, and beat until fluffy. Add nutmeg and serve chilled.

12 servings

This unusual old recipe comes from Kentucky. For a winter breakfast, prepare scrambled eggs, winter fruits (apples, pears) and *Sugared Bacon* to accompany this unique cake.

Summer Salad

Mixed herbs and greens, torn into bite-sized pieces

Ripe papaya or fresh peaches, peeled and sliced

Enoki mushrooms, in season

Fresh blueberries

Cooked bay shrimp or lump crab meat

English walnut halves

1/3 cup walnut oil

2/3 cup vegetable oil

1/3 cup blueberry vinegar

Fresh chive blossoms

Freshly ground pepper

Arrange herbs and greens on a large platter, amount depending upon number to be served. Place papaya or peaches in a fan shape on top of greens. Trim mushrooms and arrange on top. Sprinkle blueberries and shrimp or crab meat in an attractive fashion. Sauté walnuts in walnut oil until crisp. Remove with a slotted spoon and sprinkle over salad. Add vegetable oil and vinegar to walnut oil and mix well. Pour the slightly warm dressing over salad and garnish with chives and pepper.

These expensive ingredients are worth the splurge. The combination of fruit, nuts and seafood is extraordinary. Don't be afraid to use the fresh chive blossoms from your garden as an artistic touch to the presentation.

English Country Salad

2 unpeeled winesap or Granny Smith apples, sliced

1/2 pound Belgian endive

1 bunch watercress or mustard cress

4 ounces black walnuts or English walnuts

1/4 pound Stilton cheese, crumbled

Vinaigrette

2 tablespoons Grand Marnier

1 tablespoon white wine vinegar

2 tablespoons honey

1 tablespoon Dijon mustard

1/4 cup best-quality olive oil

1/4 cup vegetable oil

1 teaspoon lemon juice

Slice apples crosswise into 1/4-inch thick round slices to reveal star pattern of core. Arrange endive leaves in a spoke pattern on chilled individual salad plates. Place one round slice of apple in center of plate and dice remaining apples. Make a circle of watercress around the apple slice. Sprinkle nuts, cheese and diced apples on top of watercress. Drizzle with vinaigrette.

To prepare Vinaigrette, combine all ingredients and mix well.

4 servings

Select violets from your garden and tuck in artfully. An edible and beautiful touch, as fresh as the Cotswolds in early May! Serve this dish as a separate course.

inguine Salad

1	pound fresh linguine, cooked, drained and cooled
1/4	cup best-quality olive oil
1	cup sliced radishes
1	small green pepper, chopped finely
1	medium cucumber, peeled, seeded, cut in half lengthwise and then in 1/4-inch slices
4	scallions, including tops, minced
1/3	pound prosciutto or Missouri cured ham, cut in julienne strips
2	tablespoons wine vinegar or tarragon vinegar
1/3	cup imported grated Parmesan cheese or more
1/2	cup heavy cream or more
	Salt and white pepper to taste
	Black olives for garnish

Toss pasta with olive oil, making sure pasta is evenly coated. Add radishes, green pepper, cucumber, scallions and prosciutto. Toss. Add vinegar and cheese and toss again. Add cream and seasonings. Toss. Chill until serving time. Add more cream if necessary. Sprinkle with olives, if desired.

**6-8 servings as a main course
8-10 servings as a side dish**

Easily prepared and chilled in advance. Bring this salad to the reunion picnic in lieu of potato salad.

ea Pod Salad

12-16	ounces pea pods, cooked until tender-crisp and chilled
1	cup cherry tomatoes, halved
1	5-ounce can water chestnuts, drained and sliced
1	bunch scallions, chopped

Dressing

1/3	cup vegetable oil
1	tablespoon lemon juice
1	tablespoon white wine vinegar
1/2	teaspoon salt
1/2	teaspoon sugar
1	clove garlic, minced

Combine dressing ingredients and mix well. Place pea pods, tomatoes, water chestnuts and scallions in a salad bowl. Toss with dressing just before serving.

6-8 servings

Cool, green and crisp . . . chilled plates are a must!

Tomato Pasta with Basil Sauce

A brilliant summer salad . . . spectacular in a clear glass bowl or platter, ringed with fresh tomato wedges and basil leaves.

1	pound fresh *Tomato Pasta* (fettuccine width or wider)
2	tablespoons best-quality olive oil
1	recipe *Basil Sauce*
1/2	cup *Crème Fraîche* or sour cream
1/2	cup pine nuts, toasted 5-7 minutes at 325 degrees
1	cup pitted black olives, sliced
1-2	tablespoons capers, well drained

Cook Tomato Pasta in boiling salted water until tender but al dente (slightly resistant to the bite). Drain and rinse with cold water. Drain again thoroughly. Toss with olive oil. Refrigerate.

Prepare Basil Sauce. Transfer to a bowl and fold in *Crème Fraîche* or sour cream.

Pour half the basil sauce over tomato pasta and mix well. Add enough remaining sauce to moisten. Fold in pine nuts, olives and capers. Refrigerate.

6 servings

If you prepare this ahead of time, reserve one-fourth of the sauce to toss with the pasta just before serving.

Pasta Salad with Tomatoes and Peppers

1	pound small shell pasta (cavatelli)
2	tablespoons best-quality olive oil
1/4	cup milk
1/2	cup sour cream
1 1/2	cups mayonnaise
2	tablespoons good-quality beef bouillon crystals
	Salt to taste
2	green peppers, chopped
1	red onion, chopped
2	fresh tomatoes, peeled, seeded and chopped
6	sweet pickles, chopped
1	teaspoon white wine vinegar
2	pounds medium shrimp (optional) — boiled, shelled and deveined

Prepare salad a day ahead.

Cook pasta until tender but al dente (slightly resistant to the bite) in boiling salted water to which olive oil has been added. Rinse and drain. Transfer to a bowl, add milk to moisten and toss. Set aside.

Combine sour cream and mayonnaise. Add bouillon crystals and salt. Combine with pasta and toss. Add peppers, onion, tomatoes, pickles and vinegar. Add shrimp, if desired, and mix well. Chill, covered, overnight. Toss again before serving. Garnish with fresh dill and cracked pepper.

8 servings

Sensational with *Blackened Leg of Lamb!* Add the shrimp for a noble one-dish meal.

orn Jumble

24	ounces frozen whole kernel corn, thawed
3/4	cup diced, unpeeled cucumber
1/4	cup diced onion
2	small tomatoes, chopped
1/4	cup sour cream
2	tablespoons mayonnaise
1	tablespoon vinegar
1/2	teaspoon salt
1/4	teaspoon dry mustard
1/4	teaspoon celery seed

Combine corn, cucumber, onion and tomatoes. Blend remaining ingredients and add to corn mixture. Toss to coat vegetables and chill.

6-8 servings

A summer treat for picnics or barbecues and a pleasant respite from the usual picnic salad. Present in a bowl lined with radicchio.

icilian omatoes

1	pound tomatoes, sliced 1/4-inch thick
1/2	pound mozzarella cheese, sliced 1/4-inch thick
	Fresh spinach to cover platter
1	small red onion, sliced
1	6-ounce can pitted black ripe olives or Greek olives
	Fresh basil leaves for garnish

Dressing

3	tablespoons best-quality olive oil
1	tablespoon red wine vinegar
1/4	teaspoon salt
1/8	teaspoon pepper
1/4	teaspoon dry mustard
10	fresh basil leaves, chopped
	Juice of 1/2 lemon

Combine dressing ingredients in a jar and shake.

Slice tomatoes and cheese so that they are equal in size and place in an alternating pattern on a bed of fresh spinach. Arrange onion slices on top and mound olives in center. Tuck in fresh basil leaves and drizzle dressing over all.

6 servings

The geometric design makes this a good choice for your buffet table. Prepare this salad when tomatoes are at their peak.

Market Vegetable Salad

A spectacular use of your garden's bounty.

1	cup asparagus tips, blanched and cut in 1-inch pieces on the diagonal
1	cup snow peas, blanched
1	head broccoli florets, blanched
1	head cauliflower florets, blanched
1½	cups peas, fresh or frozen
1½	cups green beans, blanched and cut in 1-inch pieces
1½	cups celery, sliced diagonally
1	medium red onion, thinly sliced
1	cup diced green pepper
1	cup diced red pepper or 1 4-ounce jar pimiento, drained and diced
½	cup chopped parsley
1	can garbanzo beans
1	can small pitted black ripe olives or small Greek olives
1	cup sliced artichoke hearts
	Cherry tomatoes for garnish

Dressing

½	cup tarragon wine vinegar
1	cup vegetable oil
1	tablespoon salt
1	tablespoon sugar
1	teaspoon Tabasco sauce
4	tablespoons capers
2	teaspoons tarragon
2	teaspoons basil
4	tablespoons chopped shallots
2	teaspoons oregano
¼	cup minced fresh basil

Combine dressing ingredients and mix well.

Assemble all vegetables in a large container. (The blanching keeps them tender-crisp and colorful.) Pour dressing over vegetables, cover and refrigerate several hours, tossing occasionally. Salad will keep for several days.

24 servings

Display salad on a large platter. With beef tenderloin and a robust red wine, you have a complete menu.

Adjust the amount of vegetables to accommodate a smaller group.

Deli Salad

1	15½-ounce can garbanzo beans (chick peas)
⅓	pound hard salami, cut in julienne strips
¼	cup pimiento-stuffed olives, sliced
¼	cup finely chopped celery
¼	cup finely chopped scallions
¼	cup finely chopped red pepper, if available
	Lettuce leaves
3	tablespoons finely chopped scallions
2	tomatoes, peeled, seeded and diced
3	tablespoons chopped parsley

Dressing

½	cup tarragon vinegar
½	cup vegetable oil
1	clove garlic, minced
1	teaspoon salt
	Freshly ground pepper

Combine dressing ingredients and mix well. Rinse beans in cold water, drain and dry thoroughly. Mix with salami, olives, celery and peppers; toss with dressing. Refrigerate.

Before serving, drain well. Heap in a salad bowl lined with lettuce leaves and sprinkle scallions, tomatoes and parsley on the top.

6 servings

Make this an even more substantial salad by substituting tortellini for garbanzo beans. As its name suggests, this colorful and vegetable-laden salad is harmonious with picnic fare and casual suppers.

Salad Greens with Hot Bacon Dressing

	Assorted salad greens
6	slices bacon, fried and crumbled
6	tablespoons bacon drippings
6	tablespoons vinegar
6	tablespoons water
6	tablespoons sugar
3	eggs

In skillet, combine bacon drippings, vinegar, water and sugar. Heat to boiling, then cool slightly. Beat eggs in a bowl and stir slowly into warm vinegar mixture. Add bacon crumbles and cook slowly 5 minutes.

Serve hot over arugula, fresh spinach, leaf lettuce, endive or any of the more unusual lettuces. Add raisins if you wish.

Arugula (or rocket) is a lettuce look-alike with a horseradish flavor.

Molded Gazpacho Salad with Shrimp Sauce

A delicate refreshing luncheon salad with harmonious flavors.

2	envelopes unflavored gelatin
1	12-ounce can V-8 juice
2	stalks celery, finely chopped
1	14½-ounce can Italian tomatoes, chopped to a purée
½	green pepper, finely chopped
½	cucumber, peeled, chopped and seeded
½	medium onion, finely chopped
2	cloves garlic, minced
2	tablespoons Italian dressing
¾	cup beef broth
½	teaspoon basil
	Salt and pepper to taste
3-4	dashes Tabasco sauce (more if you like a spicier dish)

Shrimp Sauce

1	egg
½	teaspoon salt
¼	teaspoon dry mustard
1	tablespoon tarragon vinegar
½	teaspoon lemon juice
	Pinch of sugar
¾-1	cup oil
½	teaspoon Italian seasoning
¼	small onion, chopped
⅓	pound small shrimp, cooked, peeled and deveined

Dissolve gelatin in V-8 juice. Heat to boiling and set aside. In large bowl, combine remaining ingredients. Stir in gelatin mixture. Pour into well-greased 6-cup mold. Refrigerate several hours or overnight. Unmold and serve with Shrimp Sauce.

To make Shrimp Sauce, blend egg, salt, mustard, vinegar, lemon juice and sugar in food processor, using steel blade. With machine running, pour oil slowly down chute and process until mixture is thick. Add Italian seasoning. Stir in onion and shrimp.

10-12 servings

Place salad on a bed of unpeeled cucumber slices and serve with *English Muffins Melba Style* which have been sprinkled with paprika.

Chicken Taco Salad

1/2 medium head lettuce, shredded

2 cups cooked chicken, cubed

1 tomato, seeded and chopped

1/2 cup sliced ripe olives

1/4 cup sliced scallions

8 slices bacon, fried and crumbled

3/4 cup grated Cheddar cheese

1 cup crushed corn chips

Dressing

1 medium avocado

1 tablespoon fresh lemon juice

1/2 cup sour cream

1/4 cup vegetable oil

1 clove garlic, minced

1/2 teaspoon sugar

1/2 teaspoon chili powder

1/4 teaspoon salt

1/4 teaspooon hot pepper sauce

Mix dressing ingredients until smooth. This may be done in a blender. Chill. Layer salad ingredients, beginning with lettuce and ending with cheese, in a 2-quart glass dish. Spread chilled dressing over top and sprinkle with crushed corn chips.

4-6 servings

This main-dish salad may be made early in the day and chilled, if the corn chips are added last. Substitute tuna for a hurry-up meal. The beauty is in the layering, so use a glass bowl or dish and resist the temptation to toss.

Frozen Slaw

1 teaspoon salt

1 medium cabbage, chopped

3 ribs celery, chopped

1/2 green pepper, chopped

1 cup white vinegar

2 cups sugar

1 teaspoon celery seed

1 teaspoon mustard seed

Sprinkle salt over chopped cabbage and let stand 1 hour. Squeeze out all liquid and mix cabbage with celery and green pepper. Place remaining ingredients in saucepan and boil for 1 minute. Cool and pour over cabbage mixture. Stir, then put into container and freeze. Before serving, let stand several minutes at room temperature; amount of time will vary depending upon size of container.

8-10 servings

Slaw is crisp when defrosted and is perfect for a pot luck or barbecue.

Bibb and Endive Salad

2 to 3 heads bibb lettuce

1 head Belgian endive or watercress

Vinaigrette

1 clove garlic

1 teaspoon salt

1/2 teaspoon white pepper

1/2 teaspoon dry mustard

1 teaspooon Dijon mustard

2 tablespoons best-quality olive oil

Juice of 1 lemon

2 tablespoons tarragon vinegar

4 tablespoons vegetable oil

Tear lettuce and endive into bite-sized pieces and place in bowl.

Combine vinaigrette ingredients in a jar and shake well. Prepare in advance to promote an exchange of flavors. Remove garlic before using. Toss with lettuce.

Makes 1/2 cup dressing

The fine quality of the vinaigrette makes this combination a success. To embellish the salad, you might like to add chopped fresh herbs, chopped shallots, toasted nuts or quartered artichoke hearts.

California Salad

1 medium head leaf lettuce

1 medium head red lettuce

2 avocados, peeled and sliced

2 cups fresh grapefruit sections

12 large black ripe olives, sliced

Dressing

1/2 cup vegetable oil

1/4 cup red wine vinegar

1/4 cup sugar

1/2 teaspoon salt

1/2 teaspoon celery seed

1/2 teaspoon dry mustard

1/2 red onion, grated

Combine dressing ingredients and mix well.

Combine salad ingredients in a large bowl. Just before ready to serve, add dressing and toss gently.

8-10 servings

Accentuate this salad with rings of chilled red onion.

White Lake Salad

¾	pound romaine lettuce
¼	pound fresh spinach
¼	pound mushrooms, sliced
2	ounces alfalfa sprouts
8-10	slices bacon, fried and crumbled
4	ounces blue cheese, crumbled
2	hard-cooked eggs, sliced
6-8	cherry tomatoes, halved

Dressing

	Generous ¾ cup sour cream
¼	cup mayonnaise
2	tablespoons fresh lemon juice
1	teaspoon Worcestershire sauce
1	beef bouillon cube, dissolved in 4 teaspoons warm water
	Salt to taste
3½-4	teaspoons cracked pepper
	Milk, if necessary

Combine all dressing ingredients except milk in a bowl and whisk to blend. Thin with milk, if desired. Refrigerate, tightly covered at least 3 hours before serving. Dressing may be refrigerated up to 10 days.

Mix romaine and spinach in a large salad bowl. Add mushrooms, then dressing and toss well. Top with alfalfa sprouts, crumbled bacon, blue cheese, egg slices and tomato halves, arranging toppings in concentric circles. If you prefer, simply place all salad ingredients in a large bowl, mix and toss with dressing.

6-8 servings

This is peppery!

Missouri Spring Salad with Walnuts

exceptionally lovely dinner salad.

1	bunch red leaf lettuce
1	bunch watercress
½	pound arugula leaves
1	cup walnut halves

Dressing

½	cup walnut oil
½	cup best-quality olive oil
⅓	cup red wine vinegar
2	teaspoons salt
2	teaspoons sugar
¼	teaspoon pepper

Put greens in a bowl, sprinkle with walnuts, cover and chill.

Combine dressing ingredients and beat until thick. Let stand at room temperature, then beat again before tossing with salad.

8 servings

Missouri's streams and springs are full of fresh watercress in April and May.

Sonoran Salad

1	large head romaine lettuce, finely chopped or shredded
1	large tomato, chopped
1	medium red onion, chopped
1	large avocado, chopped
3	ounces blue cheese, crumbled
6	slices bacon, fried and crumbled

Dressing

3/4	cup vegetable oil
1/4	cup vinegar
1	clove garlic, minced
1	teaspoon salt
4	teaspoons sugar
	Pepper to taste

Combine dressing ingredients in a jar and shake well.

Place romaine on bottom of an oval or rectangular bowl. Chop all vegetables in uniform size. Arrange each vegetable in a colorful row on top of the lettuce to make a "composed" salad. Add dressing just before serving and toss.

Picture perfect with a minimum of effort. Definitely present this salad to your guests before tossing.

Calcutta Salad

1/2	pound fresh spinach
1	head romaine lettuce
1	bunch scallions, chopped
1	cup broken cashews

Dressing

3/4	cup vegetable oil
1/4	cup vinegar
1/4	cup plain or pineapple yogurt
1	teaspoon salt
1	tablespoon Dijon mustard
1	tablespoon chopped chutney
1/2	teaspoon curry powder
1	tart apple, grated

Combine dressing ingredients and mix well.

Combine spinach, romaine and scallions. Toss with dressing. Add nuts and toss again lightly.

8 servings

The unusual flavor of this slightly different green salad complements grilled fish or meat. Try it with *Broiled Shrimp Saffron*.

Feta Cheese Salad

3/4	pound spinach
1	medium cucumber, thinly sliced
1/2	cup sliced radishes
3	hard-cooked eggs, sliced
1/4	cup sliced scallions
1/3	cup currants
1/3	cup pine nuts, toasted
1	ounce feta cheese, crumbled

Feta Cheese Dressing

1	ounce feta cheese, crumbled
1/2	cup mayonnaise
1/2	cup sour cream
1	teaspoon lemon juice
1/2	clove garlic, minced
	Fresh pepper
1	tablespoon grated Parmesan cheese

Arrange spinach in bottom of shallow dish. Top with cucumbers, radishes and eggs. Spread Feta Cheese Dressing over top. Cover and refrigerate overnight. Before serving, sprinkle top with scallions, currants, pine nuts and cheese.

To make Feta Cheese Dressing, combine all ingredients and blend well.

4 servings

Dressing is useful on other salads as well, but sensational with this combination of ingredients.

Hearts of Palm Salad with Herb Dressing

1	14-ounce can hearts of palm
1	clove garlic
	Mixed salad greens
2	cups cherry tomatoes, halved
3	tablespoons freshly grated Parmesan cheese
	Freshly ground black pepper

Dressing

1/3	cup best-quality olive oil
2-3	tablespoons red wine vinegar
3/4	teaspoon salt
1/4	teaspoon salad herbs

Mix dressing ingredients together and let stand. Slice hearts of palm into 1-inch pieces; drain and chill. Rub wooden salad bowl with cut garlic clove and discard garlic. Toss greens with hearts of palm and tomatoes. Sprinkle with Parmesan cheese, pour dressing over salad and toss again. Grind fresh black pepper over top.

8 servings

Hearts of palm make this an exceptional dinner salad.

Strawberry Spinach Salad

10	ounces fresh spinach
1	jicama, peeled and cut in julienne strips
1	basket strawberries, halved
2-3	cups bean sprouts

Strawberry Dressing

1	cup strawberries, halved
2	tablespoons red wine vinegar or raspberry vinegar
2	tablespoons sugar
1/4	cup vegetable oil
	Few drops sesame oil
	Salt and pepper to taste

Combine spinach, jicama, strawberries and bean sprouts in a large bowl. Purée dressing ingredients in food processor, using steel blade. Toss with salad ingredients just before serving. Sprinkle with violets for a beautiful effect!

6 servings

Bring new style to your summer entertaining with this deliciously different salad.

Cloisonné Salad

1	large head romaine lettuce
1	pound bacon, fried and crumbled
4	large avocados, peeled and sliced
1	small red onion, thinly sliced
1	11-ounce can mandarin oranges, drained
1	Jerusalem artichoke, peeled and thinly sliced, or 1 can water chestnuts, sliced

Dressing

1/3	cup chopped shallots
1/4	cup sugar
1/4	cup ketchup
1/4	cup white wine vinegar
1/2	cup vegetable oil
1	teaspoon salt
1	teaspoon paprika

To make dressing, mince shallots in food processor, using steel blade. Add remaining ingredients and blend well.

Tear lettuce. Combine salad ingredients and toss with dressing.

8-10 servings

Varied in textures and colors, this salad is enhanced by its sweet and tangy dressing. Show it off in a transparent salad bowl.

urried Chicken alad in a Pastry hell

Curried Chicken Salad

1²/₃	cups mayonnaise
¹/₄	cup heavy cream
2	tablespoons lemon juice
1	teaspoon curry powder or to taste
	Salt to taste
³/₄	cup rice, cooked
1	cup diced celery
2	tablespoons chopped parsley
3	whole chicken breasts, cooked and diced
1	can water chestnuts, drained and sliced
¹/₄	pound pea pods, blanched for 1¹/₂ minutes and chilled (optional)

Pastry Shell

²/₃	cup water
5	tablespoons butter
¹/₄	teaspoon salt
²/₃	cup all-purpose flour
3	eggs

At least 30 minutes before using, combine mayonnaise, cream, lemon juice, curry powder and salt to make a dressing. Combine cooked rice with celery and parsley, using forks to toss. Add chicken and toss again to distribute. Gradually add dressing and water chestnuts. Mix lightly.

To prepare Pastry Shell, combine water, butter and salt in a 2-quart saucepan. Bring to a boil quickly, stirring to melt butter. Add flour all at once. Remove pan from heat and beat mixture with wire whisk until smooth. Transfer to a food processor, fitted with a steel blade. With machine running, add eggs through the feed tube, one at a time, and process until mixture is smooth and glossy.

Pour into ungreased 10-inch springform pan and, using a rubber spatula, spread evenly over bottom of pan and three-fourths up the sides. Bake at 400 degrees for 40 minutes or until brown and puffed. Turn oven off. Prick shell in 10 places and return to cooled oven for 10 minutes. Remove pan from oven and cool completely. Remove shell from pan. Note: Should center of shell puff up, simply push down before filling.

Use pea pods, if you wish, as a layer on the bottom and up the sides of the pastry shell before filling with Curried Chicken Salad. Embellish the salad with grated egg yolk, tomato wedges or radish roses and more pea pods.

6-8 servings

Shell may be made a day in advance. Cover with foil and store at room temperature. Re-crisp by warming at 250 degrees for 15 minutes.

Steak Salad

2	pounds boneless sirloin, 2 inches thick
	Salt and freshly ground pepper to taste
1/2	pound mushrooms, sliced
6	scallions, sliced
1	14-ounce can hearts of palm, drained and sliced 1/4-1/2 inch thick
2	tablespoons chopped chives
2	tablespoons chopped parsley
2	tablespoons chopped fresh dill

Mustard Vinaigrette

1	egg, beaten
1/3	cup best-quality olive oil
2	teaspoons Dijon mustard
1 1/2	teaspoons fresh lemon juice
3	tablespoons tarragon vinegar
1	teaspoon Worcestershire sauce
1	teaspoon salt
1/4	teaspoon freshly ground black pepper
	Dash of Tabasco sauce

Combine Mustard Vinaigrette ingredients and blend well. Season steak with salt and pepper. Broil to desired doneness (medium rare to rare is preferable). Cool and slice thinly into bite-sized pieces. Combine steak, mushrooms, scallions, hearts of palm and herbs. Toss gently. Pour mustard vinaigrette over salad and refrigerate overnight. The marinade will continue to cook the meat.

8-10 servings

This hearty salad is substantial enough for an entrée. Serve over romaine leaves with garden fresh tomatoes, fresh sugar snap peas and sliced white mushrooms.

Aspic Piquante

A pleasantly sharp salad with a south-of-the-border flavor.

2	3-ounce packages lemon gelatin
2	cups boiling water
2	10-ounce cans Ro-tel tomatoes and green chilies
1	teaspoon celery salt
	Juice of 1/2 lemon
1/2	cup diced celery

Dissolve gelatin in boiling water. Add tomatoes and green chilies, celery salt and lemon juice. Refrigerate until slightly thickened, about 30 minutes. Add celery and pour into a 1 1/2-quart mold or individual molds.

8-10 servings

This aspic welcomes a dollop of guacamole for flavor and garnish.

Cold Poached Chicken with Basil Sauce

6	whole chicken breasts, poached
	Boston lettuce
1	bunch broccoli florets, blanched 4 minutes
4	large tomatoes, peeled and cut into wedges
1	can pitted ripe black olives, drained
1/4	pound feta cheese, crumbled

Basil Sauce

1	large clove garlic
2	eggs
1/2	teaspoon dry mustard
2	tablespoons lemon juice
1/2	teaspoon salt
2	dashes white pepper
3/4	cup best-quality olive oil
3/4	cup vegetable oil
3	tablespoons fresh basil, chopped, or 1 tablespoon dried

Remove skin from poached chicken and pull meat from bones in long strips. Cover with plastic wrap; refrigerate chicken and vegetables until ready to use.

To make Basil Sauce, mince garlic in food processor. Add eggs, mustard, lemon juice, salt and pepper; blend. Pour oils slowly down feed tube, blending until thick. Stir in basil.

Arrange lettuce on chilled plates or platter. Mound chicken in center and surround with broccoli, tomato wedges and olives. Pour sauce over chicken and sprinkle with feta cheese.

The basil sauce and feta cheese are the secrets to this beautiful dish. A lovely alternative to chicken salad in the summer, when basil is plentiful. Use sauce later on cold rare roast beef or vegetables, over pasta, in a cold rice salad or on a cocktail-buffet table with crudités. Keeps 12-14 days in the refrigerator.

Dill and Sour Cream Potato Salad

3	pounds unpeeled new potatoes
2/3	cup mayonnaise
1	cup sour cream
1	tablespoon chopped fresh dill or 1 teaspoon dried
2	teaspoons chopped fresh parsley
	Salt and pepper to taste

Boil potatoes until tender. Cut into bite-sized pieces, leaving skins on. Combine remaining ingredients and mix with potatoes while they are still hot. Refrigerate overnight.

8-10 servings

When summer hospitality calls for potato salad, try this contemporary version.

For a complete departure, slide potato chunks on wooden skewers, garnish with fresh lovage and serve with cold pork.

Red Snapper on a Bed of Limes

2-3 limes or lemons, cut in 1/4-inch slices

1 1/2 pounds red snapper fillets

Salt

Lemon Herb Butter

1/2 cup whipped butter

2 tablespoons lemon juice

2 tablespoons minced parsley

2 tablespoons minced chives

2 tablespoons minced scallions

Line a shallow baking dish with a layer of lime or lemon slices. Arrange red snapper fillets on top in a snug, single layer. Sprinkle lightly with salt and top each fillet with 2 slices (1/2 inch thick) of Lemon Herb Butter.

Bake, uncovered, at 350 degrees for 12-15 minutes, depending on thickness of fish.

To make Lemon Herb Butter, combine ingredients and mix thoroughly. Shape into a roll approximately 1 1/2 inches in diameter. Wrap and freeze at least 30 minutes.

4 servings

Lemon Herb Butter is excellent with any fish, but is essential to the success of this dish. Leftover fish should not be left on lime or lemon bed, as the bitter oil will ruin the flavor of the snapper.

Calamari Italian Style

2 pounds squid, cleaned and cut into 1-inch ringlets

1/4 cup best-quality olive oil

2 cloves garlic, chopped

1/4 teaspoon thyme

1/4 teaspoon dried red pepper

1 cup canned Italian plum tomatoes or equal amount fresh, chopped

1 tablespoon chopped parsley

1 medium unpeeled zucchini, cut into medium-sized chunks

Salt and pepper to taste

Cook squid in oil with garlic, stirring, for 5 minutes. Add thyme and red pepper. Cover and cook over low heat for 10 minutes. Add remaining ingredients, cover and cook 15 minutes.

4 servings

This dish has such glorious colors that it needs little garnish. Serve with pasta or rice and a sprinkling of grated Parmesan cheese.

Ask your fish monger for help in cleaning squid if you have never tried it.

Baked Catfish

An absolutely foolproof recipe to please your fisherman's palate.

4	fresh catfish, heads removed
	Salt and pepper to taste
1/2	cup vegetable oil
25	saltine crackers, crushed

Wash, drain and thoroughly dry catfish. Season with salt and pepper. Roll fish in oil, making sure it is completely covered, then roll in cracker crumbs, coating thoroughly. Place on cookie sheet or baking dish and bake for 1 hour and 15 minutes at 325 degrees.

4 servings

Crab Gratin

1	cup sour cream
1/3	cup Parmesan cheese
1	tablespoon fresh lemon juice
1	tablespoon grated onion
1/8	teaspoon salt
	Dash of Tabasco sauce
13	ounces crab meat
3/4	cup bread crumbs
2	tablespoons butter, melted
	Paprika

Combine sour cream, Parmesan, lemon juice, onion, salt and Tabasco. Add crab meat and stir together gently. Spoon into 6 buttered scallop shells or ramekins. Mix bread crumbs with butter and sprinkle on top. Dust lightly with paprika and bake at 350 degrees for 30 minutes or until lightly browned. Remove from oven and entwine with fresh fennel.

6 servings

Rich and creamy, this lovely first course can be prepared a day in advance and chilled until ready to bake.

Open-Faced Crab Sandwich

4	slices pumpernickel bread
8	ounces crab meat
2	stalks celery, chopped fine
4	scallions, chopped
5-6	mushrooms, sliced
1	teaspoon caraway seeds
3-4	tablespoons mayonnaise
2-3	tablespoons sour cream
8	slices bacon, fried and drained
4	slices Cheddar cheese

Toast bread under the broiler on one side only. Place toasted side down on cookie sheet.

Combine crab meat, celery, scallions, mushrooms, caraway seeds, mayonnaise and sour cream. Spread mixture on untoasted side of bread; top with 2 slices of bacon and a slice of cheese. Broil until cheese melts and bubbles.

4 servings

The perfect Sunday supper sandwich! Caraway seeds are very important to the flavor of this dish.

Salmon Soufflé with Green Herb Sauce

3	tablespoons butter
3	tablespoons flour
1	cup milk, heated to boiling
4	eggs, separated
	Salt to taste
1/4	teaspoon dry mustard or to taste
1	teaspoon Worcestershire sauce
1/2	teaspoon lemon juice
1	cup fresh salmon, cooked, or 1 7³/₄-ounce can red salmon, drained

Green Herb Sauce

1	cup mayonnaise
1 1/2	tablespoons chopped chives
2	teaspoons fresh tarragon or 1 teaspoon dried
1/4	cup chopped parsley
1	teaspoon dill weed
1	teaspoon minced onion

Melt butter in saucepan and stir in flour, blending with a whisk. Add milk all at once, stirring until smooth and thickened. Cool. Beat in egg yolks, one at a time, and season with salt, dry mustard, Worcestershire and lemon juice. Flake salmon and blend into sauce.

Beat egg whites until stiff, but not dry. Fold gently into salmon mixture with wooden spoon. Do not over blend. Pour into buttered 2-quart soufflé dish. Place on center rack of pre-heated 400-degree oven and immediately reduce temperature to 375 degrees. Bake 30-40 minutes or until golden brown and puffed.

4 servings

For Green Herb Sauce, place all ingredients in a blender or food processor and blend on high speed for several seconds.

Serve soufflé immediately, table-side, using 2 spoons to apportion servings. Pour a little Green Herb Sauce onto each plate and top with a serving of soufflé. Sprinkle with capers or chopped chives.

Green Herb Sauce is also a nice dipping sauce for crudités.

Scallops with Mushrooms and Cognac

A sophisticated, delicately flavored appetizer that can be made in minutes.

2	pounds scallops, drained
1	pound mushrooms, sliced
1	cup butter
	Salt and freshly ground pepper to taste
1	tablespoon sugar
	Juice of 1 lemon
1	cup buttered bread crumbs
1/2	cup Cognac

Divide scallops among 8 buttered coquille shells or any small, shallow oven-proof dishes. Add sliced mushrooms. Place 2 tablespoons butter on top of each. Season with salt, pepper and a pinch of sugar; sprinkle with lemon juice. Cover top with buttered bread crumbs and bake in a 400-degree oven for 20 minutes. Add 1 tablespoon Cognac to each shell. Return to oven and broil for 5 minutes.

8 servings

Serve with baskets of crisp *Parmesan Sticks*.

Scallops Capri

Tomato is the pivotal ingredient in this memorable dish.

1/3	cup chopped shallots
2	tablespoons butter
2	pounds scallops, rinsed
3	tablespoons Cognac
3	tablespoons white wine
2	cups peeled, seeded and chopped tomatoes
1 1/2	cups heavy cream
2	egg yolks
	Juice of 1/2 lemon
1/4	cup chopped parsley

Sauté shallots briefly in butter; add scallops and cook briefly. Add Cognac and flame. When flame is extinguished, remove scallops; set aside and keep warm.

Add wine to the butter mixture and cook until liquid is reduced by half. Add tomatoes and cook until thick. Stir in cream and cook 5 minutes. Add a little of the sauce to the yolks and return mixture to the pan. Stir in lemon juice, parsley and scallops; heat briefly.

6 servings

Serve in a shell for a first course or over *Spinach, Tomato* or *Egg Pasta* as an entrée with lightly sautéed julienne vegetables.

Seafood Rusk

1	8-ounce package cream cheese, room temperature
1/2	teaspoon Worcestershire sauce
4-6	Holland rusks
1-2	tomatoes, sliced
2	avocados, sliced
3	hard-cooked eggs, sliced
	Crisp lettuce
2	cups mayonnaise
1 1/2	cups chili sauce
2	teaspoons cider vinegar
2	teaspoons grated onion
1/2	teaspoon anchovy paste
	Dash Tabasco sauce
24	ounces crab meat or lobster

Mix cream cheese with Worcestershire and spread on rusks. Top each with a tomato slice, 2 slices of avocado and 3 slices of egg. Place the rusks on a bed of lettuce and top with sauce made by mixing the mayonnaise, chili sauce, vinegar, onion, anchovy paste, Tabasco and crab or lobster.

This dish may be prepared ahead and assembled at the last minute.

4-6 servings

For a glorious luncheon, serve with a cup of *Iced Tomato-Lime Soup.*

Caribbean Seafood Medley

An outstanding blend of colors, textures and flavors.

2	cups mayonnaise
1/2	cup horseradish, drained
2	teaspoons dry mustard
2	teaspoons lemon juice
1/2	teaspoon salt
1	pound raw sea scallops, quartered and heated in butter
1	pound medium shrimp, cooked and peeled
1	8-ounce can sliced water chestnuts, drained
1	box cherry tomatoes, halved or whole
1	cup pitted ripe olives, drained
1/2	head cauliflower florets

Combine mayonnaise, horseradish, mustard, lemon juice and salt. Add remaining ingredients and mix well.

Serve slightly chilled.

6-8 servings

Heap generous portions into chilled avocado halves or fill an artichoke for an outstanding luncheon offering. Olives, shrimp or tomatoes may be reserved for garnish. Choose a light dessert of *Lemon Mousse.*

This seafood medley is also an obvious choice for a sumptuous first course. Small portions, please . . . it's rich.

Herb Shrimp

2	pounds large shrimp, rinsed but not peeled (may slit and devein, if desired)
1	recipe *Basil Sauce*

Marinade

3/4	cup best-quality olive oil
2	tablespoons lemon juice
1	tablespoon minced parsley
2	cloves garlic, crushed
1	teaspoon salt
1/2	teaspoon oregano
	Pepper to taste

Combine marinade ingredients in long shallow dish. Thread shrimp onto six 10-12-inch flat skewers. Lay skewers in the marinade, turning to coat, and marinate 2 hours, turning every 30 minutes.

Grill shrimp over hot coals for 3 minutes on each side or until they are just cooked. Remove shrimp from skewers. Heap on a platter and garnish with lemon slices and fresh basil. Prepare *Basil Sauce.* Peel shrimp and use sauce for dipping.

4 servings

Let this be the basis for a casual summer "finger food" party. Accompany shrimp with baskets of crunchy raw vegetables, a loaf of *Old World Peasant* bread, fresh fruit and *Decadent Chocolate Cookies.*

Grilled Mexican Shrimp

1	pound large shrimp in the shell

Garlic-Butter Sauce

1/2	cup butter, melted
6	cloves garlic, minced
1/2-1	tablespoon chili powder
1/4	cup minced parsley
1/2	cup minced scallions

Cook shrimp in 2 gallons of boiling water for no more than 2 minutes and drain immediately. Do not peel. (This may be done early in the day.)

Combine Garlic-Butter Sauce ingredients in saucepan. Bring to a simmer and turn off heat.

When ready to serve, grill shrimp for no more than 4-5 minutes. Do not overcook. (For a smokier taste, cover the grill.) Place grilled shrimp in a large bowl and "drown" with Garlic-Butter Sauce.

3-4 servings

The best way to eat grilled shrimp is with your fingers. For a casual party, bring out your seashells to decorate the table and individual sand buckets to hold crushed ice with beer or wine. Serve shrimp with *Sonoran Salad*, chunks of crusty bread to soak up the last of the Garlic-Butter Sauce and bowls of freshly churned *Peach Ice Cream*.

Broiled Shrimp Saffron

2	pounds large shrimp, peeled and deveined, leaving tail sections attached
1/2	cup butter

Marinade

1/2	teaspoon salt
1/4	teaspoon pepper
1/2	teaspoon saffron
1	large shallot, chopped
2	cloves garlic, chopped
1/4	teaspoon thyme
3	tablespoons best-quality olive oil
1/4	cup lemon juice

In large bowl, combine marinade ingredients. Add shrimp; marinate in refrigerator for at least 2 hours, turning once or twice. Remove shrimp and reserve marinade.

Broil shrimp on rack 2-3 minutes per side; remove to heated platter. Combine pan drippings, remaining marinade and butter in a saucepan and heat to boiling. Pass separately.

4 servings

For buffet presentation, thread shrimp onto small skewers before cooking. Arrange skewers in a spoke pattern on a platter and fill center with fresh thyme. Serve with *Creamy Lemon Rice*.

107

Shrimp in Beer Louisianne

¹/₂	cup sliced almonds
7	tablespoons butter, divided
1	tablespoon oil
2	pounds large shrimp, peeled and deveined
¹/₄	cup minced scallions
1	green pepper, cut into strips
¹/₂	pound small whole mushrooms
1	tablespoon Hungarian paprika
	Salt and pepper to taste
1	teaspoon tomato paste
1	cup light beer
1	cup *Crème Fraîche* or sour cream

Sauté almonds in 1 tablespoon butter and oil until golden. Drain on paper towels and sprinkle with salt.

Cook shrimp in 4 tablespoons butter over moderate heat, tossing lightly, until they turn pink. Transfer shrimp and pan juices to a bowl. Cover and set aside.

Add 2 tablespoons butter to the pan and sauté scallions and green pepper until just soft. Add mushrooms, paprika, salt and pepper. Cook, stirring, until mushrooms are tender. Stir in tomato paste, beer and pan juices from the shrimp. Cook over high heat until liquid is reduced to ¹/₂ cup. Lower heat, add *Crème Fraîche* or sour cream and the reserved shrimp. Simmer until hot.

6-8 servings

Ladle from a bowl or deep platter onto steaming rice and sprinkle toasted almonds on top for added crunch.

Springtime Shrimp

Beautiful colors and flavors!

¹/₄	cup butter
1	pound asparagus, peeled and cut into 2-inch pieces (or substitute 28-32 fresh snow peas; pull off stems, string, blanch 1-2 minutes, refresh in cold water)
¹/₄	teaspoon salt
1	bunch scallions, green tops only, chopped
	Grated zest of 1 lemon
24-28	large shrimp, peeled and deveined
1-2	tablespoons dry sherry

Melt butter in skillet or wok. Toss asparagus in butter and sprinkle with salt. Cover and cook over low heat 4-5 minutes. (If using snow peas, cook 1-2 minutes.) Add scallion tops, lemon zest, shrimp and sherry; cook 3-4 minutes or until shrimp are just done. Prepare *Creamy Lemon Rice* to serve on the side.

4 servings

Shrimp Nantucket

As classic as Moby Dick! *A truly superior first course.*

1	cup dry white wine
1/2	teaspoon salt
1/8	teaspoon pepper
1/2	bay leaf
1	pound shrimp, peeled and deveined
1/2	pound mushrooms, sliced
2	tablespoons chopped scallions
3	tablespoons butter
4	tablespoons flour
3/4	cup milk
2	egg yolks
1/2	cup heavy cream
	Salt and pepper to taste
2	teaspoons lemon juice
1/2	cup grated Swiss cheese (Gruyère or Emmenthal)
	Butter

Simmer wine, salt, pepper and bay leaf for 5 minutes. Add shrimp, mushrooms, scallions and enough additional wine to cover. Simmer 5 minutes, covered. Remove shrimp and mushrooms with slotted spoon; boil liquid until it is reduced to 1 cup and strain.

Melt butter and add flour, stirring over low heat for 2 minutes. Remove from heat and add strained, hot cooking liquid and milk. Return to heat and boil 1 minute.

Blend egg yolks and cream in a bowl. Gradually beat the hot sauce into this mixture. Return sauce to the pan and boil, stirring, for 1 minute. Thin with more cream, if desired. Season with salt, pepper and lemon juice.

Cut shrimp into bite-sized pieces. Blend two-thirds of the sauce with shrimp and mushrooms. Divide among 8 buttered individual au gratin dishes or scallop shells. Cover with remaining sauce, sprinkle with cheese and dot with butter. (May be refrigerated at this point until ready to heat.) Bake at 350 degrees for 15-20 minutes.

8 servings

Island Shrimp

3-4	small white onions, chopped
1	green pepper, chopped
1/2	cup butter
2	pounds shrimp, boiled, peeled and deveined
1/4	cup slivered almonds
1/2	teaspoon each ginger, cinnamon, mace and pepper
1	teaspoon curry powder
1	cup raisins

Sauté onions and green pepper in butter until they are tender-crisp. Add shrimp, almonds, spices and raisins. Simmer briefly until shrimp are pink.

4-6 servings

A lively last-minute dish. Serve over hot rice — or, bring out the real island flavor by presenting in a hollowed pineapple, papaya or melon with rice on the side. Choose fruit slices, raisins, cinnamon sticks or almonds for additional garnish.

Shrimp Caneel

A spicy, colorful dish that is easily doubled or tripled for a large group.

- 2 medium onions, finely chopped
- 1 large green pepper, seeded and finely chopped
- 1/2 cup diced celery
- 1/3 cup vegetable oil
- 1 16-ounce can Italian plum tomatoes, chopped
- 1 cup tomato purée
- 1/4 teaspoon basil
- 1/8 teaspoon cayenne pepper
- 1 large clove garlic, mashed
- 2 bay leaves
- Salt and pepper to taste
- 2 tablespoons curry powder
- 3 pounds shrimp, peeled and deveined

Condiments

- Golden raisins
- Coconut
- Slivered almonds

In a large saucepan, sauté the onions, green pepper and celery in oil, stirring often, until soft. Add tomatoes, purée, basil, cayenne, garlic, bay leaves, salt and pepper. Bring to a boil; add curry powder and lower heat. Simmer, covered, about 20 minutes. If sauce is too thick, thin with water or chicken broth. (Dish may be prepared to this point and frozen up to one week.) Add shrimp and simmer until shrimp are cooked. Serve over rice with condiments.

6-8 servings

Make the most of the lovely red-orange color by centering Shrimp Caneel in a ring of *Creamy Lemon Rice* or a bed of *Orange Pasta* with condiments on the side.

Fillet of Sole Parmesan

- 1/2 cup grated Parmesan cheese
- 1/4 cup butter, room temperature
- 3 tablespoons mayonnaise
- 3 tablespoons chopped scallions
- 1/4 teaspoon salt
- Dash Tabasco sauce
- 2 pounds skinless sole fillets (or any fresh white fish)
- 2 tablespoons lemon juice

Combine cheese, butter, mayonnaise, scallions, salt and Tabasco. Set aside. Place fish fillets (serving size) in a single layer in a buttered baking dish. Brush with lemon juice and let stand 10 minutes. Broil fillets 3-4 inches from heat for 4-5 minutes. Spread with cheese mixture and broil 2-3 minutes longer or until golden.

6 servings

What could be quicker? Arranged on a platter with *Green Beans and Pears*, it is equally successful as family or company fare.

Sole Giovanni

The light refreshing flavor of garden mint combines delightfully with the smoky aroma of the grill.

2	medium-sized sole, boned, or 2 large fillets of sole
	Salt and pepper to taste
2	tablespoons butter, room temperature
1	tablespoon chopped parsley
2	tablespoons chopped fresh mint
1	small clove garlic, crushed

Season sole with salt and pepper. On each side, make two crosswise incisions. Mix butter, parsley, mint and garlic. Press this mixture into the slits. Grill sole on the barbeque 3-4 minutes on each side for fillets or 7 minutes on each side for whole sole. (If using fillets, place on foil to prevent fish from falling into grill.) Serve on large platter garnished with sprigs of fresh mint.

2 servings

Trout with Rosemary and Prosciutto

1	fresh trout per person, boned

For each trout, you will need:

1	sprig fresh rosemary, about 2 inches long
1/2	ounce prosciutto, cut in 1-inch julienne strips
2	teaspoons butter
	Flour
	Paprika
	Dry white wine

In cavity of each trout, place a sprig of rosemary, half the allotted amount of prosciutto and 1 teaspoon butter. Place in a buttered baking dish and dot each fish with 1 teaspoon butter and a dusting of flour and paprika. Cover trout with a cake-cooling rack or something similar to help keep its shape. Bake in a 350-degree oven for 10 minutes per inch of thickness. (Fish is measured at thickest part.) Baste with pan juices. Remove cake rack and top the trout with remaining prosciutto. Drizzle with white wine and broil for about 1 minute to crisp.

Serve on warmed plates and add more fresh rosemary for color and fragrance.

Marinated Grilled Swordfish

Swordfish and your outdoor barbecue team up with great results. The firm, meat-like texture of this fish lends itself to grilling.

6	swordfish fillets, 1/2 inch thick or more (fresh tuna may be substituted)

Marinade

1/2	cup soy sauce
1/2	cup sherry
1	tablespoon lemon juice
1/4	cup vegetable oil
1	clove garlic, crushed

Combine marinade ingredients and blend well. Pour over fish and marinate in refrigerator for no longer than 3 hours.

Brush barbecue grill with oil and cook fish until the white milk starts to flow, about 5-8 minutes per side, depending on the heat of the coals. Garnish with julienne scallions and a twist of fresh lime.

6 servings

Halibut on the Grill

1/2	cup butter
2	cloves garlic, minced
	Freshly ground white pepper to taste
3	tablespoons chopped parsley
1	large halibut fillet to serve 3 to 4, skin on
	Vegetable oil

Melt butter and add garlic and pepper. Remove from heat and add chopped parsley. Reserve.

Brush both sides of fish with oil. Place on a greased grill. Grill 10 minutes per inch of thickness. (Fish is measured at the thickest part.) Baste with the parsley-butter mixture. Turn fillet half way through the cooking time, using a large spatula.

3-4 servings

This method of grilling is adaptable to many fish steaks, large fillets or whole small fish. Bluefish, sea bass, salmon and trout are especially good fish to use. The same technique can be applied to the broiler.

Seafood Crepes

This outstanding recipe sets the standard for all seafood crepes.

1/2	pound mushrooms, sliced
1/2	pound small shrimp, peeled and deveined
1/4	cup butter
1	small onion, finely chopped
1/2	cup finely chopped celery
1/2	cup chopped fresh broccoli
2	beef bouillon cubes
4	tablespoons white wine
1/4	teaspoon salt
1/8	teaspoon pepper
1	cup sour cream with chives
2	tablespoons lemon juice
1/4	cup chopped pimiento
7	ounces crab meat
1/2	cup cooked scallops (optional)
8	crepes

Sauté mushrooms and shrimp in butter for 5 minutes; remove from pan. Sauté onions, celery and broccoli until tender; remove from pan. Add bouillon cubes, wine, salt and pepper; simmer 5 minutes. Stir in sour cream and lemon juice. When well-combined, add remaining ingredients, reserved shrimp and vegetables. Heat through.

Prepare your favorite crepe recipe. Fill each crepe with sauce, roll up and top with a dab of sour cream or *Crème Fraîche*.

Fills 8-10 crepes

Serve either as a first course or with fresh fruit and *Sesame Asparagus* for a brunch or light dinner.

Flavored Butters

to serve with broiled or grilled fish

Horseradish Butter

4	tablespoons unsalted butter, room temperature
1	teaspoon freshly grated horseradish

Green Peppercorn Butter

1/2	cup unsalted butter, room temperature
1	teaspoon crushed green peppercorns
	Salt and pepper to taste

Red Pepper Butter

2/3	cup roasted peppers, diced
1	cup plus 2 tablespoons unsalted butter, room temperature
6-7	cloves garlic, unpeeled
2	tablespoons lemon juice
	Salt and pepper

To make Horseradish Butter, combine all ingredients thoroughly.

To make Green Peppercorn Butter, combine all ingredients.

To make Red Pepper Butter, sauté roasted peppers in 2 tablespoons butter for 5 minutes. Place garlic in pan with boiling water to cover and blanch 5 minutes. Drain, peel and pat dry.

Using food processor, purée sautéed peppers and blanched garlic. Add lemon juice and seasonings and combine. Cream remaining butter with mixer until light and fluffy. Beat pepper-garlic mixture into butter, half at a time. Put in crock and cover. Chill at least 1 hour.

Shape butter into cylinders and chill. When ready to serve broiled or grilled fish, top each serving with a medallion of butter for added interest and zest.

Two Mustard Sauce

2	egg yolks, room temperature
1/2	teaspoon Dijon mustard
1/2	teaspoon dry mustard
	Pinch of cayenne pepper
1/8	teaspoon mace
1/8	teaspoon nutmeg
1/4	teaspoon minced garlic
1	tablespoon tarragon vinegar
1/2	teaspoon salt
2	teaspoons Cognac
1	cup oil
3	tablespoons sour cream
1/2	cup heavy cream, whipped

Combine egg yolks, mustards, cayenne, mace, nutmeg, garlic, vinegar, salt and Cognac in food processor and mix thoroughly. With machine running, dribble oil down the chute in a slow, steady stream. Process until mixture becomes the consistency of mayonnaise.

Remove from processor. Gently stir in sour cream and whipped cream. Chill.

This new version of the traditional mustard is wonderful with shrimp, crab, cold seafood salads, turkey and *Summer Baked Ham.* Add it to your next buffet table as a nice complement to other mustards.

POULTRY & GAME

POULTRY & GAME

Chicken with Summer Berries

20	strawberries, washed and hulled
4	chicken breasts, skinned, boned and split
2	tablespoons unsalted butter
1/2	cup framboise (raspberry liqueur)
1/4	cup raspberry vinegar
3	tablespoons peeled, seeded and chopped tomatoes
1/8	teaspoon finely chopped garlic
2	tablespoons chicken base
1	teaspoon tomato paste
3/4	cup heavy cream, divided
1/2	teaspoon salt
	Freshly ground pepper
1/2	cup raspberries (optional)
1/4	cup scallions, very thinly sliced (green part only)
8	basil leaves for garnish

Cut 12 strawberries into quarters, leaving 8 whole for garnish. Cook chicken in butter for 2 minutes on each side or until chicken is white but not brown. Remove from heat. In small pan, heat framboise. Ignite the framboise and carefully pour it over the chicken while still flaming. Shake pan gently to extinguish flames. Transfer chicken to a platter and keep warm.

Pour vinegar into skillet and stir over high heat with a wooden spoon to loosen any particles from bottom of pan. Add tomatoes, garlic, chicken base, tomato paste and 1/2 cup heavy cream. Stir and bring to a boil; cook for 1 minute or until thickened. Season with salt and pepper.

Return chicken and any accumulated liquid to the skillet. Add quartered strawberries, raspberries, if desired, and remaining cream. Cook 2 minutes until chicken is almost cooked through. Add 2 tablespoons scallions and cook 1 minute longer.

4 servings

To present this unique and memorable entrée, divide sauce among 4 warm dinner plates. Place breasts on each plate; arrange 2 basil leaves in the center of each plate and garnish with 2 whole strawberries. (Pomegranate seeds cooked whole cranberries can be added to the sauce.) Sprinkle with chopped scallions.

Szechwan Chicken

1	tablespoon cornstarch
3	tablespoons soy sauce, divided
2	large chicken breasts, boned, skinned and cut into 1/2-inch cubes
1	tablespoon dry sherry
2	teaspoons sugar
1	teaspoon vinegar
1/4	cup oil
1	teaspoon crushed red pepper (or less)
2	scallions, sliced
1/2	teaspoon ground ginger
1/2	cup salted peanuts

Combine cornstarch and 1 tablespoon soy sauce in bowl. Add chicken, stir to coat and set aside. Combine 2 tablespoons soy sauce, sherry, sugar, and vinegar; set aside.

Heat oil in wok; add red pepper and cook until black. Add chicken and cook two minutes; remove chicken and set aside. Add scallions and ginger; stir-fry for 1 minute. Return chicken to wok and cook 2 minutes, stirring constantly. Add soy sauce mixture and stir 1 minute. Add peanuts. Serve over rice.

4 servings

Szechwan is a province in southwest China which is noted for its fiery hot pepper dishes. However, you will not find Szechwan Chicken too spicy for most palates.

While the wok is hot, prepare *Spinach and Bamboo Shoots* to serve with this dish.

Note: **You may want to reduce amount of crushed red pepper if you are not accustomed to hot foods.**

Chicken in Cream

2	whole chicken breasts, split and boned
6	tablespoons butter
1/2	medium onion, minced
3/4	pound mushrooms, sliced
1	cup heavy cream
3/4	cup grated Parmesan cheese
	Salt
	White pepper

Cut chicken into strips and sauté in butter 3-5 minutes. Add onion and mushrooms and sauté 3-4 minutes. Pour in cream and cook over medium heat until sauce reaches desired thickness. Add cheese and season to taste with salt and white pepper.

4 servings

So simple! Try using your kitchen scissors to cut the chicken easily into strips. Serve over *Almond Rice* or one of the flavored pastas. Chopped fresh tarragon over the top would be pleasant.

Southern Grilled Chicken

2	tablespoons crunchy peanut butter
5	tablespoons fresh lemon juice
4	tablespoons grated onion
1/4	cup best-quality olive oil
1/2	teaspoon salt
1/4	teaspoon freshly ground pepper
2	chickens, split in half or cut into pieces

Heat peanut butter and lemon juice until melted. Add onion. Slowly add olive oil, stirring constantly. Season with salt and pepper.

Broil chicken on the grill, 15 minutes per side, basting several times with sauce. Any remaining sauce may be heated and served with the chicken.

4-6 servings

Two childhood favorites, peanut butter and chicken, are combined with surprisingly delicious results. *Corn Jumble* or *Dill and Sour Cream Potato Salad* complete a picnic menu.

Chicken Romano

4	chicken breasts, split
	Flour
1	cup butter, melted
1	cup grated Romano cheese
1	cup sherry or white wine

Dust chicken with flour. Pour melted butter into a 9x13-inch pan and add chicken, plump side up. Bake 30 minutes at 350 degrees, basting once. Sprinkle chicken with cheese and add sherry or wine; return to oven and bake another 30 minutes, basting twice.

4-6 servings

Overlap breasts down the center of serving platter, cover with sauce and surround with *Sesame Asparagus* or *Zucchini and Walnuts.*

Chicken in Lemon and Cream

3	chicken breasts, split, skinned, boned and pounded
	Salt and pepper to taste
3/4	cup butter, divided
2	tablespoons vermouth, sherry or white wine
2	teaspoons grated lemon zest
2	tablespoons lemon juice
1	cup heavy cream
	Grated Parmesan cheese to taste

Salt and pepper breasts. Sauté 5-8 minutes in 1/2 cup butter, turning once. Transfer chicken to oven-proof platter. Combine vermouth, lemon zest and juice in a saucepan and cook 1 minute, stirring constantly. Season with salt and pepper. Add cream slowly and stir. Pour sauce over chicken. Put a pat of butter on each piece of chicken and sprinkle with Parmesan cheese. Brown under broiler and serve.

6 servings

Garnish with fresh lemon balm.

Roasted Lemon Chicken

2	fryers (about 2½ pounds each)
	Salt
	Freshly ground pepper
	Juice of 1 lemon
4	whole lemons
	Garlic and rosemary (optional)

Dry chickens with paper towels. Sprinkle the inside of the chickens with salt and pepper. Squeeze lemon juice over chickens and rub with additional salt and pepper.

Prick each lemon 20 times with a round toothpick. Place 2 lemons in the cavity of each bird. Add rosemary and garlic, if desired. Close the opening with toothpicks and tie legs together loosely.

Place chickens in a roasting pan, breast side down, and bake for 20 minutes in the upper third of a 350-degree oven. After 20 minutes, turn chickens over. Bake for another 20 minutes. Increase heat to 400 degrees and continue baking for another 20 minutes or until the chicken is golden. Garnish with fresh chervil.

6-8 servings

Lemon juice gives this chicken its crispy crust. Serve with *Summer Creole* and *Cloisonné Salad*.

Orange Tarragon Chicken

1	tablespoon grated orange zest
1	cup fresh orange juice
¼	cup fresh lemon juice
⅓	cup honey
2	tablespoons Worcestershire sauce
1	tablespoon fresh tarragon or 1 teaspoon dried
1	teaspoon dry mustard
	Salt and pepper to taste
4	chicken breasts, skinned, boned and split
2	teaspoons cornstarch, dissolved in 1 tablespoon water

Combine orange zest, juices, honey, Worcestershire, tarragon, mustard, salt and pepper. Pour over chicken breasts and marinate, covered, for 2 hours in the refrigerator. Bring to room temperature and place chicken and marinade in a large flat baking dish. Bake, covered, at 350 degrees for about 30 minutes or until done. Thicken sauce with cornstarch mixture and ladle sauce over chicken when serving.

4 servings

Pull a sprig of tarragon through the center of an orange slice for a colorful garnish and top chicken with grated orange zest.

Chicken and Artichoke Buffet

3	whole boneless, skinned chicken breasts, split and cooked (4 cups meat)
2	cups carrots, cut in 1-inch julienne strips
4	tablespoons butter, divided
4	cups cooked wild rice (about 2 cups dry)
10	medium mushrooms, sliced
10	scallions, chopped
2	cans cream of chicken soup
1/2	cup heavy cream
1/2	cup sherry
1	teaspoon salt
2	14-ounce cans artichoke hearts, drained and quartered
10	slices thick bacon, fried and crumbled
3	cups grated mozzarella cheese
	Parmesan cheese (for top)

Cut split chicken breasts in half. Blanch carrots for 5 minutes. Rinse with cold water and drain well.

Grease 9x13-inch casserole with 2 tablespoons butter and spread cooked rice over bottom. Sauté mushrooms and scallions in remaining butter. Add soup, heavy cream, sherry and salt. Mix well. In large bowl, combine the mushroom mixture, chicken, artichokes, bacon blanched carrots and mozzarella; mix well, spread over rice and sprinkle with Parmesan. Bake at 35 degrees for 45 minutes (covered for the first 30 minutes, uncovered for the last 15).

8-10 servings

This entrée, with a loaf of *Swiss Braided Bread,* is terrific for a large gathering.

Chicken en Brochette

3	chicken breasts, skinned, boned and split
	Salt and pepper to taste
1-1 1/2	pounds Italian sausage, link-type, cut in 1-inch pieces
1	cup white wine
12	large mushrooms
2	tablespoons butter

Cut chicken in 1-inch pieces and season with salt and pepper. Set aside. Simmer sausage in wine 5-1 minutes. Set aside. Simmer mushrooms in butter and enough water to cover for 3-4 minutes to soften.

Arrange sausage, chicken and mushrooms in an alternating patte on skewers. Grill 7-8 minutes on each side.

4 servings

Serve this unique combination with *Sherried Tomatoes* on a bed of *Saffron Rice* and garnish with red, yellow and green pepper rings.

Chicken Teriyaki

¹/₂	cup soy sauce
¹/₂	cup sugar
¹/₄	teaspoon garlic powder
¹/₈	teaspoon ground ginger
¹/₈	teaspoon onion powder
	Salt to taste
12	chicken thighs, skinned, or similar amount of chicken
¹/₂	cup chopped cashews

In a large saucepan, combine soy sauce, sugar, garlic powder, ginger, onion powder and salt. Bring to a boil over medium heat. Add chicken and simmer over low heat, uncovered, for 45-60 minutes. (For a deeper flavor, marinate chicken in the sauce for up to 4 hours before proceeding with cooking instructions.)

Transfer chicken to a serving platter and sprinkle with chopped cashews.

6 servings

Cashews give this excellent buffet dish a unique texture and rich taste. Serve with *Snow Peas with Shallots and Basil* and garnish with feathered scallions.

Oriental Chicken in Clay

1	clove garlic, crushed
1	teaspoon sesame seeds, toasted
¹/₄	cup soy sauce
3	tablespoons sherry or dry vermouth
1	whole chicken (3¹/₂-5 pounds)
1¹/₂	cups uncooked rice
1	8-ounce can water chestnuts, drained and sliced
1	14-ounce can mixed Chinese vegetables, drained
1	small piece lean ham, diced
¹/₈	teaspoon cracked black pepper
¹/₃	cup peanuts or cashews

Combine garlic, sesame seeds, soy sauce and sherry or vermouth. Marinate chicken in mixture for 12 hours. Drain and reserve marinade for stuffing.

Soak clay cooker and lid in cold water for at least 10 minutes before assembling. Cook rice until slightly underdone. Combine rice, water chestnuts, Chinese vegetables, diced ham, pepper, marinade liquid and nuts, tossing lightly. Stuff chicken with mixture and place leftover stuffing in bottom of cooker. Place chicken in cooker, breast side up, and bake, covered, at 450 degrees for 1 hour and 15 minutes.

4-6 servings

By all means bring the clay cooker to the table. Transfer the beautifully browned chicken to a platter lined with colorful kale or bok choy and carve.

Country Chicken with Cream Biscuits

1	chicken, cut up
2	teaspoons salt
1	stalk celery
1	medium onion, quartered
5	carrots, cut in chunks
3/4	cup flour
2	cups half and half
2	egg yolks, beaten

Cream Biscuits

2	cups Bisquick
1	cup heavy cream
1/4	cup butter, melted

Place chicken in a kettle with enough water to cover. Add salt, celery and onion. Simmer, covered, until tender. Add carrots the last 30 minutes of cooking.

Drain broth from chicken. Skim fat, reserving 1/4 cup for gravy. Strain broth; save carrots. Measure 2 cups broth for gravy and pour remaining broth back into kettle with chicken to keep hot.

Heat chicken fat in a saucepan and blend in flour. Cook 2 minutes. Gradually add the 2 cups chicken broth and cream, cooking and stirring with a wire whisk until thick and smooth. Add a small amount of hot gravy to egg yolks, then return yolks to gravy. Cook 2 minutes more.

Place chicken and carrots in serving dish or soup tureen; cover with gravy and top with Cream Biscuits.

To make Cream Biscuits, combine Bisquick and cream. Turn out on a floured board. Flour hands and knead dough a few times. Pat or roll out to 1/2-inch thickness. Cut into rounds with a floured cutter, 1 to 2-inches in diameter. Dip each biscuit in butter and place on a cookie sheet, 9-inch square baking pan or iron skillet. Bake at 450 degrees until light brown, 12-15 minutes.

4-6 servings

This is a refinement of an old favorite country recipe that is worth every little change from your usual method. Remember to pass more Cream Biscuits and *Honey-Orange Butter.*

These melt-in-your-mouth biscuits perk up family suppers. Serve them directly from a heavy iron skillet for a great country look. Use them for unforgettable strawberry shortcake.

Breast of Chicken Piccata

4	chicken breasts, boned and split
	Flour, seasoned with salt, pepper and garlic
1/4	cup butter
3	lemons (1 for garnish)
3	ounces capers
1/4	cup chopped parsley

Pound chicken breasts lightly, dredge in seasoned flour and brown in butter. Pour juice of 2 lemons over chicken. Reduce heat, cover and cook 8-10 minutes. Add capers and parsley; stir and baste chicken with pan juices.

4 servings

Slice a lemon or lime for garnish and arrange chicken and citrus slices on a serving platter. Serve with *Almond Rice* and sautéed vegetables.

Picnic Stuffed Chicken Breasts

8	slices bacon
1	large onion, finely chopped
1	10-ounce package frozen chopped spinach, thawed and squeezed dry
1	egg, lightly beaten
1/2	cup seasoned croutons, lightly crushed
1/2	teaspoon garlic salt
4	whole chicken breasts (about 1 pound each), skinned, boned and split
	Salt and pepper to taste
3	tablespoons oil

Stuffing Variation

1/2	pound fresh spinach, washed and chopped
1/2-1	cup chopped fresh basil
4	ounces mozzarella cheese, shredded
1/2	pound ricotta cheese
	Salt and pepper to taste
3/4	teaspoon fresh thyme or 1/4 teaspoon dried
1 1/2	teaspoons fresh tarragon or 1/2 teaspoon dried

Fry bacon; drain and crumble. Reserve 2 tablespoons drippings. Sauté onion in bacon drippings until soft. Remove from heat and stir in spinach, egg, croutons, garlic salt and crumbled bacon. Cut pocket in thick side of each chicken breast. Stuff with spinach mixture and close with wooden pick. Sprinkle with salt and pepper. Brown breasts in oil until cooked through, about 12-15 minutes. Remove and drain on paper towels. Cool slightly, cover with foil. Serve hot or cold.

Perfect fare for a summery setting. Arrange on a bed of spinach leaves and serve with *Sicilian Tomato Salad* and *Stuffed Artichokes*.

For a beautiful hors d' oeuvre , cut breasts crosswise and arrange slices on a basket tray lined with grape leaves.

To make Stuffing Variation, combine all ingredients. Divide among breasts and stuff. Bake at 350 degrees for 1 hour. Serve hot or chilled.

Chicken Breasts in Cognac and Cream

4	chicken breasts, split, boned and skinned
	Salt and pepper to taste
	Lemon juice to taste
2	tablespoons butter
2	tablespoons oil
2	tablespoons chopped shallots
$1/4$	cup Cognac
$1/2$-$3/4$	cup beef broth
$1/4$	teaspoon thyme or 1 sprig tarragon
$1/2$	cup heavy cream
2	teaspoons cornstarch, dissolved in 1 tablespoon water (optional)

Sprinkle chicken breasts with salt, pepper and lemon juice. Sauté in butter and oil over medium heat 3-4 minutes on each side or until cooked through. Transfer to a warm platter.

Pour off oil, leaving 1 tablespoon; sauté shallots until just brown. Add Cognac and flame. Add beef stock and thyme or tarragon. Simmer 3 minutes to reduce liquid. Add cream. If desired, thicken with cornstarch mixture. (If using tarragon, remove sprig.) Serve with *Almond Rice*. (Chicken may be covered with foil and kept warm in a 300-degree oven for a short time.)

4 servings

Mound *Almond Rice* in enter of serving platter, arrange chicken around the perimeter and drizzle some of the sauce over the chicken. Garnish with toasted almonds and sprigs of thyme or tarragon. Pass additional sauce.

Chicken Persillade

A nice recipe for herb garden enthusiasts. Braid the stems of a parsley bouquet and tie with a scallion "string" for the platter.

3	chicken breasts, split and skinned
6	chicken thighs, skinned
4-6	tablespoons Dijon mustard
6	large cloves garlic
10	sprigs Italian parsley (persillade)
10-15	fresh basil leaves
$1 1/2$	teaspoons fresh tarragon or $1/2$ teaspoon dried
1	cup chicken broth
4	tablespoons red wine vinegar
$2/3$	cup heavy cream
2	teaspoons cornstarch, dissolved in 1 tablespoon water (optional)

Dry chicken and paint with mustard. Chop garlic, parsley, basil and tarragon in food processor. Combine broth and vinegar in a baking dish large enough to hold all the chicken. Pour in half the parsley mixture.

Arrange chicken in dish and sprinkle with remaining parsley mixture. Cover lightly with foil and bake at 375 degrees for 40 minutes. Transfer chicken to serving platter, cover with foil and keep warm.

Pour cooking liquid into saucepan. Add cream; bring to a boil, reduce heat and cook for 9-10 minutes or until sauce is reduced to 1 cup. For thicker sauce, add dissolved cornstarch.

6 servings

Chicken-Cream Cheese Enchiladas

2 large onions, thinly sliced

2 tablespoons butter

2 cups diced cooked chicken

1/2 cup chopped pimiento

2 3-ounce packages cream cheese, diced

Salt and pepper to taste

12 6-inch Corn Crepes or tortillas

2/3 cup heavy cream

2 cups shredded Monterey Jack cheese

Sliced ripe olives for garnish

Lime wedges for garnish

Corn Crepes

2 eggs

1 tablespoon vegetable oil

2 tablespoons flour

3/4 cup milk

1/2 cup Masa Harina flour

1/4 teaspoon salt

Separate onions and sauté in butter over medium heat until clear and beginning to brown, about 20 minutes. Remove pan from heat and add chicken, pimiento and cream cheese. Mix lightly and season.

Prepare Corn Crepes or tortillas. To make Corn Crepes, blend all ingredients in blender or food processor. Fry crepes, using about 1/3 cup batter for each one.

To prepare tortillas, heat about 1/3 cup vegetable oil in a small skillet and, using tongs, dip each tortilla into oil just long enough to soften, about 45 seconds. Remove from pan and press between paper towels to remove excess oil.

Spoon about 1/2 cup chicken filling in center of each crepe or tortilla and roll. Place seam-side down in buttered casserole. Pour heavy cream down sides of dish about 1/2 inch deep. Bake, uncovered, in a 375-degree oven for 20 minutes. Remove and sprinkle with cheese. Return to oven and bake until cheese is melted but not brown. Serve with a garnishing of ripe olives and lime wedges.

6 servings

Hobo Sandwich

18-inch loaf French or Italian bread, unsliced

2 ounces blue cheese, crumbled

Mayonnaise

1/2 pound summer sausage or beef salami, thinly sliced

12 ounces mozzarella or Swiss cheese, sliced

3/4-1 pound turkey white meat, cooked and thinly sliced

Romaine lettuce, shredded

Sweet and Sour Dressing

2 cups vegetable oil

1/2 cup vinegar

2 teaspoons dry mustard

2 teaspoons paprika

2 teaspoons salt

2 teaspoons chopped onion

3/4 cup sugar

2 teaspoons celery seed

Cut loaf in half lengthwise and hollow out some of the center. Mix blue cheese with enough mayonnaise to cover both halves of the bread and spread mixture to the edges.

On bottom half of the bread, layer meat, cheese, turkey and lettuce. Cover generously with Sweet and Sour Dressing. Top with bread and cut into slices 2 inches wide.

To make Sweet and Sour Dressing, combine all ingredients and mix well.

The savory blend of Sweet and Sour Dressing and blue cheese makes this a delicious portable sandwich. Present on a wooden board and surround with a variety of crudités and pickles.

Chicken Breasts with Prosciutto

1/4 cup butter

Juice of 1 lemon

Salt and pepper to taste

3 chicken breasts, boned, skinned and halved

1/3 pound mushrooms, sliced

6 thin slices prosciutto, cut in julienne strips

1/4 cup chicken broth

1/4 cup brandy

1 teaspoon grated lemon zest

2 tablespoons heavy cream

Melt butter in a skillet and add lemon juice, salt and pepper. Add chicken and cook over medium heat 3-4 minutes on each side. Remove from pan and keep warm.

Add mushrooms and prosciutto to pan and cook a few minutes. Remove and keep warm. Add chicken broth and brandy; bring to a boil and cook until liquid is reduced by one-third. Stir in lemon zest and cream. Return chicken, mushrooms and prosciutto to pan. Reheat slightly and serve warm with rice.

4-6 servings

Sautéed Quail in Cream

6-8	quail (1½-2 birds per serving)
	Flour, seasoned with salt and pepper
	Clarified butter
1	clove garlic, minced
½	pound mushrooms, sliced
¼	cup minced shallots
¼	cup white wine
2	cups heavy cream
	Salt and pepper to taste

Dredge birds in flour and brown in butter. Transfer to a warm oven. Add garlic, mushrooms and shallots to pan and sauté 3-5 minutes. Add wine, cook 2 minutes, then stir in cream. Season with salt and pepper. Return birds to pan. Cover and cook 15 minutes. Remove lid and reduce sauce.

Serve on a croute or shredded potato basket. Spoon sauce over and garnish with fresh thyme.

4 servings

Split Game Hens with Red Currant Glaze

6	Cornish game hens
	Salt and pepper to taste
½	cup butter, melted

Red Currant Glaze

1	10-ounce jar red currant jelly
2	tablespoons lemon juice
1	teaspoon allspice
1	tablespoon Worcestershire sauce
	Salt and pepper to taste

Additional Ingredients

3	tablespoons red wine vinegar
3	tablespoons Marsala wine

Split game hens in half by cutting with shears along the back and breast bones. Season with salt and pepper and arrange in a layer in a large roasting pan. Roast at 350 degrees, basting with butter. After hens have roasted 40 minutes, cook an additional 10-20 minutes, basting frequently with Red Currant Glaze. Remove hens from pan and set aside to cool.

To make Red Currant Glaze, combine all ingredients in a saucepan. Bring to a boil; cool.

Skim fat from roasting juices and combine juices with any remaining Red Currant Glaze. Add vinegar and wine. Boil until thick and reduced to 1 cup. Pour over cooled hens. Serve at room temperature.

6 servings

Perfect for a sophisticated tailgate picnic. Wrap servings in cellophane and tie with ribbons of your school's colors. This lovely-to-look-at dish is also delightful for porch and garden entertaining. Accent with a spray of rosemary and fresh fruit and serve with *Pea Pod Salad*.

Buttered Barbequed Cornish Game Hens

4	stalks celery
1	onion, quartered
4	Cornish game hens
1½	cups butter
1	teaspoon thyme
½	teaspoon oregano
2	cloves garlic, crushed
¼-⅓	cup fresh lemon juice
1	teaspoon paprika
1	tablespoon soy sauce
½	teaspoon freshly ground black pepper

Place celery and onion in each hen cavity. Tie wings and legs. Skewer hens securely on a spit lengthwise. Make basting sauce by combining remaining ingredients and heating until butter is melted. Roast birds on the spit, basting frequently. Cook over moderate coals until fat runs yellow (not pink) when pierced, about 1-1½ hours. (You may use a barbeque grill or the oven if you don't have a spit.)

4 servings

Using a large circular platter, place hens on a bed of radicchio leaves and tuck fresh thyme or oregano in the center. Serve with *Dill and Sour Cream Potato Salad.*

Roast Pheasant Madeira

2-3	pheasants
1	lemon, cut in half
	Salt pork or bacon
	Flour
1	cup Madeira wine

Stuffing

½	pound mushrooms, sliced
1	cup minced onion
3	tablespoons butter
2	slices bacon, fried and crumbled
1	cup chopped fresh parsley
4	cups diced bread
1	teaspoon salt

Rub pheasants inside and out with lemon halves. Fill cavities with stuffing mixture; truss and cover breasts with thin slices of salt pork or bacon. Sprinkle lightly with flour. Place birds side by side in roasting pan, add wine and roast in a 375-degree oven for 40-45 minutes or until juices run clear, basting frequently.

To make Stuffing, sauté mushrooms and onions in butter until onions are softened. Remove from heat and add bacon, parsley, bread and salt. Mix well.

4-6 servings

These are moist and delicious. Garnish with tokay grapes and ivy leaves.

Smoked Wild Duck with Orange Sauce

Nestle a jar of Orange Sauce into a terra cotta duck for a gift that will be appreciated by wild game enthusiasts.

6 wild ducks

Brine

2 cups canning salt

5 quarts water

1/2 cup molasses

1/2 cup brown sugar

1/2 teaspoon garlic salt

1 teaspoon celery salt

1 teaspoon pepper

Juice of 1 lemon

Dry rubbing mixture

1/2 cup brown sugar

1 tablespoon garlic powder

4 tablespoons pepper

Orange Sauce

1 cup currant jelly

3/4 cup orange juice

1 tablespoon Worcestershire sauce

1 tablespoon dry mustard

Salt and pepper to taste

1 tablespoon cornstarch, dissolved in 3 tablespoons orange juice

Mix brine ingredients in a large plastic container. Soak ducks in brine at least 24 hours in the refrigerator. Rinse and air dry 1 hour. Combine ingredients for Dry Rubbing Mixture and rub into ducks. Smoke 12-24 hours.

To make Orange Sauce, blend jelly, orange juice, Worcestershire, dry mustard, salt and pepper and boil until jelly is dissolved. Add cornstarch mixture and cook over medium heat until sauce is thickened and clear.

6 servings

Arrange ducks on a wooden platter with watercress and orange slices. Pass the Orange Sauce.

For an appetizer, slice the duck thinly, serve on cocktail rye or pumpernickel and top with sauce. You may also sliver duck into bite-sized pieces for dipping.

Duckling with Orange and Cognac

Surround duckling with kumquats (leaves intact) and watercress.

Juice of 4 oranges

1/3 cup Cognac

Salt and pepper

1 duckling, about 4 pounds

Combine orange juice and Cognac. Salt and pepper duckling inside and out. Roast on a rack in a foil-lined pan for 1 1/4 hours at 350 degrees, basting with orange mixture every 10 minutes. Roast for another 45 minutes. Carve. Spoon juice over each serving.

4 servings

Winter Steak with Tarragon Butter

1	2-inch thick sirloin steak, second or third cut
	Salt and pepper to taste
1 1/2	tablespoons butter
1 1/2	tablespoons oil

Tarragon Butter

2	medium shallots
2 1/2	tablespoons chopped fresh parsley
4	teaspoons tarragon vinegar
1 1/2	teaspoons fresh tarragon or 1/2 teaspoon dried
1/2	teaspoon freshly ground pepper
1/2	cup butter, well chilled and cut into small pieces

Pat steak dry. Salt and pepper steak on both sides. Sear in butter and oil for 2-4 minutes on each side or until dark brown. Transfer meat to large baking dish and bake at 350 degrees for 25 minutes for medium rare. Transfer to a warm platter.

4-6 servings

Top each serving of beef with a pat of Tarragon Butter and garnish with sprigs of fresh tarragon.

To make Tarragon Butter, mince shallots in food processor, using steel blade. Add parsley, vinegar, tarragon and pepper; process briefly. Add butter and blend well. Transfer to waxed paper and form a roll. Refrigerate or freeze until firm.

Peppercorn Roast Beef

5-6	pound boneless rib eye roast
1/2	cup coarsely cracked green or black peppercorns
1/2	teaspoon ground cardamom seed
1 1/2	tablespoons cornstarch, dissolved in 1/4 cup cold water (optional)

Marinade

1	tablespoon tomato paste
1/2	teaspoon garlic powder
1	cup soy sauce
3/4	cup vinegar

Rub meat with peppercorns and cardamom. Combine ingredients for marinade. Add meat and marinate in refrigerator for 24 hours. Bring meat to room temperature. Remove meat from marinade and wrap in foil. Place in shallow pan and roast at 300 degrees for 2 hours for medium rare. Open foil. Remove drippings and reserve. Brown roast, uncovered, at 350 degrees.

Strain pan drippings, skimming off fat. To each cup meat juice, add 1 cup water. Bring to a boil. If desired, add more marinade for flavor. Serve roast au jus or thicken gravy with dissolved cornstarch.

8-10 servings

This is compatible with all the traditional prime rib accompaniments . . . freshly grated horseradish, Yorkshire pudding and a hearty dessert of *Plum Duff*.

Dill Pot Roast

3-3½	pounds rump, arm or chuck roast
1	teaspoon salt
¼	teaspoon pepper
1	teaspoon dill seed
¼	cup water
1	tablespoon wine vinegar
3	tablespoons flour
1	teaspoon dill weed
1	cup sour cream

Season beef with salt, pepper and dill seed. Place in an ovenproof dish; add water and vinegar. Cook, covered, in a 200-degree oven for 5 hours. Remove meat. To the liquid in the pan, add flour and dill weed. Cook and stir to thicken. Add sour cream. Spoon sauce over sliced beef.

6-8 servings

Wonderful family fare. Delicious with noodles or rice . . . there's plenty of sauce to cover. Add additional dill for decoration and include the bright yellow dill flowers in season.

French Market Sandwiches

12	croissants
1	cup butter, room temperature
¼	cup prepared mustard
½	teaspoon poppy seeds
2	tablespoons finely minced onion or shallots
2	pounds shaved ham
12	slices Swiss cheese, cut to fit shape

Slice croissants in half horizontally. Mix butter, mustard, poppy seeds and onion together. Spread on half of each croissant. Top with 2½ ounces ham and a slice of cheese. Put halves together. Wrap each sandwich in foil and warm in 325-degree oven for 15 minutes.

These sandwiches may also be frozen in foil and warmed, unwrapped, at 325 degrees for 25-30 minutes.

12 servings

Party Sandwiches by the Yard

This party sandwich is a good choice for the teen-age set or a football crowd.

1	unsliced 18-inch loaf pumpernickel bread, approximately 3½ inches in diameter
1	bunch scallions, chopped
1	8-ounce package cream cheese, room temperature
3	pounds cooked beef brisket or thinly sliced rare roast beef
4	tomatoes, sliced
1	pound bacon, fried crisp
	Mayonnaise

Slice bread in half lengthwise, hollowing out some of the top and bottom pieces. Add chopped scallions to cream cheese and spread mixture about ¼-inch thick on bottom half of loaf. Cover to edge of bread. Layer meat and tomato slices twice, topping with bacon slices. Spread top half of loaf generously with mayonnaise and put sandwich halves together. Slice sandwich diagonally at 2-inch intervals with a serrated knife.

8-10 servings

Meat Loaf Burgundy

2	pounds ground beef (top round or sirloin)
1	pound ground veal
1	pound ground pork
1	cup cottage cheese
1	cup bread crumbs
1	cup chopped onion
1/2	cup chili sauce
3	eggs, beaten
3	tablespoons chopped green pepper
	Salt and pepper to taste
1/2	cup Burgundy
1	cup tomato sauce

Combine beef, veal and pork and mix thoroughly. Add cottage cheese, bread crumbs, onion, chili sauce, eggs and green pepper and season to taste with salt and pepper. Shape into a loaf and place in a roasting pan.

Pour wine over meat loaf and spread tomato sauce on top. Bake at 400 degrees for 30 minutes, basting frequently with pan juices. Reduce heat to 350 degrees and bake 30 minutes more.

8 generous servings

A "French" style meat loaf, uncommon enough for company and delicious hot or cold. Serve with green bean bundles, tied with blanched red pepper strips.

Tenderloin of Beef with Red Wine Sauce

Search the market for particularly attractive fresh garden vegetables, perhaps miniature varieties, to surround this classic dish.

1	whole tenderloin, fat and silver skin removed
1/2	cup clarified butter
3	ounces Cognac
1/4	cup water, wine or beef broth
1	tablespoon butter
Red Wine Sauce	
2	shallots, chopped
1 1/2	tablespoons butter
1/2	cup red wine
1	cup beef stock
1	tablespoon cornstarch, dissolved in 1/4 cup wine, stock or water
1/3	cup tomato sauce
	Salt and pepper to taste
	Dash Maggi

Coat beef with clarified butter. Bake at 350 degrees for 45 minutes. Remove meat from oven, pour Cognac over beef and flame. When flame is out, place tenderloin on serving platter and cover with foil to keep warm.

To make Red Wine Sauce, sauté shallots in butter. Add wine and cook until liquid is reduced by three-fourths. Add beef stock and bring to a boil. Stir in dissolved cornstarch, tomato sauce and seasonings.

To juice in pan, add water, wine or broth and cook over medium heat, scraping brown bits from bottom of pan. Add Red Wine Sauce, simmer and add 1 tablespoon butter. Nap roast with some of the sauce and serve remaining sauce separately.

8 servings

Hot and Spicy Orange Beef Szechwan Style

1½	pounds flank steak, partially frozen
3	tablespoons dry sherry, divided
1	egg white
3½	tablespoons cornstarch, divided
8	ounces bamboo shoots, cut in 1½-2 inch slices
2	tablespoons grated orange zest
2	scallions, including green stems, cut in 1½-2 inch slices
1	tablespoon minced ginger
3	tablespoons water
¼	cup chicken broth
3	tablespoons soy sauce
2	tablespoons sugar
1	teaspoon sesame oil
2	tablespoons peanut oil
½	teaspoon Szechwan chili flakes

Cut meat on the diagonal into strips ⅛-¼ inch thick and 1½-2 inches long.

Combine beef, 1 tablespoon sherry, egg white and 1½ tablespoons cornstarch. In a separate bowl, combine bamboo shoots, orange zest, scallions and ginger. In a third bowl, combine 2 tablespoons cornstarch, water, 2 tablespoons sherry, broth, soy sauce, sugar and sesame oil.

Heat peanut oil in skillet or wok to 350-375 degrees or until oil begins to smoke. Add meat mixture and chili flakes. Cook 3-4 minutes or until lightly browned. Remove meat with slotted spoon and drain on paper towel. Heat skillet again; add vegetable mixture and cook 1-2 minutes. Return meat and stir for 1 minute. Add liquid mixture and cook 1-2 minutes.

4-6 servings

Serve with steamed rice and punctuate the orange flavor by topping with little knots fashioned from orange zest.

Picnic Skewers

reat guests to a sophisticated al resco dining experience by serving his cold marinated kebob.

Marinade for 12 skewers

1	cup vegetable oil
	Juice of 1 lemon
1	clove garlic, crushed

For each skewer

2-3	ounces beef tenderloin, rare and sliced thinly
3	medium to large shrimp, cooked, peeled and deveined
1	large mushroom
1	canned artichoke heart
1	cherry tomato

Combine all the marinade ingredients. Add salt to taste. Divide marinade into thirds. In one third, marinate the beef; in another third, marinate the shrimp; in the remaining third, marinate the mushrooms and artichoke hearts. Set overnight in the refrigerator.

Thread the tenderloin, shrimp, artichoke heart, mushroom and cherry tomato onto a bamboo skewer. Chill. Allow 2 skewers per person.

Serve with rich, creamy *Zucchini and Almond Soup* and conclude with *Summer Fruit in Cassis.*

135

Festive Pork Roast

1	5-pound boneless rolled pork roast
4	teaspoons cornstarch

Marinade

1½	cups dry red wine
⅔	cup brown sugar
½	cup vinegar
½	cup catsup
½	cup water
¼	cup vegetable oil
3	tablespoons soy sauce
4	cloves garlic, minced
2	teaspoons curry powder or to taste
1	teaspoon ground ginger
½	teaspoon freshly ground pepper

Combine ingredients for marinade. Place meat in a plastic bag, cover with marinade, close bag and set in a shallow dish. Marinate in refrigerator 6-8 hours (or overnight), turning occasionally.

Drain meat, reserving 2½ cups marinade. Pat meat dry and place on rack in shallow roasting pan. Roast in 325-degree oven for 2½ hours or until meat thermometer registers 170 degrees. Blend cornstarch into reserved marinade; cook, stirring, until thickened and bubbly. Brush roast frequently with sauce during last 15 minutes of cooking. Heat remaining sauce and pass with meat.

12 servings

Serve this roast with bright green Granny Smith apples that have been sliced, sautéed in butter and sprinkled with cinnamon.

For a cold winter's night menu, prepare *Party Potatoes* and any of the winter vegetables — parsnips, celery root, turnips or carrots. Sauté them in a little butter, then braise in beef stock.

Summer Baked Ham

10-12	pound fully cooked ham with bone
1	cup sliced onion
2	bay leaves
¾	cup brown sugar, divided
4	sprigs parsley
6	whole cloves plus additional cloves for decoration
3	whole black peppercorns
2	cups beer
¼	cup honey

Place ham, fat side up, in shallow roasting pan. Lay onion and bay leaves on ham; sprinkle with ¼ cup brown sugar, parsley, 6 cloves and peppercorns. Pour beer around ham. Cover ham with foil and bake at 325 degrees for 3 hours. Baste every 30 minutes with the beer.

Remove from pan when done. Pour off all fat and drippings. Reserve 2 tablespoons drippings (not fat) and combine with remaining sugar and honey to make a glaze. Return ham to pan; score and insert cloves. Brush with half the honey glaze. Bake 30 minutes at 400 degrees, basting every 10 minutes with remaining glaze. Cool ham 20 minutes before carving.

Pork Tiko Tiko

4	pieces well-trimmed pork tenderloin, 8 ounces each, room temperature
	Salt and pepper to taste
1/2	pound bacon, room temperature

Sauce

2	cups chopped onion
6	tablespoons butter
1/2	cup finely chopped mushrooms
4	tablespoons cornstarch
1³/₄-2	cups chicken broth
1	cup sliced mushrooms
3¹/₂-4	tablespoons lemon juice
6	tablespoons white wine
	Dash Maggi
3-4	dashes cayenne pepper
	Salt to taste

Place a metal skewer through each piece of meat. Sprinkle with salt and pepper and wrap with bacon, overlapping strips and covering completely. Secure with toothpicks, if necessary. Broil 8-10 minutes per side, 2 sides only.

Pour sauce over pork, dust with paprika and serve.

4 servings

To make Sauce, sauté onions in butter over medium heat in deep pan, until clear. Add the finely chopped mushrooms, sprinkle with cornstarch and stir until blended, simmering a few minutes over low heat and stirring occasionally. Add chicken broth and sliced mushrooms, cooking over low heat until thickened. Add lemon juice, wine, Maggi, cayenne and salt. Simmer for 2 minutes. This will be a thick sauce; if necessary, add more broth. (Sauce may be made ahead and reheated before serving.)

Pork tenderloin is an overlooked cut of meat. Serve Pork Tiko Tiko sliced, napped with sauce, and served with curried rice and apricots.

Bavarian Pork Chops

4-6	pork loin chops, 1 inch thick
	Salt and pepper to taste
	Flour
1	cup dry white wine
2	cups whole mushrooms
1/2	cup sour cream

Trim fat from chops and use fat to oil pan. Season chops with salt and pepper; dust with flour. Sear chops and remove excess fat. Add wine and simmer, covered, for 1 hour. Add mushrooms and cook, covered, until tender. Remove meat and mushrooms from pan. Heat liquid to a boil, scraping brown bits from bottom of pan and reducing liquid to half the original volume. Lower heat to warm and stir in sour cream.

4 servings

Experiment with one of the more unusual rices now on the market. Try popcorn rice or pecan-flavored rice with hot curried fruit.

Pork Roast Rosemary

2	tablespoons oil
5-6	pounds boneless pork loin roast
2	cups sherry
2	cups water
1½	tablespoons rosemary or to taste
1	teaspoon salt
¼	teaspoon freshly ground pepper
¼	cup butter
½	cup flour

Heat oil in roasting pan; brown mea on all sides. Add sherry, water and seasonings. Cover and bake at 300 degrees for 4-5 hours or until tende Transfer meat to platter. Strain juices and skim off fat; set aside.

Melt butter in saucepan and blend i flour; cook, stirring constantly, for 3 minutes. Add pan juices slowly, stirring until blended. Add additional sherry or hot water to desired consistency. Serve with *Wil Rice Casserole.*

8-10 servings

Blackened Leg of Lamb with Mint Sauce

	6-pound leg of lamb
3-4	cloves garlic, slivered
⅓	cup vinegar
⅓	cup catsup
⅓	cup Worcestershire sauce
1	cup water
1	teaspoon prepared mustard
1	teaspoon salt
	Dash pepper

Mint Sauce

¾	cup chili sauce
1	cup currant jelly
½	cup butter
2-3	tablespoons bottled mint sauce

Mint Butter

½	cup butter, room temperature
½	cup mint leaves, minced
2	tablespoons lemon juice

With a sharp instrument, such as a ice pick, punch small holes randon in lamb. Insert garlic slivers into holes, leaving tips showing. Combine remaining ingredients ar marinate lamb for at least 6-8 hou Bake uncovered in a 300-degree oven for approximately 40 minutes per pound. Baste every 30 minute If you prefer lamb less done, reduc cooking time. The lamb will have black crusty appearance, but will tender and moist on the inside. Remove garlic slivers; serve lamb with Mint Sauce.

To make Mint Sauce, combine ingredients and heat in double boiler. Serve warm. This sauce keeps indefinitely in the refrigera

6 servings

Fresh mint is the traditional garnish for lamb. Serve this succulent mea dish with *Summer Creole* and, for added flavor, top each slice of lam with a dab of Mint Butter.

For Mint Butter, combine all ingredients. Form into a log and chill thoroughly or freeze.

Grilled Leg of Lamb with Onions

1	4-6 pound leg of lamb, boned and butterflied with as much fat and tendon removed as possible.
6	whole yellow onions, peeled and pricked with fork

Marinade

1	cup peanut oil
2	cups red wine
6	cloves garlic, slivered
2	teaspoons freshly ground pepper
2	teaspoons salt
2	tablespoons lemon juice
3	teaspoons fresh tarragon or 1 teaspoon dried
1/2	teaspoon basil

Combine all marinade ingredients.

Place lamb and onions in a large pan and cover with marinade. Cover and refrigerate at least 6 hours, turning meat and onions often. One hour before serving, wrap onions in heavy-duty aluminum foil and place on grill to cook. They are done when they yield slightly to pressure.

Grill lamb to desired degree of doneness, about 15 minutes on each side, over medium coals. Slice on the diagonal.

6-8 servings

Leg of lamb summer style! Place each slice on a bed of collard or mustard greens and serve with skewered and grilled baby onions, carrots, chunks of corn-on-the-cob and unpeeled zucchini.

Lamb Chops with Cream and Capers

2	shallots, finely chopped
6	tablespoons butter, divided
1	cup peeled, seeded and chopped tomatoes
	Salt and white pepper to taste
1/4	cup flour
1	cup milk
4	lamb chops
4	toast rounds
1	tablespoon capers
	Cayenne pepper for garnish

Sauté shallots in 2 tablespoons butter. Add tomatoes and cook 10 minutes over medium heat. Season with salt and pepper.

In separate pan, prepare white sauce by melting 4 tablespoons butter and stirring in flour, blending well. Do not allow to brown. Gradually add milk, stirring constantly until thickened. Season with salt.

Broil lamb chops 3 inches from heat, 7 minutes per side.

For each serving, spoon some tomato mixture onto a serving plate and cover with a toast round, lamb chop and white sauce. Finish with capers and a dash of cayenne.

4 servings

Prepare *Broccoli and Cherry Tomatoes* as a fresh and colorful complement.

Marinated Lamb Chops

6-8 lamb loin chops, about 1 inch thick, trimmed

Marinade

1 teaspoon dry mustard

1/2 teaspoon salt

1/4 teaspoon paprika

2 cloves garlic, pressed, or 1 tablespoon garlic powder

3 tablespoons vinegar

5 tablespoons best-quality olive oil

Combine ingredients for marinade. Marinate lamb chops for at least 3 hours. Cook over hot fire on grill, basting with marinade. For medium rare lamb, cook approximately 5 minutes on each side.

6-8 servings

Create a springtime menu by serving chops with *Sesame Asparagus* and *Creamy Lemon Rice*. Garnish meat with a sprinkling of chopped fresh mint or a sprig of watercress.

Veal Roast Pommery

1 veal roast, approximately 3 pounds (rolled boned leg or loin)

Herbes de Provence

Salt and cracked pepper to taste

Grated zest and juice of 1 lemon

1/4 cup butter, melted

1 cup white wine

Pommery grain mustard

Herb Crumbs

1 cup fresh bread crumbs

1 teaspoon minced garlic

1/4 cup chopped parsley

6 tablespoons butter, melted

Season roast liberally with Herbes de Provence, salt, pepper, lemon zest and juice. In roasting pan, heat butter and brown veal well on all sides. Roast in 375-degree oven. After 30 minutes, add wine to pan; baste veal frequently until cooked, approximately 45-60 minutes total cooking time. (When done, juices should run pink when a metal skewer is inserted.) Remove from oven and strain off juices.

Combine Herb Crumb ingredients and mix well. Cover veal with mustard and pat Herb Crumbs evenly on surface of the roast. Return roast to the pan and place 450-degree oven to glaze, approximately 10 minutes, or until crust is crisp and golden.

8 servings

Herbes de Provence is a blend of herbs typical of those used in the South of France and includes marjoram, thyme, summer savory, basil, rosemary, sage, fennel and lavender. It is available at specialty food stores.

Veal Scallops with Green Peppercorns

Veal scallops (allow about 1/4 pound per person)

Salt and pepper to taste

1/2 cup flour

3 1/2 tablespoons butter, divided

3 1/2 tablespoons oil, divided

2 cups thinly sliced mushrooms

1 cup dry white wine

1 cup heavy cream

1 1/2 teaspoons Dijon mustard

1 rounded tablespoon green peppercorns, drained

Sprinkle scallops with salt, pepper and flour. Heat 1 1/2 tablespoons each of butter and oil until it stops foaming. Sauté mushrooms until tender. Transfer mushrooms to another dish. Add remaining butter and oil and heat until it stops foaming. Lightly brown scallops, a few at a time, and remove from pan. Add wine, scraping brown bits from bottom of the pan and reducing liquid to about 1/2 cup. Add cream, mustard and peppercorns, stirring constantly until slightly thickened. Return scallops and mushrooms to pan and heat with sauce for about 2 minutes.

4-6 servings

Serve with sautéed leeks, *Missouri Spring Salad with Walnuts, Swiss Braided Bread* and *Fresh Peach Flan.*

As a seasonal variation, substitute 6 tablespoons fresh tarragon (or 2 tablespoons dried) for the mustard and peppercorns when making the sauce.

Lemon Veal with Parmesan

8 large or 12 medium veal scallops, pounded thin

1/4 cup lemon juice

1/2-3/4 cup flour

2 tablespoons grated lemon zest

2 tablespoons grated Parmesan cheese

1 teaspoon freshly ground pepper

1 teaspoon salt

6 tablespoons unsalted butter, preferably clarified

3 tablespoons oil

8-12 lemon slices

2 tablespoons chopped parsley

Lightly flour scallops, shaking off any excess. Dip scallops in lemon juice and then in flour which has been mixed with lemon zest, Parmesan, pepper and salt. In skillet, heat butter and oil until it stops foaming. Sauté scallops quickly over high heat until lightly browned. Add lemon juice, lemon slices and parsley. Transfer scallops to a warm platter and spoon pan juices over veal.

6 servings

Asparagus with hollandaise sauce is an excellent vegetable choice. If veal scallops are not available, substitute boneless chicken breasts.

Medallions of Veal Almondine

1½	cups almonds, toasted and ground
⅔	cup chopped parsley
1½	cups bread crumbs
12	veal scallops, cut from sirloin tip or round, pounded
4	egg whites, beaten with a little water until frothy
½	cup clarified butter
¾	cup grated Parmesan cheese
2-3	tablespoons butter
2-3	tablespoons slivered almonds
1	clove garlic
¼	cup white wine
	Juice of ½ lemon
	Crème Fraîche (optional)
	Soft butter

Combine ground almonds, parsley and bread crumbs. Dip scallops into egg white mixture, then into parsley-almond mixture, coating both sides well. Chill several hours to set coating.

When ready to prepare, melt clarified butter over medium-high heat. Sauté scallops quickly until brown and crisp on each side. About 30 seconds before removing from pan, sprinkle 1 tablespoon Parmesan cheese on each scallop. Remove from pan and keep warm.

In same pan, melt butter and stir to loosen any particles remaining on the bottom. Add slivered almonds and whole garlic clove; sauté until almonds are brown. Add wine and lemon juice, cooking until liquids have been reduced by about half. You may add a little cream or Crème Fraîche, if desired. Remove from heat and add a little soft butter. Remove garlic, pour sauce over scallops and serve immediately.

4-6 servings

Veal Chops with Three Herb Butter

6	veal loin chops, 1½ inches thick
	Flour for dredging
	Salt and pepper to taste
	Clarified butter or oil
	Three Herb Butter
¾	cup unsalted butter, room temperature
	Grated zest of 2 lemons
2	tablespoons finely chopped dill
1	tablespoon each chives, shallots and tarragon
	Salt and pepper to taste

Have butcher make an incision into the side of each chop, creating a pocket. Fill each pocket with about 2 tablespoons Three Herb Butter, using either a spoon or a pastry bag with a ½-inch tip. Close pocket with toothpick. Refrigerate 1 hour to harden butter.

To make Three Herb Butter, combine all ingredients and blend well.

Season chops with salt and pepper and flour lightly. Sauté in clarified butter or oil for 1-2 minutes per side. Place in a 350-degree oven and continue the cooking process for 6-10 minutes.

6 servings

Curry of Veal

1½	pounds boneless veal, cubed
4	cups chicken broth
1	onion, stuck with cloves
3	stems parsley
2	bay leaves
1	teaspoon thyme
¼	cup butter
½	cup coarsely chopped onion
2	apples, peeled and sliced
1	clove garlic, minced
3	tablespoons flour
1½	tablespoons curry powder
1	cup sliced bananas, almost green
1	cup white raisins
	Salt and white pepper to taste
	Juice of ½ lemon
2-4	tablespoons heavy cream

In a large pot, combine veal, broth, onion with cloves, parsley, bay leaves and thyme. Simmer 45 minutes or until veal is tender. Strain, reserving 2 cups veal stock. Melt butter in a heavy saucepan; add chopped onions, apples and garlic; cook 2-3 minutes. Add flour and curry; cook 1 minute. Add 1½-2 cups reserved veal stock. Bring to a boil and cook until thickened. Add bananas, veal, raisins, salt, pepper and lemon juice. Chill. Reheat over low heat, adding heavy cream to moisten.

Can be prepared 2-4 days in advance, if bananas are added at the last reheating.

4-6 servings

Serve from a chafing dish and use the following condiments in separate dishes for an "eight boy curry": toasted almonds, grated coconut, chopped chutney, chopped scallions, peanuts, crumbled bacon, chopped cucumber and chopped hard-cooked eggs.

Lamb may be substituted successfully.

Quesadillas

Quesadillas (kehs-ah-dee-ahs) are a variety of Mexican turnover combining tortillas and melted cheese.

1	teaspoon salt
1	pound ground beef
½	cup finely chopped onion
1	clove garlic, minced
½	teaspoon oregano
8	ounces tomato sauce
½	cup butter or more
12	6-inch flour tortillas
¾	pound Cheddar cheese, grated

Sprinkle salt in skillet and add meat and onion. Sauté over high heat until meat is crumbly. Drain fat. Add garlic, oregano and tomato sauce and simmer, uncovered, 10 minutes or until liquid evaporates.

In another skillet, melt 2 tablespoons butter and place tortilla in skillet. Sprinkle with ½ cup cheese and ½ cup meat mixture. Top with another tortilla, sandwich-style, and cook 1-2 minutes on each side until golden brown. Repeat procedure until all sandwiches are made. You may need to use more butter; do not let butter get too hot.

Surround with shredded lettuce and top with guacamole and sour cream.

"Mizzou" Barbecue Sauce

2 cups catsup

1 cup water

1/4 cup vinegar

1/2 cup brown sugar

1 teaspoon each salt, chili powder and celery seed

1 onion, chopped

1 tablespoon liquid smoke or to taste

1 tablespoon prepared mustard

Several dashes Tabasco sauce

1/4 teaspoon each nutmeg, ginger and allspice

1 clove garlic, minced

1 tablespoon Worcestershire sauce

Combine all ingredients and cook over low heat until onions are clear and flavors combined. Keep refrigerated and reheat as needed

1 1/2 pints

Barbecue sauce should be used on during the final 5-10 minutes of grilling. If applied too soon, the sauce will turn black before the mec is done. Many barbecue experts do not use sauce for basting but merely serve sauce with the meat.

Tarragon Mayonnaise

Keep this versatile mayonnaise on hand to add distinctive flavor to cold beef, pasta salads, chicken salad or cold poached chicken.

1/3 cup plus 1 teaspoon white wine vinegar

2 shallots, finely minced

1/4 cup dried tarragon

1/2 teaspoon salt

Freshly ground pepper

2 egg yolks

1 tablespoon Dijon mustard

1 1/3 cups vegetable oil, divided

Using a non-aluminum saucepan, combine 1/3 cup vinegar, shallots, tarragon, salt and pepper. Cook over medium-high heat until liquid reduced by half, about 5 minutes. Cool slightly.

Combine egg yolks, mustard, 1 teaspoon vinegar and 2 tablespoc oil in a food processor, using steel blade. Blend about 30 seconds or until it begins to thicken. With machine still running, add remain: oil slowly until it thickens to the consistency of mayonnaise. Add tarragon mixture and blend for 5 seconds; scrape sides of bowl and blend 5 more seconds. Taste for seasoning.

1 1/2 cups

To make a sherry mayonnaise, om tarragon and shallots and substitu sherry vinegar . . . an ideal mayonnaise for sandwiches.

Aioli Sauce

3	medium-sized cloves garlic, peeled
1	egg
2	tablespoons white wine vinegar
1	teaspoon salt
1	teaspoon Dijon mustard
1	cup vegetable oil

Mince garlic in food processor, using steel blade. Add remaining ingredients except oil and combine. With machine running, add oil in a thin stream until mixture thickens to the consistency of mayonnaise. Chill.

1 cup

Those who favor garlic will welcome a bit of this mayonnaise on sliced cold beef or with chilled or crisply steamed vegetables, especially artichokes, asparagus, new potatoes or blanched green beans.

Creamy Blue Sauce

3/4	cup dry white wine
1	cup heavy cream
4	ounces blue or Roquefort cheese, crumbled
1/2	cup butter, cut in small pieces
	Dash white pepper

Heat wine in a small saucepan and cook over high heat until liquid is reduced to 1 tablespoon. Add heavy cream and cook over moderate heat until liquid is reduced by half. Add cheese and butter; simmer about 3 minutes. Season with white pepper.

1¼ cups

Enlivens a grilled hamburger. This meat accompaniment also can be used successfully as a dipping sauce for raw vegetables.

Sweet Hot Mustard

1/2	cup plus 1 tablespoon dry mustard
1/2	cup plus 1 tablespoon sugar
1/2	cup cider vinegar
3	eggs
3	tablespoons butter, room temperature

Combine mustard, sugar and vinegar in top of a double boiler. Add eggs, one at a time, and mix well. Cook over hot water until thick. Remove from stove and beat in butter with a wire whisk, stirring until thickened. Pour into sterilized 1-pint jar and refrigerate.

Keeps indefinitely in the refrigerator and also makes a thoughtful gift.

Zucchini and Walnuts

Fabulous with lamb or beef tenderloin.

1/3	cup English walnut pieces
1/4	cup butter
2	small zucchini, coarsely shredded
	Lemon juice
	Salt and pepper to taste

Sauté walnuts in butter until lightly browned. (Be careful not to burn.) Remove nuts. Sauté zucchini briefly — about a minute — in the same pan. Sprinkle with a few drops lemon juice; season. Add walnuts. Toss and serve.

Double the recipe and heap around the periphery of an oval platter lined with tenderloin slices for an elegant buffet presentation.

4 servings

Zucchini in Dill Cream Sauce

2 1/4	pounds unpeeled zucchini, cut into thick strips
1/4	cup finely chopped onion
1/2	cup chicken broth
1	teaspoon salt or to taste
1 1/2	teaspoons chopped fresh dill or 1/2 teaspoon dried
2	tablespoons butter, melted
2	teaspoons sugar
1	teaspoon lemon juice
2	tablespoons flour
1/2	cup sour cream

In saucepan, combine zucchini, onion, broth, salt and dill; bring to boil. Reduce heat and simmer, covered, until zucchini is tender-crisp. Do not drain. Add butter, sugar and lemon juice. Remove from heat. Blend flour into sour cream. Stir about half the hot cooking liquid into sour cream, then return all to saucepan. Cook and stir until thickened and bubbly. Serve immediately.

8 servings

Julienne Zucchini and Carrots

Simply beautiful!

3/4	pound unpeeled zucchini, cut in 1/4-inch julienne strips
3/4	pound carrots, cut in 1/4-inch julienne strips
1/2	cup unsalted butter, melted
	Salt and pepper to taste

Arrange carrots in a vegetable steamer over 1 inch boiling salted water; put zucchini on top of carrots and steam until vegetables are tender-crisp. Transfer to a heated dish, toss with butter and season.

6 servings

For a delicious variation, steam vegetables with 2 tablespoons melted butter, 2 tablespoons dry vermouth and a pinch of thyme! Serve in a red cabbage leaf.

Spaghetti Squash Monterey

Here's a great way to add pizazz to your next dinner of broiled meat.

1	spaghetti squash
1	large onion, chopped
1/4	cup butter
1/2	cup sour cream
	Salt and pepper to taste
2	cups grated Monterey Jack cheese, divided
	Paprika

Cut squash in half lengthwise and remove seeds. Place cut side down in a pot with 2 inches of water; cover and boil 20 minutes. After cooked, remove squash from shell with a fork and reserve these spaghetti-like strands.

Sauté onion in butter until transparent. To the reserved squash, add onion, sour cream, salt, pepper and 1 cup of the cheese. Place in buttered casserole and sprinkle with remaining cheese and paprika. Bake at 325 degrees for 30 minutes.

For an impressive buffet dish, bake and serve this in its own squash shell. Add color by garnishing with slivers of red pepper.

6-8 servings

Turnip Soufflé

1 1/2	pounds turnips, tops removed
1/3	cup butter
1/3	cup flour
1/2	cup heavy cream
1/4	teaspoon each salt and white pepper or to taste
1/4	cup minced onion
4	eggs, separated

Peel and cut turnips into cubes. Cook in one inch of boiling salted water, covered, until tender, about 15-20 minutes. Drain, mash well and set aside. Melt butter in saucepan; gradually add flour, stirring until smooth. Cook 2 minutes. Add cream gradually and cook, stirring constantly, until mixture is smooth and thickened. Add salt, pepper and onion. Cool. Beat egg yolks slightly and add to mixture. Stir in mashed turnips. Beat egg whites until stiff and gently fold into turnip mixture. Pour into greased 2-quart casserole. Bake at 350 degrees for 30-35 minutes or until a knife inserted in middle comes out clean. Serve immediately.

8 servings

The delicate flavor of this soufflé will surprise you and just may change your opinion of turnips forever. A golden-hued fall dish, this goes well with pork and duck.

Spinach and Bamboo Shoots

1/2	cup vegetable oil
1	8-ounce can bamboo shoots, rinsed and drained
1	pound fresh spinach, stemmed
1/2	teaspoon salt or to taste
2	teaspoons sugar

Heat oil in a wok or large heavy skillet over medium-high heat until hot. Add bamboo shoots. Cook, stirring, 30 seconds. Add spinach; cook and stir 1 minute. Add salt and sugar and continue to stir 2 minutes more. Using slotted spoon, place mixture on serving dish. Serve immediately.

6 servings

The contrast of bamboo shoots and bright green spinach makes this decorative in itself.

Snow Peas with Shallots and Basil

Beautiful!

1	pound fresh snow peas, strings removed
2	tablespoons minced shallots
1/4	cup butter
1/4	cup beef bouillon
	Salt and freshly ground pepper to taste
2	tablespoons chopped fresh basil

Steam snow peas 2-3 minutes or until tender-crisp. Sauté shallots in butter. Add bouillon and cook until soft. Add snow peas and heat through over medium-high heat for about 1 minute, tossing well. Season with salt and pepper. Sprinkle with basil and serve.

Snow peas are also elegant when steamed and tossed with clarified butter and freshly grated nutmeg.

4 servings

Summer Creole

1	cup minced green pepper
1/2	cup minced scallions
1/2	cup butter
1	cup fresh corn or thawed frozen corn
1	cup sliced fresh okra, cut crosswise
3	tomatoes, peeled, seeded and chopped
1	teaspoon tomato paste
1/4	teaspoon thyme
	Salt and pepper to taste

Sauté green pepper and scallions in butter for 5 minutes or until scallions are soft. Add corn and okra and cook over medium heat, stirring, for 10 minutes. Add tomatoes, tomato paste and seasonings. Cover and simmer for 20 minutes, stirring occasionally.

Okra puts its best foot forward in this colorful, fresh dish. Goes nicely with *Blackened Leg of Lamb*.

You can serve individual portions of Summer Creole in hollowed red bell pepper halves, topped with a sprig of fresh thyme.

4 servings

Green Beans and Pears

2	pears, peeled and diced
1/4	pound bacon, fried and crumbled
1	tablespoon bacon drippings
1	tablespoon butter
1	tablespoon flour
1/4	cup white wine
1	cup chicken broth
2	pounds fresh green beans, blanched

Sauté pears in bacon drippings and butter until tender. Remove pears. Stir in flour and cook 2 minutes. Add wine and chicken broth and simmer until thickened. Add blanched green beans and cook until tender. Stir in pears and simmer for 1 minute. Serve immediately, topped with crumbled bacon.

Your guests will be intrigued by this interesting marriage of flavors, textures and colors. Serve with grilled chicken or game.

8 servings

Sherried Tomatoes

Here it is — our very favorite vegetable recipe!

	Fresh tomatoes
	For each tomato:
1	tablespoon sherry
1/8	teaspoon dill weed
1/8	teaspoon or 2 twists black pepper
1	tablespoon mayonnaise
1	tablespoon finely grated Cheddar cheese

Remove core from each tomato and slice tomato in half. Place cut side up on a cookie sheet. Pierce each tomato several times with a fork. Sprinkle each half with sherry, dill weed and pepper. Broil for 2-3 minutes. (May be prepared to this point 1 hour before serving.) Top each half with a mixture of mayonnaise and cheese. Broil for 2-3 minutes or until bubbly and slightly browned. Serve immediately.

Sesame Asparagus

2 1/2	pounds fresh asparagus, cut diagonally into bite-sized pieces
1/4	cup butter
2	tablespoons lemon juice
2	tablespoons sesame seeds, lightly toasted
2	teaspoons Oriental sesame oil
	Salt and pepper to taste

Cook asparagus until just tender. Drain and rinse well with cold water; pat dry. (This may be done several hours ahead, storing the asparagus in refrigerator.) Melt butter and stir in lemon juice, sesame seeds, sesame oil, salt and pepper. Add asparagus and toss until coated. Serve hot.

8 servings

A great way to take advantage of early spring's most aristocratic vegetable. Delicious with tenderloin or leg of lamb, it has a definite sesame flavor.

Fabulous Fried Onion Rings

1¹/₂	cups flour
1¹/₂	cups beer
3	large yellow or Bermuda onions, sliced ¹/₄-inch thick and separated into rings
3-4	cups shortening

Sift flour into a large bowl. Gradually stir beer into flour with a wooden spoon. (Beer can be flat or active.) Cover bowl and let mixture "rest" at room temperature for 3 hours.

Coat each onion ring with batter and fry in hot fat until brown and crisp. To keep warm, place in 200-degree oven on heavy brown paper.

The alcohol in the beer breaks down the gluten in the flour, creating a light, delicate batter. There is little greasiness, and the batter does not separate from the onion rings. A popular addition to family suppers and cookouts. Any leftover rings can be reheated the next day for snacks — just pop into a 400-degree oven for 4-6 minutes.

Leeks in Cream

8	leeks, thoroughy washed and cut into 2-inch julienne strips
¹/₄	cup butter
	Nutmeg to taste
	Salt and pepper to taste
1	cup heavy cream
	Freshly grated Parmesan cheese

Sauté leeks in butter until just wilted. Add freshly grated nutmeg, salt, pepper and cream. Cook for about 1 minute. Strain leeks, reserving liquid, and place in a buttered gratin dish. Pour cream mixture back into sauté pan and cook over high heat until it is reduced slightly. Pour cream over leeks and sprinkle with cheese. Place gratin dish into another baking pan which has a small amount of water in it and bake at 350 degrees for 30-35 minutes.

This onion-like garden vegetable takes on new dimensions as an accompaniment to lamb, pork or beef. To make ahead, reduce the baking time by about 5 minutes. Leave gratin dish in its "bath" and reheat at dinner time.

Cauliflower Walnut Casserole

1	medium head cauliflower (2 pounds), broken into florets
1¼	cups sour cream
1	cup grated Cheddar cheese
1	tablespoon flour
2	teaspoons seasoned chicken stock base
1	teaspoon dry mustard
¼	cup coarsely chopped walnuts
¼	cup fine dry bread crumbs
1	tablespoon butter, melted
1	teaspoon dried marjoram leaves, crumbled
¼	teaspoon onion salt

Cook cauliflower in 1 inch salted water until tender; drain and place in a baking dish. Combine sour cream, cheese, flour, stock base and mustard and spoon over cauliflower. Mix walnuts, bread crumbs, butter, marjoram and onion salt. Sprinkle over casserole. Bake at 400 degrees until hot and bubbly, 15 to 20 minutes.

4-6 servings

A beautiful creamed dish with texture. Delicious with brisket. The crumb-nut topping is its own garnish.

Cucumbers in Cream

2	medium cucumbers
1	teaspoon finely chopped onion
¼	teaspoon minced garlic
2	tablespoons butter
½	cup heavy cream
	Salt and white pepper to taste
1	tablespoon lemon juice

Peel cucumbers, slice in half lengthwise and scoop out seeds with spoon. Then, cut into half-inch slices (they resemble half moons). Blanch in boiling salted water for 2-3 minutes; drain. Sauté onion and garlic in butter. Add cucumbers and cream. Simmer gently 15-20 minutes, stirring occasionally. Season. Cream should be reduced and clinging to cucumbers. Add lemon juice just prior to serving.

4 servings

Although fabulous by itself, this dish can also be served in a baked tomato half, artichoke bottom or puff pastry shell. This under-used vegetable makes an excellent accompaniment to broiled salmon or any fish.

Asparagus Souffle

2/3	cups Parmesan cheese, divided
3	tablespoons butter, melted
4	tablespoons flour
1 1/2	cup milk
6	eggs, separated
2	egg whites
1	tablespoon freshly chopped parsley
1	tablespoon freshly chopped chives
1	cup asparagus, cooked and pureed

Butter a 1 1/2 quart souffle dish. Sprinkle inside with 1/3 cup Parmesan cheese. Make a foil co butter it and tie on souffle dish.

Melt butter in heavy saucepan. A flour and cook whisking 2 minute Add milk slowly and stir until thickened. Remove from heat and add yolks, whisking in one at a ti Add seasonings and asparagus. Beat all whites with a pinch of sa until light and stiff but not dry. Fa all ingredients together. Pile gen into dish. Bake at 350 degrees fo 35-40 minutes. Remove collar an serve immediately.

Serves 6-8

Carrots in Orange Sauce

1	pound carrots, peeled and coarsely grated
	Grated zest and juice of 1 navel orange
1/2	cup unsalted butter
	Salt and freshly ground pepper to taste
	Dash of freshly grated nutmeg

Sauté carrots and orange zest in butter over high heat for 2 minute tossing frequently. Add orange ju and cook until liquid is almost completely absorbed, about 2 minutes. Add seasonings and ser

4-6 servings

A lovely, colorful addition to almos any dinner plate, this recipe is particularly special because it is no sweet. Especially delicious with roasted poultry or pork.

Pike County Hominy

Goodbye potatoes . . . hello hominy!

1/4	cup butter
4	tablespoons flour
2	cups half and half
2	teaspoons horseradish
	Salt and white pepper to taste
2	15-ounce cans white hominy, drained
1/3	cup grated Parmesan cheese

Melt butter, stir in flour and cook minutes. Gradually add cream a cook until thickened, about 5 minutes, stirring constantly. Add horseradish, salt and pepper. Ble in hominy and place in a greased 2-quart casserole. Sprinkle with cheese. Bake, covered, at 300 degrees for 1 hour and 20 minute

4-6 servings

Add a little Pike County goodness your next meal of charcoaled mea ham or pork chops.

Parmesan Eggplant Sticks

1/2	cup freshly grated Parmesan cheese
1/4	cup seasoned bread crumbs
1	tablespoon chopped parsley
1/4	teaspoon salt
1/8	teaspoon pepper
2	eggplants, about 1 pound each, peeled and cut in finger slices
1/4	cup flour
2	eggs, slighty beaten
2	tablespoons butter

Combine cheese, bread crumbs, parsley, salt and pepper in a dish. Dust eggplant slices in flour, dip in egg and dredge in crumb mixture. Melt 1 tablespoon butter in each of two jellyroll pans. Tip to coat. Arrange eggplant on pans and bake, uncovered, at 400 degrees for 25 minutes.

6 servings

Next time you serve hamburgers, arrange a platter of these with a batch of *Fabulous Fried Onion Rings.*

Broccoli and Cherry Tomatoes

1	large bunch broccoli
1/4	cup butter
3	tablespoons fresh lemon juice
1/2	teaspoon basil
1/2	pint cherry tomatoes, sliced in half
	Salt and freshly ground pepper to taste

Steam broccoli until tender-crisp. Rinse under cold water, pat dry and cut into small florets. (This may be done early in the day.) Melt butter; add lemon juice and basil. Put broccoli into a skillet over high heat and pour lemon butter over it. Toss for 1 or 2 minutes. Add cherry tomatoes, salt and pepper and toss briefly. Serve immediately.

4-6 servings

New Potatoes with Dill

2	pounds new potatoes
1/3	cup sour cream
2	tablespoons chopped fresh dill
	Salt and pepper to taste

Boil potatoes until tender, approximately 20 minutes. Drain. Cut into quarters or halves, leaving skins on, to make uniform bite-sized pieces. Add sour cream and seasonings and toss gently. Serve hot.

6-8 servings

Make a wreath of dill flowers to surround this tribute to spring.

Roasted Potato Wedges

4 medium-sized baking potatoes, peeled

1/4 cup butter, melted

Salt

Cut potatoes in half lengthwise and then slice each half in thirds down the length, making 3 wedge-shaped pieces. Blanch wedges in rapidly boiling water to cover for 3 minutes. Drain and pat dry.

Grease a baking dish large enough to hold potatoes and place wedges side by side in a single layer. Drizzle melted butter over potatoes and sprinkle liberally with salt. Roast in center of 450-degree oven for 15 minutes, turn potatoes and roast another 15 minutes.

4-6 servings

Country Garden Potatoes

This hearty dish knows no season. A great combination of flavors!

12 medium-sized red potatoes

1/3 cup milk

1 green or red bell pepper, diced, or a combination of both for color

1 onion, diced

1 tablespoon minced fresh parsley

1/2 cup grated sharp Cheddar cheese

1/4 cup butter, melted

Salt and freshly ground pepper to taste

Boil potatoes in jackets until just tender, about 25 minutes. Dice potatoes, leaving skins on, into bite-sized chunks and place in shallow casserole. Moisten with milk. Mix together bell pepper, onion, parsley and cheese and place on top of potatoes. Drizzle with melted butter and season. Bake uncovered at 400 degrees for 30-45 minutes.

Bake in a decorative oven-proof casserole and bring directly to the table. The colors and textures blend well with grilled meats for a summer barbecue or a winter supper.

6-8 servings

Potato Shells

There's a good reason why this tasty, infinitely versatile dish has enjoyed such popularity. Although it could be dubbed "the appetizer of the '80's," don't hesitate to serve it with grilled meats or barbeque as a side dish.

4	large baking potatoes
2	tablespoons vegetable oil
6	drops Tabasco sauce
1/4	cup unsalted butter, melted
	Salt and freshly ground pepper to taste

Rub unpeeled potatoes with oil, prick with a fork and bake at 425 degrees until tender, about 45 minutes. Cut potatoes into quarters lengthwise. With a spoon, remove all but a thin layer of the pulp. Spread quartered shells on an oiled baking sheet and brush with mixture of Tabasco, butter, salt and pepper. Bake 8-10 minutes more until crisp. Serve at room temperature as is or cut into bite-sized pieces.

Variations: Here are just a few; the possibilities are endless.

Arrange in a pinwheel around a bowl of sour cream and chopped onion.

Cut shells into halves instead of quarters and fill with mixture of diced ham, green pepper and onion; fill with chili and top with grated cheese.

Top quarters with crumbled fried bacon and grated Cheddar cheese; reheat to melt cheese.

Party Potatoes

Holiday dinners are a breeze with these easy, do-ahead potatoes.

5	pounds potatoes, peeled
1/2	pint sour cream
1	8-ounce package cream cheese
1/4	teaspoon pepper
1/8	teaspoon garlic salt
1	teaspoon salt or to taste
1/4	teaspoon onion salt
2	tablespoons butter

Cook peeled potatoes in boiling salted water until tender. Drain and mash until smooth. Add sour cream, cream cheese, pepper and salts and beat until light and fluffy. Place potatoes in greased 2-quart casserole and bake at 350 degrees for 30 minutes.

8-10 servings

Swirl potato mixture with the back of a spoon to make a circular or meringue-like pattern. Sprinkle with paprika and run briefly under the broiler. For an autumn touch or your Thanksgiving buffet, heap potatoes into a hollow pumpkin or squash shell.

Note: This dish may be refrigerated for two weeks or frozen.

Basic Egg Pasta

2¼ cups all-purpose flour

3 large eggs, room temperature

1 teaspoon best-quality olive oil

Combine all ingredients in food processor and process with steel blade until dough is smooth and elastic and forms a ball. Remove and cover with a cloth or bowl for 3(minutes. Proceed with kneading, rolling and cutting instructions according to the manufacturer's suggestions for your pasta machine

4 servings

To a certain extent, estimating the amount of pasta to cook is a matter of personal preference. Many people like their pasta lightly sauced while others prefer a larger proportion of sauce. The generally accepted rule is this: Cook twice the amount called for when substituting fresh pasta for dried. We used fresh pasta except where noted in testing these recipes. If you decide to use packaged, you will probably want tc decrease the amount of pasta by one-fourth or one-half according to your personal taste.

Broccoli Pasta

12 ounces fresh broccoli, chopped

3 cups all-purpose flour

2 eggs, room temperature

1 tablespoon best-quality olive oil

½ teaspoon salt

Cook broccoli until tender. Drain well and squeeze in towel until fair dry. In processor, using steel blade process broccoli until almost puréed. Add flour, eggs, oil and sc and continue processing until doug is smooth and elastic and forms a ball. Remove and cover with a clot or bowl and let rest for 30 minutes. Proceed with kneading, rolling and cutting instructions according to th manufacturer's suggestions for you pasta machine.

4 servings

A green pasta with a very delicate flavor.

Orange Pasta

1¹⁄₂	cups all-purpose flour
2	small eggs
2	tablespoons strained fresh orange juice
1	tablespoon minced orange peel
1¹⁄₂	teaspoons best-quality olive oil
¹⁄₄	teaspoon salt

Combine all ingredients in a food processor, using steel blade. Process until dough forms a smooth elastic ball. Remove and cover with a cloth or bowl. Let rest for 30 minutes. Proceed with kneading, rolling and cutting instructions according to the manufacturer's suggestions for your pasta machine.

4 servings

Just a hint of citrus flavor . . . nice with pork chops or ham.

Spinach Pasta

¹⁄₂	pound spinach, cleaned and stemmed
2	large eggs, room temperature
1	teaspoon best-quality olive oil
2	cups all-purpose flour

Cook spinach in 2 tablespoons water, covered, over medium heat, stirring occasionally, until tender. Drain well in colander. When cool, squeeze in a towel until dry as possible. Combine spinach, eggs, olive oil and flour in a food processor and, using steel blade, process until dough is smooth and elastic and forms a ball. Remove and cover with a cloth or bowl and let rest for 30 minutes. Proceed with kneading, rolling and cutting instructions according to the manufacturer's suggestions for your pasta machine.

4 servings

Packaged spinach pasta is readily available in stores everywhere, but we think homemade is best.

Tomato Pasta

2¹⁄₂	cups all-purpose flour
3	eggs, room temperature
4	tablespoons tomato paste
1	tablespoon best-quality olive oil
¹⁄₂	teaspoon salt

Combine all ingredients in a food processor. Process with steel blade until dough is smooth and elastic and forms a ball. Remove and cover with a cloth or bowl. Let rest 20 minutes. Proceed with kneading, rolling and cutting instructions according to the manufacturer's suggestions for your pasta machine.

4 servings

Four Cheese Sauce for Pasta

1/4	cup butter
1/4	cup grated fontina cheese
1/4	cup grated mozzarella cheese
1/4	cup grated Gruyère cheese
1/2	cup grated Parmesan cheese
1	cup heavy cream
	Salt and white pepper to taste

Melt butter in heavy pan or double boiler and add the fontina, mozzarella and Gruyère cheeses. Cook over low heat until just melted. Do not overcook or cheese will become stringy. Add Parmesan cheese. Slowly add cream, whisking until sauce is smooth. Season to taste.

The essence of Northern Italian cooking is captured in this rich blend of premium cheeses. Homemade pasta is essential. Serve as a first course.

Cavatelli with Broccoli

2	cups coarsely chopped fresh broccoli
1	teaspoon salt
5	ounces small shell pasta (cavatelli)
1/4	pound mushrooms, sliced
1/2	cup butter, divided
1	cup grated Parmesan cheese

Cook broccoli in boiling, salted water until tender-crisp. Remove broccoli and set aside. Add enough water to broccoli water to make 2 quarts. Bring to a rolling boil, add pasta shells and cook until tender but al dente (slighty resistant to the bite). Drain pasta and combine with broccoli.

Sauté mushrooms in 3 tablespoons butter until tender and add to pasta and broccoli. Add remaining butter and grated cheese. Toss lightly with 2 forks. Serve immediately.

6 servings

Creamy Ricotta Pasta

Unusual pasta shapes . . . bow ties or wagon wheels . . . are possibilities with this recipe. Add chopped prosciutto, sautéed in butter, or fried and crumbled bacon for a heartier dish.

2	eggs, lightly beaten
8	ounces ricotta cheese
1	cup heavy cream
12-16	ounces fresh pasta
1/4	cup butter
1/2	cup grated Parmesan cheese
	Salt and freshly ground pepper to taste

Combine eggs, ricotta cheese and cream in bowl. Cook pasta until tender but al dente (slightly resistant to the bite). Drain. Melt butter in pot in which pasta was cooked. Return pasta to pot and mix with butter. Add cream mixture to pasta, stirring well over low heat until cream is mostly absorbed by ricotta and pasta. Stir in Parmesan cheese, salt and ground pepper. Serve immediately. Pass extra Parmesan cheese.

4-6 servings

Fettuccine with Shrimp

1	clove garlic, minced
1/2	cup sliced scallions
1/4	cup butter
2	pounds medium shrimp, shelled and deveined
1/2	teaspoon oregano
	Pinch rosemary
1	pound fresh fettuccine
4	eggs, beaten
	Grated Parmesan cheese

Sauté garlic and scallions in butter until scallions are transparent. Add shrimp, oregano and rosemary. Sauté about 3 minutes.

Cook fettuccine until tender; drain and transfer to a large warm serving bowl. Add shrimp mixture and toss gently. (Reserve several shrimp for garnish, if desired.) Add beaten eggs and toss again. Sprinkle with Parmesan cheese. Serve immediately.

4 servings

Fettuccine with Zucchini and Mushrooms

3/4	pound mushrooms, thinly sliced
1	clove garlic, minced (optional)
3/4	cup butter, divided
2	pounds unpeeled zucchini, cut in small julienne strips
1	cup heavy cream
1	pound fresh fettuccine, cooked and drained
1	cup grated Parmesan cheese
1/2	cup chopped parsley
	Freshly ground black pepper

In a large skillet, sauté mushrooms and garlic, if desired, in 1/4 cup butter over moderately high heat for 2 minutes. Add zucchini (reserving a few strips for garnish), cream and remaining butter. Bring to a boil, lower heat and simmer for 3 minutes. Add hot pasta to skillet with Parmesan cheese, parsley and pepper. Toss well to combine and serve immediately. Pass additional cheese.

4 servings as a main course
8 servings as a side dish

For a substantial entrée, add 1 cup finely minced ham or prosciutto, sautéed briefly.

Fettuccine with Pine Nuts

1/2	cup pine nuts
3/4	cup unsalted butter, divided
1	pound fresh fettuccine, cooked until tender and drained
1/2	cup grated Parmesan cheese
	Freshly ground pepper to taste (optional)

Gently brown pine nuts in skillet in 1 tablespoon butter and set aside. Add remaining butter to pasta. Toss well. Add pine nuts and grated cheese and toss again. Grind black pepper over top, if desired.

6-8 servings

Choose a tomato or broccoli-flavored fettuccine for a change. Easy and delicious.

Tomato Fettuccine with Asparagus

1 cup heavy cream

2 egg yolks, lightly beaten

1/2 cup grated Parmesan cheese

3 tablespoons butter, room temperature

Salt and pepper to taste

1/2 pound pencil-thin asparagus tips, blanched or steamed 1 minute

1 pound *Tomato Fettuccine*, cooked until tender but al dente (slighty resistant to the bite) and drained

Heat cream in saucepan; add egg yolks and beat with whisk. Add remaining ingredients and toss with warm fettuccine. Serve immediately.

4 servings

Blanching or steaming green vegetables brings out the dramatic color. Don't limit yourself to asparagus . . . try broccoli florets or snow peas for an equally delicious combination.

Spinach Pasta with Artichokes

1/2 cup butter

1 clove garlic, minced

1 1/2 pounds mushrooms, sliced

1/2 pound Canadian bacon, cut in julienne slices

2 tablespoons flour

1/3 cup dry white wine

1 cup artichoke hearts, quartered

1/4 cup sour cream

2 cups heavy cream

1/3 cup grated Parmesan cheese

12 ounces *Spinach Pasta*, cooked until tender but al dente (slightly resistant to the bite) and drained

Melt butter in a large skillet with garlic. Sauté mushrooms until light brown. Remove from pan and reserve. In same pan, sauté bacon until lightly browned. Add flour and wine. Cook for five minutes or until sauce is reduced. Add reserved mushroom mixture, artichoke hearts, sour cream, heavy cream and Parmesan cheese. Heat thoroughly. Do not boil. Toss sauce with hot pasta until blended.

8 servings as a first course
4 servings as a main course

This splendid first course is also an exceptional companion to veal, pork and fish.

pinach Pasta ith Mushrooms

2	cloves garlic, minced
1½	cups thinly sliced mushrooms
½	teaspoon freshly ground pepper
6	tablespoons butter
6	ounces *Spinach Pasta*, cooked until tender but al dente (slightly resistant to the bite) and drained
¼	cup heavy cream
	Salt to taste
½	cup grated Parmesan cheese

In a large skillet, sauté garlic and mushrooms with pepper in butter over high heat. Add pasta and toss. Pour in cream and toss again. Season with salt and cook for 2 minutes. Add cheese and toss until blended. Serve immediately on warm plates.

3-4 servings as a side dish

Top each serving with a few sliced mushrooms, slivered red pepper or shredded spinach for added interest.

hrimp with egetables and asta

1½	cups butter, divided
2½	pounds jumbo shrimp, shelled and deveined
1½	cups chopped onion
1	cup chopped scallions
½	pound mushrooms, sliced
1½	cups chicken broth
½	cup white wine
5	ounces small shell pasta (cavatelli)
2	cups canned Italian plum tomatoes with juice
	Salt and pepper to taste
½	cup grated Parmesan cheese

Melt ¾ cup butter in a 3-quart saucepan. Add shrimp and sauté over medium-high heat until shrimp turn pink. Stir in onions, scallions and mushrooms; sauté until vegetables are tender, about 6 minutes. Transfer shrimp mixture to a separate dish and keep warm. Add chicken broth and wine to the pan and bring to a boil. Stir in pasta shells and cook for 15 minutes, stirring occasionally. Stir in tomatoes, salt and pepper. Simmer for 5 minutes. (The recipe can be prepared ahead to this point.) Return shrimp to pan and heat. Check seasonings. Add ¾ cup butter, which has been melted, and grated Parmesan cheese.

6-8 servings

More like a soup, this should be served in shallow pasta bowls. Pass more Parmesan cheese.

Pasta with Red and Green Vegetables

1	pound asparagus, sliced on the diagonal
1	cup unpeeled zucchini, sliced 1/4-inch thick
2	cups broccoli florets
2	cups snow peas
1	cup unpeeled yellow summer squash, sliced 1/4-inch thick
2	cloves garlic, minced
2	tablespoons vegetable oil
4	large tomatoes, peeled, seeded and chopped, or 2 cans Italian plum tomatoes, drained and chopped
1/4	cup chopped parsley
1	tablespoon chopped basil
	Salt and pepper to taste
1 1/2	cups finely chopped smoked ham or shredded prosciutto
3/4	cup butter, divided
1/2	pound mushrooms, whole or quartered if large
1	pound fresh pasta, either linguine or fettuccine
1 1/2	cups heavy cream
2/3	cup grated Parmesan cheese
	Salt and pepper to taste
1/3	cup pine nuts, toasted at 350 degrees for 10 minutes

Cook the asparagus, zucchini, broccoli, snow peas and summer squash (each separately) in boiling salted water until tender-crisp. Do not overcook. It is important that the vegetables remain crisp. Set aside.

Sauté garlic in oil briefly and add tomatoes. Cook until tomatoes have made a sauce but are not mushy. Add parsley, basil, salt and pepper. Reserve the sauce.

Sauté ham briefly in a small amount of butter. Set aside. Sauté mushrooms in 1/4 cup butter. Add the reserved vegetables and simmer until vegetables are hot. Do not allow vegetables to overcook.

Cook the pasta until tender but al dente (slighty resistant to the bite) and drain. Add 1/2 cup melted butter, cream, Parmesan cheese, reserved ham, salt and pepper; mix gently.

To serve, put the pasta and ham mixture in the center of a platter. Surround with the vegetables and top vegetables with the tomato sauce. Sprinkle with toasted pine nuts.

8-10 servings

A sensational pasta dish in Italian flag colors, certain to please all vegetable fans.

Spaghetti Sauce

1/2	cup chopped onion
2	cloves garlic, minced
1/2	cup chopped celery
1/4	cup best-quality olive oil
2	20-ounce cans undrained Italian plum tomatoes, chopped
2	12-ounce cans tomato paste
1	tablespoon salt
2	teaspoons sugar
1	tablespoon chopped fresh oregano or 1 teaspoon dried
1/4	teaspoon pepper
1/2	cup chopped parsley
1/2	cup grated Parmesan or Romano cheese
2	cups mushrooms, sliced and sauteéd
1 1/2	pounds Italian sausage, cooked, drained and seasoned
1/2	pound ground beef, cooked, drained and seasoned

Sauté onion, garlic and celery in oil. Add tomatoes, tomato paste, salt, sugar, oregano, pepper, parsley and cheese. (Add water or white wine if sauce is too thick.) Cover and simmer 1 hour. Add mushrooms and meat and simmer 30 minutes.

8-10 servings

We tested many basic spaghetti sauces and liked this one best. Some cooks prefer to reduce the acidity of the tomatoes by adding 3/4 teaspoon baking soda to the sauce during the last 10 minutes of cooking.

Fettuccine Alfredo

8	ounces fresh fettuccine
1/4	cup butter
1/3	cup grated Gruyère cheese
1/3	cup grated Parmesan cheese
1/2	cup heavy cream
1/2	teaspoon salt
	Freshly ground black pepper

Cook fettuccine until tender but al dente (slightly resistant to the bite) and drain. Return pasta to pan over medium heat. Add remaining ingredients. Toss lightly with 2 forks to blend. Serve immediately in a warm serving bowl.

4 servings

This classic dish will not be as good if you skimp on quality ingredients. By all means, use fresh pasta and top quality cheeses.

Pasta Pesto

1	pound spiral spaghetti (fusilli)
1/2	cup Pesto Sauce
	Salt and pepper to taste
1/2	sweet red pepper, slivered
1	cup broccoli florets, steamed
1	cup sliced zucchini, steamed

Pesto Sauce

1/2	cup pine nuts
4	cloves garlic, peeled
1	teaspoon kosher salt
1/2	teaspoon freshly ground pepper
3-4	cups fresh basil leaves
1/4	pound Parmesan cheese, grated
1/4	pound pecorino or Romano cheese, grated
1/2-2	cups best-quality olive oil

Cook pasta until tender but al dente (slightly resistant to the bite) and drain. While still hot, stir in Pesto Sauce. Add remaining ingredients and serve immediately.

To make Pesto Sauce, chop nuts, garlic, salt and pepper until very fine. Put in bowl, add cheese and, drop by drop, add olive oil, mixing well until smooth and creamy.

Processor method: Place pine nuts, garlic, salt, pepper, basil and cheeses in food processor with 1/2 cup olive oil and, using steel blade, process until smooth. Add remaining oil in a slow stream and process until smooth and creamy.

4 servings

Herbs are easy to grow. You can start a small kitchen garden and enjoy its bounty year around.

Spaghetti Carbonara

2	eggs, slightly beaten
2/3	cup grated Parmesan cheese
1/4	cup milk
1	tablespoon chopped fresh basil or 1 teaspoon dried
1/2	clove garlic, chopped
2	tablespoons butter
6	ounces fresh spaghetti, cooked until tender but al dente (slightly resistant to the bite)
4	strips lean bacon, fried crisp and crumbled

Combine eggs, cheese, milk and basil. Sauté garlic in butter and add the egg mixture and cooked spaghetti. Stir over low heat until sauce coats the spaghetti. Sprinkle with bacon. Serve immediately.

4 servings

Look to your herb garden for a garnishing sprig of basil, dill, Italian parsley or tarragon.

Italian Stir-Fry

2 large tomatoes, peeled

1/2 pound fresh broccoli

1 cup slivered almonds

2 tablespoons peanut oil

1 clove garlic, minced

1 small zucchini, thinly sliced or in julienne strips

1/4 pound mushrooms, thinly sliced

1/4 pound lean ham, slivered

1/4 cup sliced scallion tops

1 tablespoon fresh thyme or 1 teaspoon dried

1 tablespoon fresh basil or 1 teaspoon dried

1/4 cup minced parsley

3 tablespoons water

1 tablespoon fresh oregano or 1 teaspoon dried

1 teaspoon sugar

1 teaspoon salt

1/2 cup water chestnuts, sliced (optional)

1 cup frozen peas, thawed

1 pound fresh linguine, cooked, drained and tossed with 1 tablespoon oil

1 cup grated Parmesan cheese

Cut tomatoes in half. Remove seeds and cut into narrow strips. Pat dry. Trim broccoli, breaking florets into small pieces and slicing stems. In large skillet or wok, sauté almonds in a small amount of peanut oil. Remove from skillet. Add garlic and more oil and swirl around until browned. Discard garlic. Increase heat. When oil sizzles, add broccoli stems, zucchini and mushrooms. Stir-fry 2 minutes. Add ham, broccoli florets, scallion tops, thyme, basil, parsley, water, oregano, sugar, salt and water chestnuts, if desired. Cover and cook for about 1 minute. Remove cover and stir-fry until tender-crisp (about 2-3 minutes). Stir in tomatoes, peas, reserved almonds and pasta. Continue cooking for 2 minutes. Remove from heat and add cheese. Toss well and serve.

6-8 servings

Do all the slicing and chopping ahead of time, then invite your guests into the kitchen to watch the last minute stir-frying.

Lasagne Verde

This dish is created by layering:

1	pound *Spinach Pasta*, cut in lasagna strips
	Meat Sauce
3/4	cup grated Parmesan cheese
	Cream Sauce

Meat Sauce

2	onions, finely chopped
1/2	cup finely chopped celery
2	small carrots, finely chopped
1/4	cup butter
2	teaspoons salt
1/2	teaspoon pepper
1	teaspoon oregano
1	pound ground round or chuck, browned and drained
1	pound ground loin of pork, browned and drained
1/2	cup dry white wine
6	tablespoons tomato sauce

Cream Sauce

1/2	cup butter
1/2	cup flour
1	teaspoon salt
1/4	teaspoon white pepper
1	quart milk, heated
1	cup heavy cream
1	cup grated Swiss cheese

Cook pasta in large pot of boiling salted water until tender but al dente (slightly resistant to the bite). Drain and rinse thoroughly.

To make Meat Sauce, sauté onions, celery and carrots in butter. Cook 10 minutes. Sprinkle with salt, pepper and oregano. Add meat, wine and tomato sauce. Simmer 15 minutes, stirring frequently.

To make Cream Sauce, melt butter and stir in flour, salt and pepper. Cook 2-3 minutes. Add hot milk. Cook, stirring, until smooth and thick. On low heat, stir in cream. Add grated cheese and stir until melted.

To assemble: In a buttered 9x13-in baking dish, place a layer of spinach pasta. Top with one-third of the meat sauce and sprinkle with 2 tablespoons Parmesan cheese. Follow with a layer of spinach pasta, one-third of the cream sauce and 2 tablespoons more Parmesan cheese. Repeat these layers twice more, ending with cream sauce and grated cheese. Bake at 350 degrees 20-30 minutes or until completely heated through. Let rest 15 minutes before serving.

8-10 servings

An outstanding entrée in the finest Italian tradition.

Spaghetti Pie

1 cup ricotta cheese or sour cream

6 ounces mozzarella cheese, shredded

"Crust"

6 ounces thin spaghetti (vermicelli), cooked and drained

1/2 clove garlic, minced

1/4 cup butter

1/2 cup grated Parmesan cheese

1 large egg, beaten

1 tablespoon fresh basil or 1 teaspoon dried

Filling

1/2 pound ground beef

3/4 pound Italian sausage

1/2 cup chopped onion

1 15-ounce can tomato sauce

1 6-ounce can tomato paste

1 teaspoon sugar

1 teaspoon dried basil

1 teaspoon dried oregano

1/4 cup white wine

To make crust, combine vermicelli with other "crust" ingredients. Chop mixture with a knife and press mixture into a 10-inch pie plate.

To make Filling, cook ground beef, Italian sausage and onion together. Drain fat. Stir in remaining ingredients. Heat thoroughly.

To assemble pie, spread ricotta cheese or sour cream on "crust." Top with filling and cover with mozzarella cheese. Bake at 350 degrees for 30 minutes or until golden brown.

6-8 servings

Spaghetti Pie is the solution to many menu dilemmas. Its rich Italian flavor has universal appeal. Prepare two at a time and freeze one. Just for fun, try making bird's nest size individual pies, using 5-inch tart pans.

Jumbo Cheese-Stuffed Shells

1 pound jumbo pasta shells (conchiglie)

1 cup grated Parmesan cheese

Cheese Filling

2 pounds ricotta cheese

6 ounces prosciutto, finely minced

1 cup grated mozzarella cheese

1/4 cup finely chopped fresh parsley

2 eggs, beaten

Salt and white pepper to taste

Besciamella Sauce

1/4 cup butter

4 tablespoons flour

2 1/2 cups half and half

6 tablespoons grated Parmesan cheese

Nutmeg to taste

Salt and pepper to taste

Tomato Sauce

3 tablespoons best-quality olive oil

1 small onion, finely chopped

1 clove garlic, minced

2 pounds fresh tomatoes, peeled, seeded and finely chopped, or 2 16-ounce cans Italian plum tomatoes, drained and finely chopped

5 large basil leaves

Salt and freshly ground pepper to taste

Prepare pasta according to package directions, reducing cooking time by about 1 1/2 minutes. Drain and plunge into cold water for a moment to stop the cooking process. Drain again and place shells on an oiled tray. Fill shells with Cheese Filling, using a pastry bag or spoon.

To make Cheese Filling, mix all ingredients together.

Prepare Besciamella Sauce by melting butter in a heavy saucepan. Stir in flour with a wire whisk and cook for 2-3 minutes. Remove from heat and stir in cream and cheese. Return to heat and stir until thickened. Add seasonings to taste. Keep warm.

Prepare Tomato Sauce by heating the oil in a heavy pan and sautéing onion until transparent. Add garlic and sauté another 2-3 minutes. Add remaining ingredients and bring to a boil. Lower heat and simmer very gently for about 15 minutes.

Prepare a 9x13-inch baking dish by putting a thin layer of besciamella sauce on the bottom. Place filled shells close together on top of sauce. Cover with more besciamella sauce and then spoon tomato sauce over the top. Sprinkle with Parmesan cheese. Bake for 20 minutes at 350 degrees. Cover during baking if it begins to look dry. Serve very hot.

12 servings as a first course
8 servings as an entrée

This is superb as an entrée, but even better as a first course, garnished with fresh basil. It may be made ahead and refrigerated, but be sure to add 15 minutes to the baking time it is cold. May also be frozen.

Florentine Stuffed Shells

12	ounces jumbo pasta shells (conchiglie)
1/2	pound Italian sausage
32	ounces favorite spaghetti sauce
2	packages frozen chopped spinach, thawed and squeezed dry
2	eggs, beaten
1	pound ricotta cheese
1/2	pound mozzarella cheese, shredded
1	teaspoon minced onion or onion salt
1/2	clove garlic, minced
1/8	teaspoon nutmeg
1/2	cup grated Parmesan cheese

Cook the shells until tender but al dente (slightly resistant to the bite). Drain, rinse with cold water and set aside. Brown sausage. Drain fat and add spaghetti sauce. Cover and simmer 15 minutes.

Combine spinach, eggs, cheeses, onion, garlic and nutmeg. Mix until blended. Pour about 1/2 cup spaghetti sauce mixture in the bottom of a 3-quart flat baking dish. Stuff each of the cooked shells with 2 rounded teaspoons of spinach-cheese filling.

Arrange shells in a single layer in baking dish. Pour remaining sauce over shells. Top with Parmesan cheese. Bake at 350 degrees for 30 minutes.

12 servings as a first course
8 servings as a main course

Devotees of lasagne will find this a satisfying substitute. Serve 3-5 shells per person and pass additional Parmesan cheese. "Florentine" signifies spinach, so emphasize this by garnishing with fresh spinach leaves.

Cold Chinese Noodles with Sesame Sauce

...otic side dish for an informal buffet.

1/4	pound Chinese egg noodles*
2	tablespoons soy sauce
2	tablespoons sesame seed paste*
1/8	teaspoon Chinese hot oil*
1	teaspoon sesame oil
1	tablespoon rice vinegar*
1	teaspoon sugar
1/2	teaspoon minced garlic
1	teaspoon chopped scallions
1	tablespoon vegetable oil
	Dash of salt

Cook noodles according to package directions and place in ice water to cool. Drain thoroughly. Combine all remaining ingredients and pour over drained noodles. Toss and serve immediately or refrigerate until ready to use.

4 servings

This rice substitute would be pretty served on a crinkled Chinese cabbage leaf or on a bed of bok choy. For additional texture, add 1 1/2 tablespoons toasted sesame seeds. Garnish with sliced scallions, sliced cucumbers and carrot curls.

*Available at Oriental grocery stores

Whole Wheat Pizza Dough

Discard your old notions about pizza. No longer solely a college dormitory staple, pizza is showing up on elegant tables everywhere. Tiny 6-inch appetizer pizzas are especially popular. Today's pizzas are usually made with very thin, crispy crusts and often omit tomato sauce altogether.

1	envelope dry yeast
3/4	cup lukewarm water, divided
1	cup all-purpose flour
3/4	cup whole wheat flour
3/4	teaspoon salt
2	tablespoons olive oil

Dissolve yeast in 1/4 cup lukewarm water. In a large mixing bowl, combine all-purpose flour, whole wheat flour and salt. Stir in 1/2 cup lukewarm water, olive oil and the yeast mixture. Combine until it forms a rough dough, then knead on a floured surface for 10 minutes until it is smooth and satiny. Put dough in an oiled bowl, turning to coat. Let it rise, covered, in a warm place for one hour or until doubled in bulk. Or, let dough rise in the bowl, covered, in the refrigerator overnight. Punch dough down.

Makes dough for three 8-inch or one 12-inch pizzas.

Here are some newer combinations.

Five Cheese Pizza: Parmesan, mozzarella, Romano, Monterey Jack and feta cheeses

Greek Pizza: feta cheese, Greek olives, tiny ground lamb balls, cherry tomatoes, fresh sage

Wild Mushroom Pizza: oyster, enoki and shitake mushrooms; mozzarella cheese

Red Pepper Pizza: roasted red pepper, Italian sausage, cheese, tomato sauce

Gardener's Choice Pizza

	Whole Wheat Pizza Dough
3/4	pound mozzarella cheese, shredded
3/4	cup sliced green pepper, sautéed to tender-crisp
3/4	cup sliced mushrooms, sautéed
6	artichoke hearts, quartered
1	small zucchini, sliced
4	tomato slices, halved
1/4	cup sliced almonds

Prepare *Whole Wheat Pizza Dough,* roll out and line bottom and sides of a 12-inch deep-dish pizza pan. Sprinkle one-third of the cheese over the bottom. Cover with green pepper, mushrooms, artichoke hearts and zucchini, reserving a few of each for the top. Add remaining cheese and top with reserved vegetables. Arrange tomato halves on top, allowing one per slice. Scatter almonds and chopped parsley over all. Bake at 425 degrees for 15-20 minutes. Cool 2 minutes before cutting.

Tomato Pizza Sauce

2	large tomatoes, quartered, seeded and drained, or 2 20-ounce cans Italian plum tomatoes, seeded and well drained
1	clove garlic, chopped
2	teaspoons dried red pepper flakes
1	cup tomato sauce
1/4	cup tomato paste
	Pinch of salt
	Freshly ground black pepper to taste
1	teaspoon sugar
1 1/2	teaspoons fresh oregano or 1/2 teaspoon dried
1 1/2	teaspoons fresh basil or 1/2 teaspoon dried

Place tomatoes in food processor and chop coarsely. Add remaining ingredients and mix. If sauce is made in advance and liquid separates, mix well before using. Do not drain off liquids.

Makes 2 cups

Eggplant, Mushroom and Tomato Pizza

1/3	cup chopped onion
1	large clove garlic, mashed
3	tablespoons best-quality olive oil, divided
1	eggplant (about 1 pound), baked at 375 degrees for 1 hour and cooled; pulp chopped
	Salt and pepper to taste
1/4	pound mushrooms, sliced
	Whole Wheat Pizza Dough
1 1/3	cups grated mozzarella cheese, divided
2/3	cup *Tomato Pizza Sauce*
	Oregano to taste

In a small skillet, sauté onion and garlic in 1 tablespoon olive oil for 5 minutes over low heat until vegetables are softened. Stir mixture into chopped eggplant and season to taste.

In the skillet, sauté mushrooms in 2 tablespoons olive oil over medium heat, stirring, for 5 minutes. Remove from heat.

Line bottom and sides of a 12-inch pizza pan with *Whole Wheat Pizza Dough*. Spread dough evenly with 2/3 cup cheese, then with tomato sauce. Spread eggplant mixture over tomato sauce and layer with mushrooms, the remaining 2/3 cup cheese and the oregano. Bake on the lowest shelf of oven at 500 degrees for 15-20 minutes or until crust is golden.

Nutty Brown Rice

2-3	tablespoons chopped shallots
2	cloves garlic, minced
2½	tablespoons butter
1	cup brown rice
1¾	cups beef broth
⅓	cup dry vermouth
¼	cup toasted slivered almonds
	Chopped fresh parsley

Sauté shallots and garlic in butter. Add brown rice and stir until it is caramel color. Add broth and vermouth, which have been heated to a boil. Cover and simmer over low heat for 30-45 minutes or until liquid is absorbed. Stir in almonds and parsley.

To hold rice, place in a glass bowl and cover with a damp cloth. Warm in a 150-degree oven with the door ajar. Will keep 45-60 minutes.

4-6 servings

Almond Rice

⅓	cup chopped onion
⅓	cup slivered almonds
2	tablespoons butter
1	cup long-grain white rice
¼	cup dry sherry
1¾	cups chicken broth
¼	teaspoon salt

In a skillet, sauté onion and almonds in butter briefly. Add rice. Sauté until rice is slightly opaque, but not brown. Add sherry, chicken broth and salt. Cover and simmer 20 to 30 minutes or until liquid is absorbed. Fluff rice with fork.

4-6 servings

Lemon Pilaf with Currants and Almonds

1	tablespoon minced onion
2	tablespoons unsalted butter, divided
1	cup long-grain white rice
1½	cups well-seasoned chicken broth
¼	cup lemon juice
	Zest of 1 lemon, finely minced
2	tablespoons currants
¼	cup lightly toasted slivered almonds

In a 2-quart saucepan, sauté onion in 1 tablespoon butter until onion is clear. Add rice and stir until all grains are coated with butter. Stir in broth, lemon juice, zest and currants; bring to a boil. Lower heat and cover. Simmer over low heat for about 20 minutes or until all liquid is absorbed. Lightly stir in remaining butter and almonds. Serve immediately.

4-6 servings

A savory, crunchy accompaniment to fish and lamb . . . a natural with *Curry of Veal.*

Creamy Lemon Rice

1/2	cup unsalted butter
2	cups long-grain white rice
	Grated zest of 2 lemons
3	cups chicken broth, boiling
1	teaspoon salt
2	tablespoons fresh lemon juice
1	cup heavy cream
	Freshly ground pepper

Melt butter in a saucepan on low heat. Stir in rice and zest. Cook over medium heat, stirring, until rice is opaque, about 5 minutes. Add broth and salt; cover and simmer 20 minutes or until liquid is absorbed. Stir in lemon juice. Slowly stir cream into rice. Continue to stir on low heat until cream is absorbed, about 5 minutes. Season to taste.

8-10 servings

The cream can be eliminated, and the rice is still delicious.

Saffron Rice

1/2	cup butter, divided
1	cup long-grain white rice
1/2	cup finely chopped onion
3/4	cup dry white wine
1	cup chicken broth
1/8	teaspoon saffron
2	ounces Parmesan cheese, grated

Melt 1/4 cup butter in heavy pan or skillet. Add rice and onion and cook over low heat until onion is clear. Add wine and broth. Bring to a boil. Add saffron, reduce heat and simmer, covered, for 30 minutes or until liquid is absorbed. When rice is tender, stir in remaining butter and Parmesan cheese.

4-6 servings

This rice is particularly good with fish.

Wild Rice Casserole

1	pound medium-hot sausage
1	pound mushrooms, sliced
1	cup chopped onions
1/4	cup flour
1/2	cup heavy cream
2 1/2	cups chicken broth
2	cups cooked wild rice (about 2/3 cup raw rice)
1	teaspoon salt
	Freshly ground pepper to taste
	Pinch of oregano, thyme and marjoram
	Chopped macadamia nuts

Sauté sausage until cooked through. Remove meat, drain and break into small pieces. Using some of the sausage fat, sauté mushrooms and onions. Return sausage to pan.

Mix flour and cream together until smooth. Add to meat mixture, along with chicken broth, and cook until thickened. Add rice and seasonings. Pour into buttered casserole, top with nuts and bake 30 minutes at 350 degrees. This may be refrigerated or frozen until ready to bake.

8-10 servings

A hollowed acorn squash makes an attractive container for Wild Rice Casserole. Serve with *Pork Roast Rosemary* for autumn entertaining.

Parmesan Sticks

1 cup freshly grated Parmesan cheese

1 cup crushed corn flakes

1 loaf very thin white bread, frozen

1 1/8 cups melted butter

Mix Parmesan cheese and corn flakes together. Keep bread in freezer and remove 2 slices at a time. Trim crusts; dip in melted butter, then in cheese mixture. Place on cookie sheet and cut into 5 stick-like pieces. Bake at 350 degrees for 7-8 minutes or until golden brown.

Arrange as in photograph or serve these cheese sticks upright in a low goblet or pewter mug. Team them with soups, salads or cocktails. Experiment with different shapes. They will keep for several weeks in the refrigerator or may be frozen.

Mini Bagels

1 1/2 cups flour

2 packages dry yeast

1 1/2 cups warm water

4 tablespoons sugar, divided

1 tablespoon salt

2 3/4-3 cups flour

1 egg yolk beaten with 1 tablespoon water

Poppy or sesame seeds (optional)

In a large bowl, mix the flour and dry yeast. Combine warm water, 3 tablespoons sugar and salt; add to the flour mixture. Beat with electric mixer at low speed for 30 seconds, scraping sides of bowl. Beat 3 minutes at high speed. By hand, or with dough hook, stir in flour to make a moderately stiff dough. Knead on lightly floured surface or with dough hook until smooth, 8-10 minutes. Cover dough and let rest for 15 minutes.

Divide dough in thirds and cut each third into 16 parts. Shape each part into a small ball and poke thumb through the center. Let stand 20 minutes.

Add 1 tablespoon sugar to 1 gallon water and bring to a boil. Drop Mini Bagels into the water, 6 at a time, and boil for 1 minute, turning once. Drain on a rack immediately. Brush with beaten egg yolk. Leave plain or top with poppy or sesame seeds. Bake in 400 degree oven for 20 minutes or until brown. Cool.

Bagels freeze well.

48 bagels

Tiny Orange Muffins

Tuck a tiny sprig of mock orange in a basket of muffins.

½	cup butter
1	cup sugar
2	eggs
1	teaspoon baking soda
1	cup buttermilk
2	cups all-purpose flour
	Grated zest of 2 oranges
½	cup golden raisins
	Juice of 2 oranges
1	cup brown sugar

In large bowl, cream butter and sugar. Add eggs and beat until well mixed. Dissolve baking soda in buttermilk and add to mixture alternately with flour. Add orange zest and raisins. Fill well-buttered tiny tart tins three-fourths full and bake at 400 degrees for 15 minutes. Remove immediately and keep warm on serving plate.

In a small bowl, mix orange juice and brown sugar and pour 1 teaspoon of the mixture over each warm muffin. Top with additional grated zest, if desired. Serve immediately.

4-5 dozen

Muffins are best when mixed quickly with a light hand, popped into the oven and served immediately. Wonderful with your morning cup of coffee, luncheon or brunch.

Old-Fashioned Honey Wheat Bread

1½	cups water
1	cup creamy cottage cheese (process in food processor until smooth)
½	cup honey
¼	cup butter
5½-6	cups all-purpose flour
1	cup whole wheat flour
2	tablespoons sugar
1	tablespoon salt
2	packages dry yeast
1	egg

Heat water, cottage cheese, honey and butter until very warm. Combine warm liquid with 2 cups of the all-purpose flour and remaining ingredients in a large bowl. Beat. Stir in remaining flour to make a stiff dough. Knead on floured board until smooth and elastic.

Place in greased bowl and cover. Let rise in warm place until doubled in size, about 45-60 minutes. Punch dough down, divide in half, shape and place in two greased 5 x 9-inch pans. Cover and let rise until doubled in size, about 45-50 minutes. Bake at 350 degrees for 40-50 minutes.

2 loaves

An excellent sandwich bread, it is nutritious enough for your family and popular enough for a bread, wine and soup party . . . one of the easiest ways to entertain.

Scones

Scones, the celebrated sweeter cousin of the American biscuit, are considered an indispensable feature of the English tea table and are always served with a bowl of clotted cream (so thick it resembles butter) and good berry jam.

Cheese Scones

2	cups all-purpose flour
1	tablespoon baking powder
1	teaspoon salt
1/4	cup butter
1	cup grated sharp Cheddar cheese
1	cup milk
1	egg beaten with 1 teaspoon water

Blueberry Scones

2	cups all-purpose flour
1/4	cup sugar
1	tablespoon baking powder
1	teaspoon salt
1/4	teaspoon cardamom
1/3	cup shortening
1/2	cup fresh blueberries (Dates, chopped peaches, apples or raisins may be substituted for blueberries and orange zest.)
1	teaspoon grated orange zest
1/2	cup milk
1/2	teaspoon vanilla
1	egg
1	egg yolk
1	egg white, beaten
	Sugar

To make Cheese Scones, combine flour, baking powder and salt in food processor. Add butter in pieces and process briefly until mixture resembles coarse meal. Place mixture in bowl; add cheese and mix. Make a well in center and pour in milk. Very quickly, as lightly as possible, mix the dough together with a fork.

Turn onto a floured surface and pat out to 1/2-inch thickness. Using a 2-inch round cutter, cut 8-9 scones. Gather dough, pat out and cut remaining scones. Place on ungreased cookie sheets. Brush beaten egg over top of scones. Bake at 475 degrees for 15 minutes. Serve warm with butter or make an open-faced sandwich by splitting scone and topping with a tomato slice, salt and pepper.

14 scones

To make Blueberry Scones, combine flour, sugar, baking powder, salt and cardamom. Cut in shortening until mixture resembles coarse crumbs. Add berries and orange zest. Blend milk, vanilla, egg and egg yolk; add all at once to the flour mixture, folding just until moistened.

Turn onto floured board and knead lightly. (Do not crush berries.) Pat into 9-inch circle. Place on cookie sheet and cut into 8-10 pie-shaped wedges. Brush with egg white and sprinkle with sugar. Bake at 425 degrees for 12 minutes or until golden.

8-10 scones

Serve with Honey-Orange Butter.

For successful baking powder doughs, remember to use a light hand when adding liquid. The lighter the hand, the lighter the results. These doughs are best if baked immediately.

Raised Waffles

1	package dry yeast
1/4	cup warm water
2	tablespoons sugar
1/2	teaspoon salt
1 3/4	cups milk, warmed
1/4	cup butter, room temperature
3	eggs, beaten
1	teaspoon vanilla
2	cups all-purpose flour

Three-Berry Sauce

1	pint raspberries
2	cups canned black currants in syrup
2	pints strawberries, sliced
3	tablespoons sugar
2	tablespoons cornstarch, dissolved in 2 tablespoons cold water
2	tablespoons Grand Marnier

Blackberry Sauce

1-1/2	pounds blackberries (if frozen, thawed)
1/3	cup Chambord, brandy or framboise
1	teaspoon lemon juice
1/4	cup confectioners sugar or to taste

Dissolve yeast in warm water. Add sugar and salt. In a large bowl, pour warm milk over butter and stir to melt. Add eggs and mix well. Add yeast mixture and vanilla. Beat in flour. (This can be done in mixer.) Place in an airtight container at least twice the size of the dough and cover with a tight lid. Refrigerate overnight or until ready to use. Note: **Dough will rise in the container before it is completely cool; therefore, stir dough down several times during the cooling process.**

To make waffles, bake in preheated Belgian or regular wafle iron. Serve with a sprinkling of confectioners sugar and Three-Berry Sauce or Blackberry Sauce.

Note: **For lighter waffles, separate eggs and beat whites until stiff; fold whites into batter as final step.**

5-6 servings

To make Three-Berry Sauce, combine raspberries, currants and half the strawberries in a medium saucepan. Cook, covered, over medium heat until fruit is soft and syrupy, about 15 minutes. Press through a fine mesh sieve. Return to saucepan; add sugar and dissolved cornstarch. Cook, stirring constantly, until it thickens and bubbles for 2 minutes. Stir in remaining strawberries and Grand Marnier.

To make Blackberry Sauce, begin by reserving a few whole berries for garnish. Combine ingredients in food processor and purée. Strain through a sieve, if desired. Serve warm or chilled.

John Wornall House Herb Butters

. . . from the gardeners who maintain the authentic herb garden at the restored 1858 brick farmhouse in Kansas City.

Summer Savory Herb Butter

1/2	cup butter, room temperature
2	tablespoons mayonnaise
1	teaspoon summer savory
1/4	teaspoon thyme
1	shallot, chopped
	Pepper to taste

Garlic-Cheese Herb Butter

1/2	cup butter, room temperature
2	cloves garlic, crushed
1/4	cup grated Parmesan cheese
1/4	teaspoon marjoram
1/4	teaspoon oregano

Parsley Herb Butter

1/2	cup butter, room temperature
1	clove garlic, crushed
2	tablespoons chopped fresh parsley
1	teaspoon lemon juice
1/4	teaspoon basil
1/4	teaspoon oregano
	Pepper to taste

Blend butter and herbs and let mellow overnight to bring out the flavors.

For a special gift, include one of these herb butters with a loaf of homemade bread. Pack in a decorative mold or ramekin, wrap in bright tissue, tie with raffia and attach a sprig of herbs.

Jayhawk Jam

The Jayhawk, a mythical bird and symbol of the University of Kansas, lends its red and blue colors to this delectable jam.

4	cups fresh raspberries
2	cups fresh blueberries
7	cups sugar
1/3	cup fresh lemon juice
6	ounces liquid pectin

Combine berries in large pot and crush lightly. Add sugar and lemon juice and blend well. Place over high heat and bring to a rapid boil, stirring constantly for 1 minute. Remove from heat. Stir in pectin, blending well. Skim foam, if necessary. Ladle jam into jars, leaving 1/2 inch at top. Seal with new, scalded, very hot lids. Store jam in cool dry place.

5 pints

Fruit Butters

Cranberry Butter

1	pound cranberries, room temperature
1	pound confectioners sugar, sifted
3/4	pound butter, room temperature
1/4	cup orange juice or 2 1/2 tablespoons lemon juice

Honey-Orange Butter

1	cup butter, room temperature
1/2	cup honey
6	tablespoons orange juice
1	tablespoon grated orange zest

Raspberry Butter

1	10-ounce package frozen raspberries, room temperature
1	cup butter, room temperature
2	cups powdered sugar

Strawberry Butter

1/2	cup butter, room temperature
1/3	cup strawberry jam
1/2	teaspoon lemon juice
1/2	teaspoon confectioners sugar

To make Cranberry Butter, place berries in food processor. Add remaining ingredients and spin.

To make Honey-Orange Butter, combine and blend well.

To make Raspberry Butter, cream butter and sugar. Add berries.

To make Strawberry Butter, combine all ingredients for spread.

Keep one or more flavors of Fruit Butter on hand as a spread for tea breads, pancakes, waffles, French toast, brioche, croissants or muffins. Press softened butter into pretty and unusual shapes, using heart-shaped molds, individual candy molds, ramekins or decorative jars.

English Muffins Melba Style

English muffins
Butter

Chill English muffins in refrigerator or freezer. Slice them as thinly as possible. Spread one side with butter and bake slowly in a 250-degree oven until they are crisp.

Freeze a quantity of these to have ready to serve with soups and salads. This method works equally well with bagels.

Beignets with Raspberry Sauce

Offer these light French crullers while they are piping hot.

1/2	cup butter
1	cup water
1	cup plus 2 tablespoons flour
1/4	teaspoon salt
2	teaspoons sugar
1	tablespoon dark rum
4	eggs
	Oil for frying

Raspberry Sauce

1	10-ounce package frozen red raspberries, thawed
2	tablespoons currant jelly
1/4	teaspoon lemon juice
	Dash salt
1	tablespoon framboise or kirsch
1	tablespoon cornstarch dissolved in 2 tablespoons water

Heat butter and water to a rolling boil. Add flour, salt and sugar all at once. Add rum. Stir over medium heat until mixture forms a ball and leaves a film on bottom of pan. Cook 2 minutes. Put in food processor and, using steel blade, add eggs, one at a time, mixing well after each addition.

Heat oil to 375 degrees in deep pan. Beignets can be tricky; make sure oil is correct temperature. Fry heaping teaspoonsful of dough until puffed and golden. Remove with slotted spoon and drain on paper towels. Sprinkle with confectioners sugar and serve warm with Raspberry Sauce. May be reheated at 350 degrees for 3-4 minutes.

To make Raspberry Sauce, heat berries. Add jelly, lemon juice, salt and liqueur. Bring to a boil; strain. Return to pan and thicken with cornstarch mixture.

18-24

Baked Apple Doughnuts

3	cups all-purpose flour
3 1/2	teaspoons baking powder
1	cup sugar
1	teaspoon salt
1	teaspoon nutmeg
1	cup shortening
2	eggs, beaten
1/2	cup milk
1	cup grated tart apples
1/2	cup chopped nuts
1/2	cup butter, melted
	Cinnamon and sugar mixture for coating

Sift together flour, baking powder, sugar, salt and nutmeg. Cut in shortening until mixture is fine. Add eggs, milk, apples and nuts to dry ingredients. Mix thoroughly. Fill well-greased tiny muffin pans almost two-thirds full. Bake at 350 degrees for 20-25 minutes or until golden brown. Roll in melted butter and then in cinnamon-sugar mixture. Reheat at 250 degrees.

6 dozen

Sugar-dusted with a hint of apple, these muffins resemble doughnut holes. Keep them on hand and have some packed in tins to send home with your guests. Be ready to share this uncomplicated recipe.

Chocolate Coffee Cake with Coffee Icing

½ cup packed dark brown sugar

½ cup raisins

½ cup chopped walnuts

2 tablespoons cocoa

1 tablespoon cinnamon

2 teaspoons instant coffee powder

¾ cup unsalted butter, room temperature

1½ cups sugar

2 teaspoons vanilla

3 eggs

3 cups all-purpose flour

1½ teaspoons baking powder

1½ teaspoons baking soda

½ teaspoon salt

2 cups plain yogurt

Chopped walnuts and raisins for garnish

Coffee Icing

1 teaspoon instant coffee powder

1 tablespoon hot water

6 tablespoons unsalted butter, room temperature

4 ounces cream cheese, room temperature

½ cup plus 2 tablespoons sifted confectioners sugar

½ teaspoon vanilla

½ teaspoon orange juice

Pinch of salt

Combine brown sugar, raisins, walnuts, cocoa, cinnamon and instant coffee in bowl. Set aside.

Cream butter in large bowl and gradually beat in sugar until mixture is light and fluffy. Stir in vanilla. Add eggs, one at a time, beating well after each addition.

Sift flour, baking powder, soda and salt together twice. Stir flour mixture, ⅓ cup at a time, into butter mixture, alternating with the yogurt. Beat just until well mixed. Do not overmix. (Batter will be thick.)

Grease and flour a 10-inch tube or bundt pan. Spoon in one-fourth of the batter. Sprinkle with one-third of the raisin-walnut mixture. Repeat layering twice, ending with batter. Bake 1 hour at 350 degrees or until tester comes out clean. Cool on rack. Unmold coffee cake and set on serving plate. Frost sides and top with Coffee Icing. Sprinkle with raisins and walnuts and refrigerate until ready to serve.

12-16 servings

To make Coffee Icing, mix coffee with water until completely dissolved. Cool. Cream butter and cream cheese until light. Gradually beat in sugar. Beat in vanilla, orange juice, salt and coffee mixture. Whip until doubled in volume, about 4 minutes.

Dazzle your guests with this "show stopper" coffee cake. Rich enough for dessert, it makes an ideal brunch cake. Serve it with hot, specially flavored coffee.

Almond-Glazed Poppy Seed Bread

3	cups all-purpose flour
1 1/2	teaspoons salt
1 1/2	teaspoons baking powder
3	eggs
1 1/2	cups milk
1/2	cup butter, room temperature
1/2	cup oil
2 1/4	cups sugar
1 1/2	tablespoons poppy seeds
1 1/2	teaspoons vanilla
1 1/2	teaspoons almond extract
1 1/2	teaspoons butter flavoring

Almond Glaze

1/2	teaspoon almond extract
1/2	teaspoon vanilla
1/4	cup orange juice
3/4	cup sugar

Combine all ingredients and beat with a mixer 2 minutes. Pour into 2 large or 5 small greased loaf pans. Bake large loaves at 350 degrees for 1 hour and smaller loaves for about 25 minutes or until brown. Cool 10 minutes and remove from pans. Spoon glaze generously over tops and sides. Cool completely. Wrap in foil to store or freeze.

To make Almond Glaze, mix ingredients together until sugar is dissolved.

2 large loaves
5 small loaves

This sweet bread can be made richer by adding 1 1/2 teaspoons butter flavoring to the batter and 1/2 teaspoon to the glaze.

Polynesian Nut Bread

Studded with cherries and nuts, this quick bread is sure to garner praise at a morning coffee or afternoon tea

1/2	cup shortening
1/2	cup butter
2	cups sugar
4	eggs, slightly beaten
6	very ripe bananas
3	cups all-purpose flour
2	teaspoons baking soda
1/2	teaspoon salt
1	cup chopped pecans
2/3	cup raisins
2/3	cup maraschino cherries, halved and dried on paper towels

Cream together shortening, butter and sugar. Add beaten eggs and bananas in chunks. Beat until bananas are broken and disappear into mixture. Sift together flour, soda and salt; stir in banana mixture. Blend in nuts and fruits. Pour into 2 large or 4 small greased and floured loaf pans. Bake at 350 degrees for 1 hour. Let stand 10 minutes, then turn out on wire rack to cool.

2 large loaves
4 small loaves

This nut bread is especially good served with a spread made by combining 8 ounces cream cheese and 8 ounces drained crushed pineapple.

Lemon Tea Bread

Wonderful on summer afternoons served with Strawberries Devonshire and minted iced tea.

6	tablespoons butter, room temperature
1	cup sugar
1	tablespoon lemon extract
2	eggs, room temperature
1 1/2	cups all-purpose flour
1/4	teaspoon salt
1 1/2	teaspoons baking powder
1/2	cup milk
	Grated zest of 1 lemon

Topping

1/2	cup super-fine sugar
3	tablespoons lemon juice

In a large bowl, cream butter and sugar. Add lemon extract and eggs, one at a time, beating well after each addition. Sift together flour, salt and baking powder. Stir 1/2 cup flour mixture at a time into butter and egg mixture, alternating with milk and lemon zest. Stir dough thoroughly, but only until blended. Pour into a well-greased 5 x 9-inch loaf pan or 3 small loaf pans. Bake at 325 degrees for 45 minutes for large loaf, 25-30 minutes for smaller loaves.

Combine super-fine sugar and lemon juice for topping. Remove loaf from oven and spoon topping over top. Return to oven for 10 minutes or until tester comes out clean and dry. Remove from oven and let cool for 10 minutes. Remove from pan and cool on wire rack.

Orange Bread Grand Marnier

2/3	cup milk
1	tablespoon vinegar
1/2	cup butter, room temperature
1	cup sugar
2	eggs, beaten
2	cups all-purpose flour
1	teaspoon salt
1	teaspoon baking soda
3	tablespoons grated orange zest
1	teaspoon vanilla
1/4	teaspoon almond extract
1	cup chopped raisins (optional)

Glaze

1/2	cup fresh orange juice
1/4	cup Grand Marnier

Combine milk and vinegar and set aside for 5 minutes. Cream butter, sugar and eggs until light and fluffy, about 5 minutes. Sift flour, salt and soda together. Add flour mixture, alternately with milk, to creamed mixture. Beat in zest, vanilla and almond extract and raisins, if desired. Pour into a greased 5 x 9-inch pan or three 5 x 3-inch pans. Bake at 350 degrees for 1 hour for large pan and about 25 minutes for smaller pans. Do not overbake.

Mix glaze ingredients together. Pierce hot bread all over with fork or toothpick and spoon glaze over bread. Let cool in pan.

This bread merits special treatment. Wrap in clear cellophane, tie with ribbons and give to your closest friends. Serve at room temperature; spread with flavored whipped cream cheese or *Cranberry Butter*. You can substitute Triple Sec or Cointreau for the Grand Marnier.

Austrian Coffee Crescents

An old family recipe, it is another holiday edible you will want to present to friends. Add a pound of freshly ground, fine fragrant coffee.

Dough

1	cup milk, scalded
1	cup butter
1	tablespoon sugar
1	teaspoon salt
1	package dry yeast
4	cups all-purpose flour
3	egg yolks, beaten

Filling

3	egg whites
2	teaspoons cinnamon
3/4	cup brown sugar
1	cup chopped nuts
1	cup flaked coconut
1	cup chopped dates or raisins

Additional Ingredient

1	recipe *Almond Glaze*

Pour scalded milk over butter, sugar and salt; stir until butter is melted. Cool to lukewarm. Dissolve yeast in lukewarm milk mixture. Add flour and beat thoroughly. Add egg yolks and mix well. Cover and refrigerate overnight.

To make Filling, beat egg whites until stiff. Combine remaining ingredients and fold into egg whites.

To assemble, divide dough into 2 sections. Roll each section into a very thin circle. Spread with filling. Roll dough over filling and place on greased baking sheet in a crescent shape. Let rise 2 hours. Bake at 375 degrees for 15-20 minutes or until tester comes out clean and crust is golden brown. Frost with *Almond Glaze* and sprinkle with additional nuts or coconut.

2 crescents

Old World Peasant Bread

A rustic bread with a tantalizing aroma. Serve it hot out of the oven.

2	cups lukewarm water
1	package dry yeast
1	tablespoon sugar
2	teaspoons salt
5	cups all-purpose flour
1	tablespoon cornmeal
	Melted butter

Combine water, yeast, sugar and salt. Stir in flour. Place dough in a large buttered bowl and cover with a damp cloth. Let rise in a warm place until doubled in bulk, about 4 minutes. Sprinkle cornmeal on greased baking sheet or French bread pan.

Flour hands and divide dough into 2 or 3 parts, shaping each into an oblong loaf. Do not knead. (For easier shaping, hold dough up and let it dangle until it forms an oblong loaf shape.) Place loaves on prepared baking sheet. Let rise another 45 minutes or until almost doubled. Brush top with melted butter and bake 10 minutes at 425 degrees. Reduce temperature to 375 degrees and bake 20 minutes more. While hot, brush with butter.

Glazed Egg Buns

*am and egg rolls are not old hat
en you make your own buns, and
s quick-mix yeast bread makes it
sy.*

1/4 cup butter

1 cup milk

1/2 cup sugar

1 teaspoon salt

1/4 teaspoon mace

2 envelopes dry yeast

1/4 cup warm water

4-4 1/2 cups all-purpose flour

4 egg yolks, beaten

Glaze

1 egg white

1 tablespoon water

1 teaspoon sugar

Combine butter, milk, sugar, salt and mace. Heat until butter melts and milk is scalded. Cool to lukewarm. Dissolve yeast in warm water; add to cooled mixture. Stir in 2 cups flour to make a smooth batter. Add beaten egg yolks. Stir in remaining flour. Do not knead. Put in a large oiled bowl, turning to coat the top. Cover with damp cloth and let rise until doubled in size, about 1 1/2-2 hours.

Punch down. Place on a lightly floured board and knead lightly 8-10 times. Shape into a ball; cover and let stand 15 minutes. Pinch or cut off dough according to size bun desired. Shape each piece into a ball with fingers. Place on a greased baking sheet and flatten. Let rise 20 minutes. Bake at 400 degrees for 10 minutes. Mix glaze ingredients together and beat until slightly foamy. Brush buns with glaze; bake 3 minutes more.

20 buns

wiss Braided read

*e of our favorites . . . fancy
ough for your most sophisticated
ests.*

1 package dry yeast

1 1/2 cups warmed milk

1/2 cup sugar

1 1/2 teaspoons salt

1/4 cup vegetable oil

4 1/2 cups all-purpose flour

Sprinkle yeast on warmed milk and add sugar and salt. Let yeast proof 5 minutes. Add oil and half the flour; beat until smooth and well blended. Add remaining flour. Knead until smooth and elastic, adding more flour if necessary. Turn into greased bowl and cover with waxed paper. Let rise in warm place until doubled in bulk, about 1 hour.

Divide dough in half. Cut each half into 6 pieces. Roll each piece into a smooth rope. Make 2 braids, using three ropes for each braid. Place one braid on top of the other; tuck in ends. Repeat procedure for second loaf. Place on a greased cookie sheet or in 2 loaf pans. Let rise again until doubled in size. Bake at 350 degrees for 30 minutes. Cool on rack.

2 loaves

Fondue Bread

Warm, melted cheese gives this middle European bread its distinctiveness.

3 1/2 teaspoons sugar

1 teaspoon salt

2 packages dry yeast

4 cups flour, divided

1/2 cup butter, melted

1 cup milk

2 eggs (reserve 1 egg white)

1 1/2-2 pounds Muenster cheese, shredded

2 teaspoons sliced almonds for garnish

Combine sugar, salt, yeast and 1 cup flour in large bowl. Over low heat, warm butter and milk. Gradually beat liquid into the dry ingredients, just until mixed; then, beat 2 minutes. Beat in 1 cup flour and then add enough additional flour to make a soft dough. Knead on lightly floured board until smooth and elastic, about 10 minutes, adding more flour if necessary. Shape into ball. Cover with bowl or towel and allow to rest 15 minutes.

In a large bowl, combine eggs (minus reserved egg white) with cheese. Set aside.

Roll dough into a rectangle about 6 x 24 inches. Place cheese down center of dough and fold dough over cheese, making a rope. Pinch to seal. Coil, seam-side down, in a greased 9-inch round cake pan, overlapping ends slightly. Cover with a towel. Rest in warm place 10 minutes. Brush with beaten egg white. Garnish with almonds. Bake at 375 degrees for 1 hour or until golden. Remove from pan immediately. Let stand 15 minutes before cutting. Cut into wedges to serve. To reheat, wrap in foil and place in a 350 degree oven for 30 minutes.

Pita Toast

3 pita loaves

6 tablespoons unsalted butter, room temperature

1 tablespoon minced parsley

2 teaspoons finely chopped fresh chives

1 1/2 teaspoons lemon juice

1 small clove garlic, minced

Salt and freshly ground pepper

Halve each pita loaf crosswise and separate into two pieces each. Cream butter, parsley, chives, lemon juice, garlic, salt and pepper together and let stand at least one hour. Spread inside of the bread with the butter mixture. Bake on a cookie sheet at 450 degrees for 5 minutes or until lightly brown and crisp.

12 servings

These are wonderful with soups or salads. Try adding fresh dill, if available.

Maple Oatmeal Bread

An all-American bread that makes mouth-watering toast. Serve as a winter's night accompaniment to hearty soups and stews.

1	envelope dry yeast
1/4	teaspoon sugar
2/3	cup warm water
2 1/2	cups all-purpose flour
1/2	cup whole wheat flour
1/3	cup oatmeal
1/3	cup maple syrup
1/4	cup instant nonfat dry milk
2	tablespoons unsalted butter, room temperature
1	teaspoon salt

Combine yeast and sugar with warm water in a small bowl and let stand about 10 minutes.

In food processor, using steel blade, combine remaining ingredients and process about 10 seconds, stopping machine once to scrape down sides of bowl. With machine running, pour yeast mixture through feed tube and blend until dough forms a ball, about 40 seconds. If dough is too wet, add more flour, 1 tablespoon at a time, until no longer sticky. Transfer to oiled bowl, turning to coat all surfaces. Cover and let stand in warm place until doubled in volume, about 1 hour.

Transfer dough to lightly floured surface and roll into rectangle. Roll up lengthwise; pinch ends and seam tightly. Place loaf, seam-side down, in oiled 5 x 9-inch loaf pan sprinkled with oatmeal. Fold ends under if necessary to fit pan. Cover with damp cloth and let stand until doubled in volume, about 45 minutes. Bake in center of oven at 375 degrees or until bread is golden brown and sounds hollow when tapped on bottom, about 35-45 minutes. Remove from pan and cool on wire rack before slicing.

Hearty Cornbread

1	cup stone-ground cornmeal
1	cup whole wheat flour
1/3	cup sugar
2 1/2	teaspoons baking powder
1/4	teaspoon salt
1	cup buttermilk
3/4	pound bacon, fried and coarsely crumbled
6	tablespoons unsalted butter, melted
1	egg, slightly beaten

Combine dry ingredients in a mixing bowl. Stir in buttermilk, bacon, butter and egg; mix until just blended. (Do not overmix.) Pour batter into a 9-inch square greased baking pan. Bake on middle rack of 400-degree oven for 25 minutes.

Bacon and whole wheat flour give this dark cornbread its unique flavor. Batter can also be baked in muffin tins. Either way, it is a "must" with *White Chili.*

Sugar Cookie Cutouts

1 1/2 cups sifted confectioners sugar

1 cup unsalted butter, room temperature

1 large egg

1 teaspoon vanilla

1/2 teaspoon almond extract

2 1/2 cups sifted all-purpose flour

1 teaspoon baking soda

1 teaspoon cream of tartar

Powdered Sugar Icing

2 cups confectioners sugar, sifted

1/2 teaspoon almond extract

1/3 cup milk

Food coloring

Beat sugar and butter until well blended. Add egg, vanilla and almond extract; beat until light and fluffy. Combine dry ingredients and add to batter, stirring to blend.

Divide dough into two balls. Roll each ball between waxed paper to flatten; refrigerate at least 3 hours or overnight.

Roll dough on lightly floured surface to about 1/8-inch thickness. Dip cookie cutters into flour; cut out shapes. Place cookies on lightly greased cookie sheets and bake at 375 degrees for 7-8 minutes.

To make Powdered Sugar Icing, combine sugar, almond extract and enough milk (about 1/3 cup) to make frosting the consistency of thin glue. Pour icing into bowls large enough for dipping cookies and add food coloring.

To decorate, dip topside of cookie into icing. Remove quickly and let icing drip. Smooth edge with knife if necessary.

Pour additional colored frosting into sterilized hair tinting bottles and gently squeeze frosting onto cookie in designs of your choice.

The stylized look of the cows, rabbits, anemones and hearts in our photograph is achieved by letting the dipped cookies dry before decorating.

The less definitive lines of the fish and plaid hearts are created by decorating while the dipped cookies are still wet, causing the colors to "bleed." Use a toothpick to swirl colors even more.

Orange Bavarian Cream

Decidedly delicate but worth the care.

1³/₄	cups milk
4	egg yolks
¹/₂	cup sugar
¹/₈	teaspoon salt
1	envelope unflavored gelatin
¹/₄	cup cold fresh orange juice
2	tablespoons Cointreau
1	cup heavy cream, whipped

Heat milk in a heavy saucepan. Beat egg yolks, sugar and salt until fluffy. Add to milk and stir with a wire whisk until custard coats spoon. Soften gelatin in orange juice and add to hot custard. Add Cointreau. Cool. Fold cream into mixture. (Reserve ¹/₂ cup of mixture for decorating, if desired.) Pour rest of mixture into a 5-cup mold and chill at least 4 hours or overnight.

4-6 servings

Unmold and circle base of mousse with a pool of *Raspberry Sauce.* Fill a pastry tube with the reserved ¹/₂ cup mixture and pipe triangles or swirls on top of the sauce. Place a knot of orange zest on top of each triangle. Garnish the top of the mold with a raspberry and sprig of mint.

Lemon Mousse

4	eggs, separated
1¹/₂	cups sugar
1	tablespoon unflavored gelatin, softened in ¹/₄ cup cold water
1	teaspoon cornstarch
	Juice of 3 lemons, divided
	Grated zest of 3 lemons
¹/₄	cup Grand Marnier, divided
1¹/₂	cups heavy cream
3	tablespoons confectioners sugar

Beat egg yolks; add sugar and beat well. Set aside. Place gelatin mixture in double boiler over hot water and stir until it is dissolved. Combine cornstarch and a third of the lemon juice. Stir until smooth. Add to gelatin with remaining juice and zest. Stir. Add beaten egg yolks. Cook until thickened, stirring constantly. Add half the Grand Marnier and cook 1 minute. Do not boil. Transfer to a larger bowl. Chill until set.

Whip cream, remaining Grand Marnier and confectioners sugar until stiff. Beat egg whites until stiff, but not dry. Fold cream mixture and egg whites into lemon mixture. Spoon into soufflé dish or individual glass soufflé dishes. Refrigerate.

8-10 servings

Line a glass soufflé dish with lemon leaves before adding the mousse. Using a large star tube, pipe a lattice of whipped cream over the top and place *Sugared Violets* or *Mint Leaves* at each intersection.

Grand Marnier Mousse with Crème Anglaise

Juice of 10 oranges (about 3 cups)

Juice of 4 lemons

1 cup sugar, divided

2 1/2 tablespoons unflavored gelatin, dissolved in 1/2 cup cold water

1/2 cup Grand Marnier

6 egg whites, room temperature

1/8 teaspoon salt

1/8 teaspoon cream of tartar

1 pint heavy cream, whipped

Crème Anglaise

2 cups heavy cream

6 egg yolks

1/2 cup sugar

Pinch salt

2 tablespoons Grand Marnier

Combine orange juice, lemon juice and 1/2 cup sugar. Add dissolved gelatin to 3/4 cup of the juice mixture and heat almost to boiling. Add to remaining juice. Refrigerate to thicken. When mixture starts to mound, stir in Grand Marnier.

Beat egg whites, salt and cream of tartar on low speed until soft peaks form. Slowly add remaining 1/2 cup sugar and continue beating until stiff.

Fold whipped cream into thickened orange mixture and then carefully fold in egg whites. Pour into a 12-cup mold that has been rinsed with cold water. Refrigerate overnight.

To serve, invert mold onto serving platter and cover with a damp, hot towel. Wait a few seconds and mousse should be released from the mold. Pour Crème Anglaise around base of mousse to serve.

To make Crème Anglaise, heat cream in a saucepan, but do not boil. Combine egg yolks, sugar and salt; beat until light yellow in color. Add hot cream to yolk mixture and mix to blend. Place mixture in heavy saucepan or double boiler. Cook until sauce thickens, stirring with a wooden spoon. Strain and cool. Add Grand Marnier. Serve warm or at room temperature.

8 servings

Marinate orange sections in Grand Marnier for several minutes and use with fresh mint to decorate the top of the mousse. For autumn entertaining arrange clusters of pomegranate seeds with English ivy.

Double Chocolate Terrine with Chocolate Rum Sauce

1	cup finely chopped walnuts
12	ounces semi-sweet chocolate
3/4	cup unsalted butter
3	tablespoons cocoa
1/3	cup sugar
4	egg yolks
5	egg whites, beaten with a pinch of salt until stiff

Chocolate Rum Sauce

1 1/4	cups sugar
1/2	cup unsalted butter
1/2	cup unsweetened cocoa
3	ounces unsweetened chocolate
	Pinch of salt
1	cup heavy cream
1	tablespoon dark rum or to taste

Butter a 1-quart glass loaf pan and line the bottom with buttered parchment paper. Cover bottom with walnuts, and press nuts onto the sides as far up as possible. Set aside.

Melt chocolate, butter and cocoa over low heat in a heavy saucepan or double boiler. Stir until blended. Let cool, but do not allow to harden. Transfer mixture to a bowl and beat in sugar. Add egg yolks, one at a time, beating after each addition. Stir one-fourth of the egg whites into the chocolate mixture and blend well. Fold in remaining egg whites. Pour mixture into prepared pan. Refrigerate until well chilled. To serve, run a knife around perimeter of terrine and invert onto serving platter. Press additional walnuts into the sides if desired.

Let stand at room temperature for an hour before serving. Top with Chocolate Rum Sauce or lightly sweetened whipped cream.

May be prepared a month in advance and frozen. Thaw in refrigerator 24 hours before serving.

8-10 servings

To make Chocolate Rum Sauce, combine sugar, butter, cocoa, chocolate and salt in a heavy saucepan and stir over low heat until melted. Mixture will not be smooth. Add cream slowly and beat until smooth. Add rum to taste. Serve warm.

3 cups

Chocolate Soufflé with Sabayon Sauce

3	tablespoons butter
3	tablespoons flour
3/4	cup milk
7	tablespoons sugar
2 1/2	tablespoons cocoa
	Pinch of salt
2	ounces bittersweet chocolate, broken into small pieces
5	egg yolks
7	egg whites
1/4	teaspoon cream of tartar

Sabayon Sauce

3	egg yolks
1	whole egg
1/3	cup sugar
1/2	cup sherry
1/2	teaspoon finely grated orange zest
1/2	cup heavy cream, whipped

Melt butter in small pan and add flour. Stir constantly until thick and smooth. Set aside. Heat milk, sugar, cocoa and salt until sugar has dissolved. Add butter and flour mixture and cook until thick. Stir in chocolate until melted, then cool slightly. Beat egg yolks into the sauce, one at a time. [Recipe can be done in advance to this point; remaining preparations must be done at the last minute.]

Beat egg whites and cream of tartar until stiff. Fold whites into chocolate mixture. Pour into heavily buttered 1 1/2-quart soufflé dish, dusted with granulated sugar. Bake at 375 degrees for 40 minutes. Sprinkle with confectioners sugar and serve hot with Sabayon Sauce.

To make Sabayon Sauce, beat egg yolks and whole egg in the top of a double boiler until thick and foamy. Add sugar and continue beating until ribbon forms. Add sherry and cook over medium heat until thick. Add orange zest. Just before serving, fold whipped cream into the warm sauce.

6-8 servings

Chocolate Ivy Leaves

Chocolate leaves make a simple dessert look elegant and a complicated dish look even more lavish. They freeze beautifully.

8	ounces bittersweet chocolate, coarsely chopped
	Scant 1/2 tablespoon Crisco
	Fresh green waxy leaves . . . camellia, ivy or gardenia are ideal. Leaves with raised veins on the underside of the leaf will be the most effective. Retain enough stem on each leaf to use as a "handle." Wash leaves and dry thoroughly.

Melt chocolate and Crisco in top of a double boiler over hot water on low heat. Holding leaf upside down in one hand, spread a generous layer of chocolate over the underside (the veined side) of the leaf, using a spoon, small spatula or pastry brush. Be careful not to let chocolate run onto the front of the leaf. Place on waxed paper, chocolate side up, and chill in refrigerator or freezer until chocolate is completely firm. When chocolate has hardened, gently peel leaf away from chocolate, starting at the stem end.

Chocolate Cake with Fudge Icing

3/4 cup butter, room temperature

2 cups sugar

2 eggs

Pinch of salt

1/2 cup cocoa

2 cups flour

3/4 cup buttermilk

1 teaspoon vanilla

1 teaspoon soda, dissolved in 1 cup boiling water

Fudge Icing

3/4 cup butter

2 cups sugar

4 rounded tablespoons cocoa

Pinch of salt

1 cup evaporated milk

1 teaspoon vanilla

Cream butter and sugar; add eggs, salt and cocoa and mix well. Add flour and buttermilk, alternately. Add vanilla. Stir in soda mixture. Pour into two buttered 9-inch round cake pans or a 9 x 13-inch cake pan. Bake at 350 degrees for about 30 minutes. Cool on wire rack.

To make Fudge Icing, melt butter and add remaining ingredients. Cook to soft ball stage, 237-245 degrees. Remove from heat. Add vanilla and beat until mixture begins to lose its luster and thickens. Spread quickly on cooled cake. Because this is a fudge icing, it can set up like fudge, so watch closely for signs of thickening. Be ready to add drops of cream, if necessary.

10-12 servings

Chocolate cake looks spectacular with a scattering of *Chocolate Ivy Leaves.*

Chocolate Truffle Cake

Dense and fudge-like, this French flourless cake would have pleased Le Roi de Soleil! Snip a single, perfect rose from your garden to grace center of cake. Magnifique!

8 ounces dark sweet or semi-sweet chocolate

1 cup butter, room temperature

1 1/2 cups sugar

5 eggs, beaten until foamy

Ganache

12 ounces semi-sweet chocolate

1 cup heavy cream

Melt chocolate and stir until smooth. Remove from heat and cool 1-2 minutes. Add butter, bit by bit; beat with wire whisk until smooth. Add sugar, beating 1 minute with whisk. Add eggs and beat until well mixed.

Butter an 8-inch round cake pan and line with parchment. Pour in batter and set pan into a slightly larger pan. Pour hot water into the larger pan about 1 inch deep. Bake at 350 degrees for 1 1/2 hours. Cool 1 hour. Cake will fall. Refrigerate until set, at least 2 hours. Invert onto cake plate and spread Ganache.

To make Ganache, boil chocolate and cream together, stirring to blend. Refrigerate until spreadable. Frost top and sides of cake.

12-16 servings

Regal Chocolate Cake with Frangelico Cream

4 ounces semi-sweet chocolate, chopped

1 1/2 teaspoons vanilla

2/3 cup sugar

1/2 cup unsalted butter, room temperature

6 eggs, separated, room temperature

1/2 cup toasted ground hazelnuts

1/4 cup frangelico (hazelnut liqueur)

1/8 teaspoon salt

1/8 teaspoon cream of tartar

3/4 cup plus 2 tablespoons all-purpose flour

2 tablespoons cornstarch

Chocolate Icing

3 ounces semi-sweet chocolate, chopped

1 teaspoon vanilla

1/2 cup unsalted butter, room temperature

Whole hazelnuts for garnish

Frangelico Cream

4 egg yolks, room temperature

1/4 cup sugar

Pinch of salt

1 cup milk

1/4 cup frangelico

Melt chocolate in top of double boiler; add vanilla. In large mixing bowl, beat sugar and butter together until pale yellow, about 5 minutes. Beat in egg yolks, one at a time. Mix in hazelnuts, liqueur and chocolate mixture. In a separate bowl, beat egg whites, salt and cream of tartar until stiff, but not dry. Fold one-fourth of whites into yolk mixture. Spoon the remaining whites over the top. Sift flour and cornstarch over the whites and gently but thoroughly fold mixture together. Pour into a buttered and floured 9-inch round cake pan. Bake in lower third of oven at 350 degrees about 25 minutes or until a tester inserted near sides comes out clean. (Center may still be moist.) Cool in pan on rack.

To make Chocolate Icing, melt chocolate in a double boiler and add vanilla. Beat in butter, 2 tablespoons at a time, until smooth. Set top of double boiler in ice and stir until thick (or place in freezer, stirring frequently until spreading consistency).

Invert cake onto platter. Spread icing over top and sides. Garnish top with whole hazelnuts. Serve with warm Frangelico Cream.

To make Frangelico Cream, combine egg yolks, sugar and salt in saucepan. Beat until light in color and creamy, about 3 minutes. Slowly add milk, stirring constantly with wire whisk. Cook over medium heat, stirring constantly, until mixture is thickened and coats a spoon. Add liqueur. Strain, if desired. Serve warm.

8-10 servings

For that final touch, add a splash of frangelico to your after-dinner coffee.

Petite Fudge Cakes

Easy, quick, yummy . . . they keep beautifully in the refrigerator.

5	ounces semi-sweet chocolate or white chocolate
1	cup butter
1	cup chopped pecans (optional)
1³/₄	cups sugar
1	cup all-purpose flour
4	large eggs, unbeaten
1	teaspoon vanilla

Melt chocolate and butter in double boiler. Add pecans, if desired, and stir until well coated. In another bowl, combine sugar, flour and eggs. Add chocolate mixture; stir until just mixed. Add vanilla.

Pour batter into greased or paper-lined petit four cups or regular sized cupcake tins. Bake in 325-degree oven for 12-15 minutes for small cakes, 30 minutes for larger ones. Be careful not to overbake. They should be gooey. Cool and dust with confectioners sugar.

68 small or 24 regular cupcakes

Use gold or silver cupcake liners. Add a dot of whipped cream to each cake and sprinkle with silver shot.

Grand Marnier Cake

1	cup butter, room temperature
1	cup sugar
3	eggs, separated
1	tablespoon Grand Marnier
2	cups flour
1	teaspoon baking powder
1	teaspoon baking soda
1¹/₄	cups sour cream
	Grated zest of 1 orange
1	cup chopped walnuts or pecans

Topping

¹/₂	cup sugar
1	cup fresh orange juice
¹/₃	cup Grand Marnier
	Slivered almonds, toasted

Cream butter and sugar. Beat in egg yolks, one at a time. Add Grand Marnier. Sift dry ingredients together and add to batter, alternating with sour cream; beat until smooth. Stir in orange zest and nuts. Beat egg whites until stiff and fold into cake batter. Pour into well-greased bundt cake pan.

Bake at 350 degrees for 50 minutes or until cake tester comes out clean. Cool before removing from pan.

To make Topping, combine sugar, orange juice and Grand Marnier. When ready to serve, pour topping over cake. Sprinkle with almonds. Tuck orange slices under base of cake to create petals. Add lemon leaves.

12 servings

This rich cake is enhanced by walnuts, orange zest and a light flavoring of liqueur.

Slivers of candied orange peel add color and taste.

The Prospect's Carrot Cake

From The Prospect of Westport restaurant, on the site of Kansas City's earliest settlement, comes this achievement of merit.

1¹/₄ cups oil

2 cups sugar

2 cups all-purpose flour

2 teaspoons baking powder

2 teaspoons cinnamon

1 teaspoon baking soda

1 teaspoon salt

4 eggs

1 pound carrots, peeled and grated

1 cup coarsely chopped pecans

1 cup dark raisins (optional)

Filling

1 cup sugar

¹/₄ cup flour

1 cup heavy cream

¹/₄ cup butter

¹/₄ teaspoon salt

1 cup chopped pecans

2 teaspoons vanilla

Frosting

4 ounces shredded coconut

1 8-ounce package cream cheese, room temperature

1 cup butter, room temperature

3 cups confectioners sugar

1 teaspoon vanilla

Combine oil and sugar in bowl; beat well. Sift together dry ingredients. Sift half the dry ingredients into sugar mixture; blend well. Sift in remaining dry ingredients, alternating with eggs; mix well after each addition. Stir in carrots, pecans and, if desired, raisins.

Pour into lightly oiled 10-inch tube pan. Bake in preheated 325-degree oven about 1 hour and 10 minutes. Cool upright in pan.

To make Filling, combine sugar and flour in small heavy saucepan. Gradually stir in cream. Add butter and salt. Cook over very low heat, stirring frequently, until mixture comes just to a simmer. (This may take 30 minutes.) Let simmer 2-3 minutes. Remove from heat and cool to lukewarm. Stir in nuts and vanilla. Cool completely, ideally overnight.

To make Frosting, toast coconut at 300 degrees for 10-15 minutes or until lightly browned. Cool. Combine cream cheese and butter in food processor or mixer. Add confectioners sugar and vanilla and mix until perfectly smooth. Refrigerate if too soft to spread immediately.

To assemble, split cooled cake into three layers. Spread pecan filling between layers. Reassemble on cake plate and frost top and sides with frosting. Pat toasted coconut onto sides of cake.

12 servings

emon
unflower Cake

*e color of Missouri sunflowers, this
ke is perfect for a summertime
hday or luncheon.*

1¹/₄	cups sugar
	Zest of 2 lemons
3	eggs
³/₄	cup unsalted butter, room temperature
³/₄	cup sour cream
¹/₄	cup plus 2 tablespoons orange juice
2	tablespoons lemon juice
1³/₄	cups cake flour
2	teaspoons baking powder
³/₄	teaspoon baking soda
³/₄	teaspoon salt

Lemon Curd

²/₃	cup sugar
	Zest of 1 lemon
5	egg yolks
¹/₂	cup lemon juice
	Pinch of salt
¹/₂	cup butter, melted and hot

Lemon Icing

3	cups confectioners sugar
	Zest of 2 lemons
	Pinch of salt
4-5	tablespoons sour cream
5	tablespoons unsalted butter
2	tablespoons Lemon Curd

Mince sugar and lemon zest in food processor until zest is very fine. Add eggs and process one minute. Add butter and process one minute more. Add sour cream, orange juice and lemon juice; mix well. Sift together flour, baking powder, baking soda and salt. Add to batter and mix just to combine. Do not overprocess.

Butter three 8-inch pans, line with waxed paper and butter again. Divide batter among the pans. Bake on the middle rack at 350 degrees for 20 minutes. Cool 10 minutes on wire racks. Remove cake from pans and cool completely.

Prepare Lemon Curd by mincing sugar and lemon zest in food processor until zest is very fine. Add yolks, lemon juice and salt; process. With machine running, pour hot butter through the feed tube. Pour into saucepan and cook over low heat, stirring constantly, until thickened. Do not boil. Cool; cover and refrigerate. Reserve 2 tablespoons for Icing.

Prepare Lemon Icing by mincing sugar and lemon zest in food processor until zest is very fine. Add remaining ingredients. Refrigerate 15 minutes. If icing is too thin, add more confectioners sugar.

To assemble, spread bottom and middle layers of cake with Lemon Curd. Cover top and sides of the cake with Lemon Icing.

12 servings

Sprinkle top of cake like "confetti" with hulled sunflower seeds. Set cake on a bed of black sunflower seeds; add clusters of miniature field sunflowers or daisies.

Lemon Curd will keep 2-3 months in the refrigerator. It is delicious in cookies, tart shells and pound cake.

Hot Fudge Pudding

1/2	cup sifted flour
1	teaspoon baking powder
1/8	teaspoon salt
1/3	cup sugar
3	tablespoons cocoa, divided
1	tablespoon butter, melted
1/4	cup half and half
1/2	teaspoon vanilla
1/2	cup chopped walnuts
1/2	cup sifted brown sugar
7/8	cup boiling water

Combine flour, baking powder, salt, sugar and 1 tablespoon cocoa; sift times. Combine butter, cream and vanilla; add flour mixture and blend lightly. Stir in nuts. Pour into a buttered 1-quart casserole. Combine brown sugar and remaining cocoa and sprinkle over batter. Pour boiling water gently over all. Bake at 350 degrees for 3 minutes. Serve warm with whipped cream.

6 servings

A superb chocolate pudding reminiscent of grandmother's good cooking.

Lemon Ribbon Pie

6	tablespoons butter, melted
1	tablespoon grated lemon zest
1/3	cup fresh lemon juice
1/8	teaspoon salt
1	cup sugar
2	eggs plus 2 egg yolks, slightly beaten
1	quart vanilla ice cream, slightly softened
	9-inch baked pie crust or graham cracker crust
3	egg whites
6	tablespoons sugar
	8-10 lemon slices for garnish
	Whipped cream for garnish

Combine butter, lemon zest, lemon juice, salt and sugar in top of a double boiler. Add eggs and egg yolks; cook over boiling water, beating constantly with wire whisk until thick and smooth. Cool.

Spread half the ice cream in pie shell. Freeze until hard. Spread h the lemon sauce over frozen ice cream; freeze until hard. Repeat layers, ending with sauce. Freeze until hard.

Beat egg whites to soft peaks. Gradually add 6 tablespoons sug and beat until peaks are stiff and glossy. Spread over pie and freez

8-10 servings

Decorate with whipped cream, placing twisted lemon slices on ea serving and adding mint leaves for color.

French Apple Pie

Crust

3½	cups flour
1	cup chilled unsalted butter, cut in small pieces
6	tablespoons shortening, chilled
2	teaspoons salt
1	egg plus enough ice water to equal ¾ cup

Filling

⅓	cup plus 2 tablespoons sugar, divided
2	tablespoons flour
1	cup milk
3	egg yolks, beaten
3	tablespoons butter, divided
1	teaspoon vanilla
2	pounds tart apples, peeled and sliced
1	tablespoon lemon juice
¼	teaspoon nutmeg
¾	cup apricot preserves, heated to melt
1	egg yolk

Combine flour, butter and shortening in food processor and process only until mixture resembles very coarse meal. Stir salt into egg and water; add to flour mixture. Process until it forms a mass. Wrap in waxed paper and refrigerate for 2 hours. Divide dough in half. (This makes enough pastry for 2 pies. Half can be frozen, if desired.)

Divide dough half into 2 parts. Roll 1 portion out for a 9-inch crust. Roll other portion and cut into strips for lattice.

To make Filling, combine ⅓ cup sugar and the flour in a small saucepan. Slowly add milk and bring to a boil, stirring constantly. Reduce heat and simmer until thickened, about 1 minute. Add a little of the hot mixture to the beaten egg yolks. Return yolks to saucepan, beating well. Cook until slightly thickened. Stir in 1 tablespoon butter and the vanilla. Pour into bowl and set aside to cool.

Sprinkle apples with lemon juice. In a skillet, melt 2 tablespoons butter with 2 tablespoons sugar and the nutmeg. Add apple slices and sauté about 5 minutes, until partially cooked.

Pour custard filling into pie shell. Arrange apples on top and spread with preserves. Make a lattice design on top with crust and brush strips with egg yolk mixed with a little water. Bake 35-40 minutes at 425 degrees, placing a cookie sheet on the bottom rack to catch spills.

8 servings

Tuck a large paisley cloth or square bandana around the pie. Place in a basket and carry to your next picnic.

Layered Pumpkin Spice Pie

3	eggs, separated
1/3	cup sugar
1 1/4	cups canned pumpkin
1/2	cup sour cream
1/2	teaspoon salt
1 1/4	teaspoons cinnamon
1/4	teaspoon cloves
1/4	teaspoon nutmeg
1/4	teaspoon ginger
1	tablespoon unflavored gelatin, softened in 1/4 cup cold water
1/4	cup sugar
1	cup heavy cream, whipped
2	tablespoons confectioners sugar
1/2	teaspoon vanilla
2	tablespoons rum
1	9-inch pie shell, baked and cooled
3/4	cup chopped pecans

Beat egg yolks with 1/3 cup sugar until lemon-colored and thick. Add pumpkin, sour cream, salt and spices. Cook over medium heat, stirring constantly, until mixture comes to a boil. Reduce heat. Continue stirring for 2 minutes. Remove from heat. Add softened gelatin and stir until gelatin is dissolved. Cool.

Beat egg whites until frothy. Gradually add 1/4 cup sugar and continue beating until stiff peaks form and sugar is dissolved. Fold into pumpkin mixture.

To whipped cream, add confectioners sugar, vanilla and rum. Spoon half of pumpkin mixture into pie shell. Spread half of the whipped cream on top. Repeat layers. Sprinkle with pecans. Chill at least 2 hours before serving.

8 servings

For Thanksgiving, cut 8 small turkey shapes from pie dough. Brush with melted butter and sprinkle with cinnamon and sugar. Bake until lightly browned. Place each turkey in a nest of whipped cream for a whimsical touch.

Coconut Cream Pie

A superb version of an old favorite.

1	cup sugar
2	cups milk
3	egg yolks, beaten
3	tablespoons cornstarch
1/4	cup butter
1	teaspoon vanilla
1	cup flaked coconut
1/4	teaspoon salt
	9-inch pie shell, baked
1	cup heavy cream

Heat sugar and milk in a 1-quart saucepan over medium heat.

Blend egg yolks and cornstarch. Add small amount of hot milk to yolk mixture. Mix well and return to the hot milk. Boil until thick, about 3 minutes. Remove from heat. Add butter, vanilla, coconut and salt. Stir until butter melts. Cool. Pour mixture into pie shell. Whip and sweeten cream; spread over pie. Garnish with grated coconut. (Leave the brown skin on the coconut when grating for more color.) Serve chilled.

8 servings

Coffee Toffee Pie

Pastry Shell

1	cup flour
1/2	teaspoon salt
1/2	cup shortening
1/3	cup brown sugar
3/4	cup finely chopped pecans or walnuts
1	ounce grated unsweetened chocolate
1	tablespoon ice water

Filling

3/4	cup butter, room temperature
1	cup plus 2 tablespoons sugar
1 1/2	ounces unsweetened chocolate, melted and cooled
2	teaspoons instant coffee powder
3	eggs

Topping

1	cup heavy cream
1	teaspoon instant coffee powder
1/4	cup confectioners sugar
1	ounce unsweetened chocolate, grated

Combine flour and salt. Cut in shortening. Stir in brown sugar, nuts and chocolate. Sprinkle with ice water and mix. Pat into 9-inch pie pan or springform pan. Bake at 375 degrees for 15 minutes. Cool.

To make Filling, beat butter until creamy. Gradually add sugar, beating until light. Blend in melted chocolate and instant coffee. Add eggs, one at a time, beating 3 minutes after each addition. Pour into cooled pie shell. Refrigerate for several hours or overnight.

To make Topping, combine cream, instant coffee and confectioners sugar in a bowl. Refrigerate for 2-3 hours. Beat until stiff and spread on pie. Grate chocolate over top.

6-8 servings

Circle top of the pie with decorative clusters of chocolate-covered coffee beans.

Strawberry Shortcake Pie

Crust

1	cup biscuit mix
1/4	cup butter, room temperature
3	tablespoons boiling water

Filling

1	3-ounce package cream cheese, room temperature
1	tablespoon half and half
1	teaspoon lemon juice
4	cups whole strawberries

Glaze

1/2	cup water
1	cup sugar
2 1/2	tablespoons cornstarch
2	cups strawberries, crushed
1	tablespoon butter

Additional Ingredients

1	cup heavy cream, whipped

In a small bowl, stir crust ingredients together until dough forms a soft ball. Press evenly into a 9-inch pie plate. Prick surface with fork. Bake 10-12 minutes at 450 degrees or until golden. Remove from oven and cool.

Prepare Filling by mixing cream cheese with half and half and lemon juice. Spread over top of baked shell. Mound 4 cups strawberries over cheese layer. Spoon warm glaze over, making sure all berries are covered. Chill.

To make Glaze, cook water, sugar and cornstarch in a saucepan until dissolved. Add crushed berries. Bring mixture to a boil and cook 3 minutes. Add butter. Press through a strainer. Decorate with whipped cream.

8-10 servings

Pull out stems of whole strawberries and insert tiny mint leaves; center berries on top of pie.

Six-Layered Mocha Chocolate Torte

8	ounces sweet baking chocolate
1/2	cup water
1/2	cup sugar
1 1/2	teaspoons instant coffee
2	teaspoons vanilla
1	10-ounce package pie crust (2 sticks)
2	cups heavy cream, whipped
	Slivered almonds, toasted, for garnish
	Shaved chocolate for garnish

Combine chocolate, water, sugar and coffee in a saucepan. Cook over low heat until smooth. Add vanilla; cool to room temperature. Blend all but 2/3 cup of the sauce into pie crust mix. Divide dough in 6 parts. Press each part over bottom of an inverted 8 or 9-inch round cake pan to within 1/2 inch of edge. Bake at 425 degrees for 5 minutes. Result should be firm. Cool and loosen with knife and slide onto waxed paper to cool completely.

Fold remaining chocolate sauce in whipped cream. Layer pastries and cream, ending with layer of whipped cream. Mound whipped cream in the center and sprinkle with almonds and chocolate. Chill.

Mocha Fudge Ice Cream Torte

In a word, divine! Pass a generous amount of additional sauce.

1 cup coconut or almond macaroon cookie crumbs (any cookie, such as a butter cookie or chocolate wafer, can be used)

2 tablespoons melted butter

1 quart chocolate ice cream, slightly softened

1/2 cup or more chocolate sauce, divided

1 quart coffee ice cream, slightly softened

4 ounces chocolate-covered toffee bars, coarsely crushed

Mix cookie crumbs and butter. Press lightly into bottom of a 9-inch springform pan. Bake at 350 degrees for 8-10 minutes or until light brown. Cool.

Spread chocolate ice cream in an even layer over the cooled crust, then drizzle evenly with 1/4 cup chocolate sauce. Freeze until firm. Top with an even layer of coffee ice cream (or scoop small balls of ice cream and arrange over the surface). Sprinkle evenly with crushed candy and drizzle remaining sauce over the top.

Cover with plastic wrap and freeze until firm. Remove from freezer a few minutes before serving to make slicing easier.

Black Bottom Cheesecake

Crust

1 1/2 cups chocolate wafer crumbs

1 cup slivered almonds, chopped

1/3 cup sugar

6 tablespoons butter, room temperature

Filling

3 8-ounce packages cream cheese

1 cup sugar

4 eggs

1/3 cup heavy cream

1/2 cup amaretto

1 teaspoon vanilla

Topping

2 cups sour cream

1 teaspoon vanilla

1 tablespoon sugar

1 cup slivered almonds, toasted

Combine crust ingredients in food processor. Pat crumb mixture onto bottom and sides of a buttered 10-inch springform pan.

To make Filling, cream together cream cheese and sugar in a food processor. Add eggs, one at a time, beating well after each addition. Add cream, amaretto and vanilla, beating until light. Pour into chocolate crust. Bake on middle rack of a 375-degree oven for 30-40 minutes. Transfer cake to a wire rack and let stand 5 minutes.

Combine all Topping ingredients except nuts. Spread evenly over cake. Bake for 5 more minutes. Cool on rack. Cover lightly with waxed paper and chill overnight.

To serve, remove sides from pan. Break off crust above cheesecake and crumble around outer edge of top. Fill center with toasted almonds.

16 servings

Italian Chocolate-Almond Cheesecake

Crust

7	ounces amaretti cookies, finely ground
2	tablespoons sugar
1	ounce unsweetened chocolate
5	tablespoons unsalted butter

Filling

6	ounces semi-sweet chocolate
4	ounces almond paste, cut into small pieces
1/3	cup amaretto liqueur
3	8-ounce packages cream cheese, room temperature
1/2	cup sugar
4	eggs
1/2	cup heavy cream
8	ounces amaretti cookies, coarsely broken

Place crumbs in a bowl and add sugar. Melt chocolate and butter; add to the crumb mixture and stir. Butter sides only of a 9-inch springform pan and press crumb mixture into the bottom of the pan. Refrigerate.

To make Filling, melt chocolate in the top of a double boiler. Set aside to cool slightly. Place almond paste pieces in a mixer and, on low speed, gradually add the amaretto. Beat until thoroughly mixed. Set aside.

In a large bowl, beat cream cheese until smooth. Add sugar and beat again until smooth. Add the almond paste-amaretto mixture and mix well. Add melted chocolate and beat. On low speed, add the eggs, one at a time, and beat only until they are incorporated. Add cream and beat only until smooth. Do not overbeat. Gently stir in the broken cookies.

Pour batter into prepared pan. Rotate the pan gently to spread batter evenly. Bake in a 350-degree oven for 45 minutes in the bottom third of the oven. Do not bake any longer — it becomes firm as it chills. Cool to room temperature. Remove sides of the pan. Refrigerate for several hours or overnight.

To remove from pan, insert and rotate sharp knife to release crust. Mound white and dark chocolate shavings on top and encircle base of cheesecake with fresh, perfect strawberries topped with whipped cream.

16-20 servings

This extraordinary cheesecake is exceedingly rich so serve small pieces, very cold. It freezes well if wrapped airtight.

Crème de Cassis Cheesecake

Crust

1/2	cup unsalted butter
2	cups finely ground vanilla wafer or butter cookie crumbs
1	ounce white chocolate, grated
1/4	cup sugar

Filling

4	8-ounce packages cream cheese, room temperature
1 1/4	cups sugar
3	tablespoons crème de cassis
	Pinch of salt
4	large eggs, room temperature
3	ounces white chocolate, shaved

Topping

2	cups sour cream
1/4	cup sugar
1	teaspoon almond extract

Melt butter over low heat; combine with crumbs, white chocolate and sugar until well blended. Press mixture on sides and bottom of an ungreased 10-inch springform pan.

To make Filling, combine cream cheese and sugar and beat with a mixer for 2 minutes until soft. Add liqueur and salt; blend thoroughly. With the mixer on lowest speed, add eggs, one at a time, mixing only until each egg has been incorporated into batter. Fold in shaved chocolate. Pour into crust and bake 40 minutes at 350 degrees. Remove cake from oven and let stand for 10 minutes before adding the topping.

To make Topping, combine sour cream, sugar and almond extract. Spread over top of cake and return cake to 350-degree oven for 10 minutes. Remove from oven and refrigerate immediately. When cool, decorate with shaved white chocolate.

16 servings

Blackberries or red currants are the perfect seasonal garnish.

Praline Cheesecake

1	cup graham cracker crumbs
3	tablespoons sugar
3	tablespoons butter, melted
3	8-ounce packages cream cheese, room temperature
1 1/4	cups dark brown sugar
2	tablespoons all-purpose flour
3	eggs
1 1/2	teaspoons vanilla
1	cup finely chopped pecans, divided
	Maple syrup

Combine graham cracker crumbs, sugar and butter. Press in bottom of 9-inch springform pan. Bake at 350 degrees for 10 minutes.

Blend together cream cheese, brown sugar and flour. Add eggs, one at a time, beating well after each addition. Add vanilla and 1/2 cup pecans; mix well. Pour into crumb crust. Bake at 350 degrees for 50-55 minutes. Loosen from rim and cool. Remove from rim. Chill. Brush with maple syrup. Sprinkle with remaining 1/2 cup chopped pecans.

8-10 servings

Fresh Strawberry Almond Tart

Tart Shell

- 3/4 cup flour
- 1/3 cup finely ground almonds
- 2 tablespoons confectioners sugar
- 1/2 cup butter, cut in pieces

Almond Filling

- 1/2 cup almond paste
- 1/4 cup confectioners sugar
- 2 tablespoons butter, room temperature
- 1 egg yolk

Apricot Glaze

- 1/2 cup apricot preserves
- 1 tablespoon Cognac or kirsch

Additional Ingredients

- 1 quart strawberries, hulled, or an assortment of fresh fruit
- 1 cup heavy cream, whipped
- 1 teaspoon vanilla
- 1 tablespoon sugar

Combine all Tart Shell ingredients. Process in food processor or work together with hands until mixture resembles coarse meal. Press into 11-inch fluted flan pan. Bake at 425 degrees for 8-10 minutes. Cool and loosen slightly.

Prepare Almond Filling by beating all ingredients together.

Prepare Apricot Glaze by heating preserves. Add liqueur and press through a sieve.

To assemble: Spread almond filling over cooled shell. Arrange strawberries or other fresh fruit over the top. Spoon apricot glaze over fruit. Chill.

Flavor whipped cream with vanilla and sugar. Put cream in a pastry bag and decorate around the fruit. This tart is best if made several hours in advance. Refrigerate. Cut in wedges to serve.

8 servings

In the spring, nestle tiny strawberry blossoms from the garden around the base of the tart.

Strawberry Meringue Torte

Meringues

4	egg whites, room temperature
1/2	teaspoon cream of tartar
1/4	teaspoon salt
2	cups confectioners sugar

Filling

12	ounces semi-sweet chocolate
6	tablespoons water
1 1/2	pints heavy cream
1/3	cup sugar
3	pints strawberries (2 pints sliced and 1 pint whole with stems)

Lemon Filling for Meringue Torte

8	egg yolks
1	cup sugar
2	tablespoons grated lemon zest
6	tablespoons lemon juice
1/4	teaspoon salt
2 1/2	cups heavy cream, whipped; reserve 1 cup for garnish
2	meringue rounds (recipe above)
2	kiwi for garnish

Beat egg whites with cream of tartar and salt until stiff. With mixer running, slowly add sugar, 1 tablespoon at a time, until mixture is stiff (about 20 minutes of beating). Draw three 9-inch circles on parchment paper on a cookie sheet. Spread one-third of the meringue mixture on each. Bake at 250 degrees for 1 hour. Turn oven off and let meringues cool in oven.

Melt chocolate with water in a double boiler. Set aside. Whip cream until stiff. Gradually add sugar to the cream and beat until very stiff.

To assemble: Place one meringue on a plate. Spread with a thin layer of chocolate. Top chocolate with one-third of the whipped cream and one pint sliced berries. Repeat the procedure. Top with last meringue and frost top with remaining whipped cream. Drizzle remaining chocolate in a random pattern over the top. Decorate with whole berries. Refrigerate at least 3 hours.

10 servings

Equally delicious, when strawberries are not available, is a torte made with Lemon Meringue Filling.

In double boiler, beat egg yolks with sugar. Stir in lemon zest, lemon juice and salt. Cook, stirring, until very thick, about 10 minutes. Cool.

To assemble: Place one meringue on cake plate and spread with half the lemon mixture and 3/4 cup whipped cream. Repeat procedure.

Using a pastry bag with a decorative tip, decorate top of the torte with reserved whipped cream. Garnish with sliced kiwi.

10 servings

Walnut Fudge Tart

Crust

1³/₄	cups flour
¹/₃	cup cocoa
¹/₈	teaspoon salt
¹/₄	cup sugar
³/₄	cup butter, chilled and cut in small pieces
¹/₃ to ¹/₂	cup strong cold coffee

Filling

12	ounces semi-sweet chocolate, melted
²/₃	cup sugar
2	tablespoons butter, melted
2	tablespoons milk
2	teaspoons kahlua
2	eggs, beaten
¹/₂	cup finely chopped walnuts, toasted

Place flour, cocoa, salt and sugar into food processor and blend by pulsing 3 to 4 times. Distribute butter over flour in processor; pulse several times until mixture resemble coarse crumbs. Transfer to a bowl. Add coffee gradually. Knead together and chill overnight. Roll out and press into 9-inch tart pan. Chill until firm.

To make Filling, mix chocolate, sugar, butter, milk and kahlua together. Add eggs and walnuts. Pour into tart shell and bake at 350 degrees for 30 to 40 minutes or unti top is dry and firm. Cool.

6-8 servings

Create your own design by sifting confectioners sugar through a pape doily or placing strips of paper in a lattice pattern on top of tart before sifting. For another occasion, garnis with whipped cream and *Fried Walnuts*.

Country Classic Rice Pudding

6	cups milk
³/₄	cup long-grain white rice
1	cup heavy cream
³/₄	cup sugar
3	egg yolks, beaten
2	teaspoons vanilla
¹/₄	teaspoon salt
1	teaspoon cinnamon

Bring milk to a boil in a saucepan over medium heat. Stir in rice and return to a boil. Reduce heat and simmer, uncovered, about 45 minutes or until rice is tender. Stir occasionally.

Combine cream, sugar, yolks, vani and salt; set aside. When rice is tender, stir in cream mixture until well blended. Heat to a boil. Remove from heat and pour into a 2-quart serving dish. Sprinkle generously with cinnamon. Chill several hours.

6 servings

Surround this heartland favorite wit a medley of fresh apricots, nectarin and cherries.

Old-Fashioned Bread Pudding

Old-fashioned in name only! This former country fare is now a cosmopolitan favorite from New York to the Pacific.

10	thin slices white bread, crusts removed
3	tablespoons butter
1	cup raisins (or combination of raisins and currants)
3	tablespoons sugar
4	eggs
2	egg yolks
2¹/₂	cups milk
¹/₈	teaspoon grated nutmeg
¹/₂	teaspoon cinnamon
¹/₂	cup apricot preserves, heated and strained

Warm Pudding Sauce

¹/₄	cup sugar
2	tablespoons all-purpose flour
1	cup water
1	tablespoon butter
¹/₄	teaspoon grated nutmeg

Warm Lemon Sauce

	Juice of 2 lemons
³/₄	cup water
¹/₂	cup sugar
1	tablespoon cornstarch, dissolved in ¹/₂ cup water
1	teaspoon vanilla

Butter the bread; cut each slice into 2 triangles. Arrange half the bread, butter side up, in a baking dish. Sprinkle with raisins and sugar and cover with remaining pieces of bread. Combine eggs, egg yolks, milk, nutmeg and cinnamon; beat lightly. Pour egg mixture over the bread. Let rest for about 20 minutes. Bake, uncovered, in a 375-degree oven for 40 minutes or until bread is lightly browned and custard has set. Spread pudding with warm apricot preserves. Serve with Warm Pudding Sauce or Warm Lemon Sauce.

To make Warm Pudding Sauce, mix together sugar and flour in a small saucepan. Add water and butter; whisk together over medium heat. When slightly thickened, remove from heat and stir in nutmeg. (This is a very thin sauce.)

To make Warm Lemon Sauce, combine lemon juice, water and sugar in saucepan and bring to a boil. Thicken with dissolved cornstarch and add vanilla. Serve warm.

6 servings

Lemon Sauce is also a lovely spring accompaniment to pound cake.

Apples Normandy with Rum Sauce

6 tablespoons butter

8 tart apples, peeled and sliced

2/3 cup raisins

1/3 cup sugar

1 teaspoon grated lemon zest

1/2 teaspoon cinnamon

1/4 teaspoon freshly grated nutmeg

Dash of ground cloves

Rum Sauce

6 large egg yolks

1 cup heavy cream, heated

1 cup milk, heated

1/2 cup sugar

2 tablespoons dark rum

2 teaspoons vanilla

Melt butter in a large pan and add apples, raisins, sugar, lemon zest and cinnamon. Sauté apples about 10 to 15 minutes or until they are soft but not mushy — the apples should retain their shape. Add nutmeg and cloves. Spoon into serving dishes and serve warm with cold Rum Sauce.

For Rum Sauce, combine egg yolks, cream, milk and sugar in top of a double boiler. Stirring frequently, cook about 30 minutes or until the sauce is thick enough to coat a spoon. Remove from heat; stir in rum and vanilla. Chill.

8 servings

Bring this autumn and winter dessert to the table in country French pottery.

Apple Strudel

9 apples, peeled, cored and thinly sliced

2 tablespoons fresh lemon juice

3/4 cup sugar

1 teaspoon cinnamon

Dash nutmeg

1/2 cup walnuts

1/2 pound phyllo dough

1 cup butter, melted

1 cup ground nuts or bread crumbs

Confectioners sugar

Sprinkle apple slices with lemon juice and toss to coat thoroughly. Combine sugar, cinnamon, nutmeg and walnuts; add mixture to apples and combine gently but thoroughly.

Brush one sheet of phyllo with some melted butter; sprinkle with nuts or bread crumbs. Place second sheet directly over first sheet. Brush with butter and sprinkle with nuts or bread crumbs. Repeat procedure until there are 5 sheets. Place half the filling on long edge, fold over extended sides of sheets and roll like a jellyroll.

Place strudel seamside down on buttered cookie sheet and brush with melted butter. Score top. Bake 30-40 minutes at 375 degrees or until golden.

2 strudels

Place warm strudel on freshly starched linen napkin and sprinkle with confectioners sugar.

Bavarian Apple Torte

Crust

1/2	cup butter, room temperature
1/3	cup sugar
1/4	teaspoon vanilla
1	cup all-purpose flour

Filling

12	ounces cream cheese, room temperature
1/4	cup sugar
1	egg
1	teaspoon vanilla

Topping

1/3	cup sugar
1/2	teaspoon cinnamon
4	cups peeled and sliced tart apples
1/4	cup slivered almonds
1	cup heavy cream, whipped

Cream butter, sugar and vanilla. Blend in flour. Spread dough on the bottom and 1 inch up the sides of a 9-inch springform pan.

To make Filling, beat together cream cheese and sugar. Blend in egg and vanilla. Pour into pastry-lined pan.

To make Topping, combine sugar and cinnamon; toss with apples. Arrange apples in concentric circles over cream cheese layer, avoiding spilling apple juice on pastry. Sprinkle with slivered almonds. Bake at 450 degrees for 10 minutes. Reduce heat to 400 degrees and continue baking for 25 minutes. Cool before removing rim of pan.

Serve with a bountiful amount of whipped cream, laced with cinnamon.

8 servings

Plum Duff

Winner of the Kansas City Gourmet Gala, this dessert surprise turns prunes into paradise. For holiday flair, add a sprig of holly.

2	cups prunes
1/2	cup butter
1	cup light brown sugar
2	eggs, beaten
1	cup all-purpose flour
1	teaspoon soda

Plum Duff Topping

1	egg
5	tablespoons butter, melted
1/2	pound confectioners sugar
1	cup heavy cream
1	teaspoon vanilla

Cover prunes with water and cook over medium heat for 10-15 minutes or until soft. Drain, chop and set aside. Melt butter and add the sugar, stirring until sugar is dissolved. Add prunes and eggs. Fold in flour and soda.

Pour into a greased 1-quart mold. Cover mold tightly with foil and place on a rack over simmering water in a covered pan on top of the stove. Steam for one hour. Serve warm with a dollop of Plum Duff Topping on each serving.

To make Plum Duff Topping, beat egg until foamy. Add butter and sugar. Whip cream until stiff; add vanilla. Fold into mixture. (Topping keeps indefinitely in refrigerator.)

Fresh Peach Flan

Caramelized Sugar

1	cup sugar
3	tablespoons water

Flan

1	14-ounce can condensed sweetened milk
5	eggs
2	tablespoons sugar
1	cup water
5-6	tablespoons brandy or Grand Marnier
1/4	teaspoon salt
1/4	teaspoon nutmeg
1/2	teaspoon lemon juice
	Grated zest of 1 lemon
4-5	ripe peaches, peeled and diced

Garnish

3	peaches, peeled and sliced
	Blueberries
	Mint leaves
2	tablespoons toasted almonds

Heat a 2-quart soufflé dish in a 150-degree oven while caramelizing the sugar.

To caramelize sugar, place sugar and water in a heavy saucepan. Swirl pan to dissolve sugar and bring to a rolling boil over medium-high heat. Cook until syrup is a nut brown. Pour into the heated soufflé dish and rotate dish to cover bottom and sides with syrup. Set aside.

To make Flan, combine condensed milk, eggs, sugar, water, liqueur, salt, nutmeg, lemon juice and zest in food processor. Add diced peaches. Pulse 3 to 4 times to chop and blend. Pour mixture into prepared soufflé dish. Set in a shallow pan. Pour hot water into pan about 2 inches deep. Bake at 350 degrees for 75 to 90 minutes. Test with a knife for doneness. Refrigerate 4 hours or overnight.

When ready to serve, run a knife around the inside of the dish and invert onto serving platter. Arrange peach slices and blueberries around base of flan with sprigs of mint. Place almonds in the center.

6-8 servings

Peaches and Blueberries Sabayon

4	peaches, peeled and halved
1	pint blueberries
	Sabayon Sauce
1/2	cup almonds, toasted

Place a peach half and several blueberries in each of 8 individual stemmed glasses. Top with *Sabayon Sauce*; sprinkle with toasted almonds and a few more blueberries.

8 servings

Sugared Violets, Rose Petals and Mint Leaves

	Violets, rose petals or mint leaves
1	egg white, slightly beaten
	Granulated sugar

With a small brush, coat each petal or leaf on all sides with slightly beaten egg white. Dip petals or leaves into granulated sugar and place on plate liberally sprinkled with sugar. Sift more sugar lightly over petals. Set in warm place to dry overnight.

Use within a few days or freeze on layers of paper towels in a tightly covered tin or plastic container. Will keep 6 months or more without color or flavor change.

Chocolate Meringue Torte

Chocolate Meringues

5	egg whites
	Pinch cream of tartar
3/4	cup sugar
1 3/4	cups confectioners sugar
1/3	cup unsweetened cocoa

Mousse

13	ounces semi-sweet chocolate
7	egg whites, beaten with 1/4 teaspoon cream of tartar
3	cups chilled heavy cream, whipped with 1 1/2 teaspoons vanilla until stiff

To prepare Chocolate Meringues, beat egg whites with cream of tartar until they hold soft peaks. Add sugar, 2 tablespoons at a time, and continue beating until very stiff. Sift sugar and cocoa together and fold into egg white mixture.

Using an 8-inch square pan as a guide, trace and cut 3 squares from parchment paper. Place on baking sheets. Divide meringue mixture evenly among the squares, spreading it evenly to the edges. Bake at 300 degrees for 1 hour, 15 minutes. Transfer meringues to racks to cool.

To prepare Mousse, melt chocolate in top of a double boiler; cool to lukewarm. Fold carefully into egg whites. Fold in two-thirds of the whipped cream. Mix carefully to blend. Reserve remaining cream.

To assemble, place one meringue on a cake stand and spread thickly with mousse. Top with a second meringue and spread with more mousse. Top with remaining meringue.

Using remaining mousse mixture and reserved whipped cream, pipe scrolls onto meringue in an alternating pattern, using a pastry tube with a decorative tip. Be sure scrolls overlap to cover meringue completely.

Chuppachuk Brownies

½ cup unsalted butter

2 ounces unsweetened chocolate

1 cup sugar

½ teaspoon vanilla

2 large eggs

½ cup sifted all-purpose flour

Pinch of salt

½ cup coarsely chopped pecans

Icing

2 tablespoons butter, room temperature

½ teaspoon vanilla

1 cup sifted confectioners sugar

1 egg

2 ounces unsweetened chocolate, melted

Line an 8-inch square pan with foil; lightly butter bottom and sides. Melt butter and chocolate over low heat. Cool 2 minutes. Stir in sugar and vanilla. Add eggs, one at a time, stirring until smooth. Add flour and salt; stir in nuts. Pour into prepared pan. Bake at 350 degrees for 20-25 minutes. Cool. Lift brownies from pan by foil edges and frost.

To make Icing, beat butter, vanilla, sugar and egg in a small bowl until smooth. Add warm chocolate and beat until smooth. Spread on brownies and refrigerate until ready to serve. Peel away foil and slice.

16   2-inch brownies

Named for the mythical creature who is soothed only by chocolate, these moist rich brownies won a "brownie bake-off" at a St. Louis cooking school. Sprinkle the finished product with finely chopped pistachio nuts, if you dare!

Decadent Chocolate Cookies

8 ounces semi-sweet chocolate

3 ounces bitter chocolate

6 tablespoons butter

⅓ cup all-purpose flour

¼ teaspoon baking powder

¼ teaspoon salt

3 eggs

1 cup sugar

2 teaspoons vanilla

1½ cups chocolate chips

1 cup pecans

1 cup walnuts

Melt semi-sweet and bitter chocolate with butter over low heat until smooth. Cool. Sift flour, baking powder and salt together. Beat eggs, sugar and vanilla until fluffy. Add chocolate and then flour mixture. Beat until blended. Stir in chips and nuts. Drop by tablespoon amounts onto lightly greased or parchment-lined cookie sheets. Bake 10-12 minutes at 350 degrees.

3 dozen

With three kinds of chocolate, these are the ultimate in chocolate cookies. This soft-centered cookie is dark, moist and fudgy.

zark Walnut ars

1/2	cup butter, room temperature
1	cup brown sugar, divided
1 1/4	cups flour
1/3	cup apricot preserves
2	eggs
1/4	teaspoon salt
1/2	teaspoon vanilla
2	tablespoons cocoa
1 1/2	cups finely chopped walnuts

Icing

6	ounces semi-sweet chocolate
2	tablespoons light corn syrup
2	teaspoons rum
2	teaspoons boiling water
1/2	cup chopped walnuts

Cream butter and 1/4 cup brown sugar. Gradually add flour and beat only until mixture holds together. Over the bottom of an unbuttered 9-inch square cake pan, spread the dough with your fingertips to make a smooth layer. Bake for 10 minutes at 375 degrees.

Stir the preserves to soften and set aside. Beat eggs at high speed for 2 or 3 minutes. Add salt and vanilla. On low speed, add 3/4 cup brown sugar and cocoa. Increase speed to high and beat for 2-3 minutes more. Fold in nuts.

Spread preserves over hot crust. Pour filling over preserves and tilt pan to level the filling. Bake at 375 degrees for 25 minutes. Let cool completely before icing.

To make Icing, melt chocolate in a double boiler. Add corn syrup, rum and boiling water; stir until smooth. Spread icing evenly over the top and sprinkle with nuts. With a wide spatula, press nuts down slightly into the icing. Let stand a few hours until icing is firm before cutting.

32 small bars

Chocolate, walnuts and apricots are teamed together in this wickedly rich triple-layered cookie. These bars and fresh fruit are a perfect duo tucked into your first spring picnic basket.

offee Cookie iamonds

1	cup butter, room temperature
1	cup brown sugar
1	egg yolk
1	cup flour
6	1.45-ounce chocolate bars (White chocolate may be used)
2/3	cup chopped pecans

Cream together butter, brown sugar and egg yolk. Add flour and stir until mixed. Spread mixture in a 10 x 15-inch jellyroll pan which has been lined with greased foil. Bake 20 minutes at 350 degrees or until brown. Immediately top with the candy bars. When melted, spread bars with a spatula and top with pecans. Cut on the diagonal into diamond shapes.

24 cookies

Chocolate Fudge Cookies

2	tablespoons sifted all-purpose flour
1/8	teaspoon baking powder
1	tablespoon butter
1	ounce unsweetened chocolate
3	ounces semi-sweet chocolate
1	teaspoon vanilla
1	tablespoon water
1	large egg
1/3	cup brown sugar
1	cup semi-sweet chocolate chips
1	cup chopped pecans
18-20	whole pecans

Sift together flour and baking powder. Set aside. Melt butter, unsweetened and semi-sweet chocolate in a double boiler. Cool. Stir in vanilla, water, egg and brown sugar. Add flour and baking powder to mixture and blend well. Stir in chocolate chips and chopped nuts. If batter is not firm enough, chill until it is ready.

Drop cookies 2 inches apart on a foil-lined cookie sheet. Press a pecan into each cookie. Bake at 350 degrees for 12 minutes or until springy.

Note: **One cup coarsely chopped white chocolate may be substituted for the chocolate chips.**

18-20 cookies

A crisp chocolate cookie, studded with pecans, that could become a family tradition.

Truffles

When the cocoa dust settles, enjoy!

8	ounces German's sweet chocolate, broken into pieces
2/3	cup heavy cream, scalded
1 1/2	tablespoons Grand Marnier or favorite liqueur
2	tablespoons unsalted butter, room temperature
1/4	cup unsweetened cocoa, mixed with a little cinnamon, or coarsely chopped toasted nuts

Melt chocolate in a double boiler, stirring until smooth. Add cream, whisking vigorously until mixture is smooth. Stir in liqueur. Refrigerate at least 4 hours or overnight.

Beat chilled chocolate mixture and butter until smooth. Form into 1-inch balls and roll in cocoa and cinnamon mixture or nuts. (Chill if mixture gets too soft.) They will look rough and uneven like real truffles. Cover and refrigerate. Truffles may be kept in refrigerator up to one month or frozen for several months.

Approximately 70 truffles

Nestle truffles in a little silver basket.

Chocolate Wafers

No one will guess the ingredients in these confections!

6	ounces semi-sweet chocolate
18-24	waffle-style potato chips

Melt chocolate in top of a double boiler over medium heat. Remove from heat; dip potato chips, one at a time, into chocolate, turning to coat completely. Place on a tray lined with waxed paper. Refrigerate to harden the chocolate, about 10 minutes.

Honey Caramels

1	cup heavy cream
1	heaping cup sugar
1/4	cup honey
1	teaspoon vanilla
2	tablespoons unsalted butter
1/4	teaspoon salt
1/3	cup almonds, pecans or walnuts, roasted and chopped (optional)

Bring cream to a boil in a heavy saucepan. Add sugar and honey. Stir until mixture comes to a boil again and boil gently until it reaches the soft ball stage (237-245 degrees on a candy thermometer). Remove from heat; add vanilla, butter and salt. Pour into a buttered 9-inch pan and cool 1 1/2 hours. Add nuts, if desired, after mixture has cooled, but before it has set. Cut candy into squares or bars with oiled knife and wrap each piece in waxed paper, twisting ends.

Placed in a well-sealed container, these caramels may be refrigerated for several weeks or frozen for several months.

Fill an old-fashioned jar with Honey Caramels for a Christmas gift and tie it with a "ribbon" of thin red licorice. Tuck fresh evergreen into the bow.

Chocolate Nutcrackers

An incredibly easy gift to make.

12	ounces semi-sweet chocolate, white chocolate or almond bark
2	cups mixed nuts

Melt chocolate or almond bark in double boiler or microwave. Add nuts, stir to coat and arrange by teaspoonfuls on waxed paper on cookie sheet. Refrigerate.

2 dozen

Chocolate Crème de Menthe Ice Cream

4	eggs
6	cups heavy cream
2	cups milk
1	cup sugar
¹/₂	cup light corn syrup
2	teaspoons vanilla
¹/₂	teaspoon salt
²/₃	cup green crème de menthe
4	ounces semi-sweet chocolate, shaved

Beat eggs until light. Stir in all other ingredients except chocolate. Freeze according to the manufacturer's instructions for your ice cream freezer. When firm, remove dasher and stir in chocolate. Allow to ripen several hours.

4 quarts

This silky ice cream with its flecks of chocolate is perfect crowned with fresh mint leaves and chocolate curls or a generous amount of hot fudge sauce.

Lime Sorbet

2	cups sugar
3³/₄	cups hot water
2¹/₄	cups lime juice (about 15 limes)
3	tablespoons lemon juice
1¹/₂	tablespoons dark rum
2	drops green food coloring
1	egg white, lightly beaten

Dissolve sugar in hot water. Add remaining ingredients. Freeze. Before serving, spoon into food processor and process just until smooth. Return to freezer until firm. (May also be made in an ice cream freezer.)

6 cups

The uncomplicated tang of fresh lime in this sorbet makes it a perfect refresher between courses. Serve in a hollowed lemon or lime, cut lengthwise and scalloped along the edge. Set on a bed of fresh lemon leaves.

Peach Ice Cream

1	cup sugar
4	eggs
1	tablespoon vanilla
2	cans condensed milk
1	cup heavy cream
3	cups peach purée
1	cup chopped peaches
1	quart whole milk

Combine sugar, eggs, vanilla, condensed milk and cream. Add purée, chopped fruit and milk. Freeze according to the manufacturer's instructions for your ice cream freezer. Allow to ripen several hours.

4¹/₂ quarts

A luscious ice cream that calls for summer's ripest peaches. It is irresistible when served with *Raspberry Sauce.*

ruit Ice

2	cups sugar
3	cups boiling water
3	lemons, peeled and seeded
3	oranges, peeled and seeded
1	banana, peeled

Mix sugar and water until sugar is dissolved. Cool. Purée lemons and oranges in a food processor. Pour the purée through a sieve and reserve the juice for another use, if desired. Mash banana in food processor. Combine banana, fruit purée and sugar water. Freeze in a 9 x 13-inch dish, stirring several times while freezing. Before serving, spoon into food processor and process just until smooth. Return to freezer until firm.

12 servings

Pale, icy scoops of this sherbet are a refreshing conclusion to a pasta dinner. Top with finely slivered orange zest or frozen orange slice halves, dipped into sugar.

aspberry herbet

1	10-ounce package frozen raspberries, thawed and mashed
1	scant cup sugar
1	cup sour cream
½	teaspoon vanilla

Mix all ingredients together and freeze.

4-6 servings

A simple but delightful sherbet. The beautiful color, creamy texture and fresh taste make it particularly enticing. A dash of whipped cream and a few of the darkest fresh berries are the final touches.

ummer Fruit in assis

1	10-ounce package frozen red raspberries, thawed
2	ounces crème de cassis
3	peaches, peeled and sliced
1	cup green grapes
1	cup bing cherries, pitted, or black grapes
1	banana, sliced
	Any colorful fresh seasonal fruit that mixes well with the above

Purée raspberries in food processor and add crème de cassis. Combine fruits. Add raspberry purée and mix gently. Chill.

A mosaic of summer fruits, bathed in a raspberry purée. Serve in pineapple shells or in shining crystal glasses, bowls or plates. Delicious with ice cream.

The Seasoned Cooks whose recipes
are presented here are
professionals in the field of the
culinary arts and have been
members of our League. Each has
submitted a sampling of her favorite
recipes.

SEASONED COOKS

Chestnut Dessert Pâté with Shortbread

Linda Davis

1   8³/₄-ounce can sweetened chestnut spread (creme de marron)

¹/₄   cup unsalted butter, room temperature

1   3-ounce package cream cheese, room temperature

2   tablespoons Cognac, Grand Marnier, Frangelico or Chambord, divided

¹/₄   cup pecans, hazelnuts or English walnuts, chopped and toasted

4   ounces semi-sweet chocolate

3   tablespoons heavy cream

Shortbread

³/₄   cup butter

4   tablespoons sugar

Few drops vanilla

1³/₄   cups all-purpose flour

2   tablespoons rice flour

Chocolate Shortbread

¹/₂   cup sugar

3   ounces semi-sweet chocolate, room temperature, cut in pieces

1   cup unsalted butter, cut in pieces

2   cups all-purpose flour

Place chestnut spread, butter, cream cheese and 1 tablespoon liqueur in the food processor; process until smooth. Stir in nuts.

Melt chocolate over low heat and stir in cream and 1 tablespoon liqueur. Beat with a wooden spoon until smooth.

Spoon one-third of the mixture into a 1³/₄-cup French canning jar or glass soufflé dish. Cover this layer with half of the chocolate (about ¹/₄ cup). Repeat layers. Top with chestnut layer. Cover and chill several hours.

Serve at room temperature with apples, pears, Shortbread or English semi-sweet biscuits.

To make Shortbread, cream butter. Add sugar and beat until well mixed. Add vanilla. Sift all-purpose flour with rice flour and stir into butter mixture, making a dry dough.

Press or roll onto a floured board to ¹/₄-inch thickness. Cut with cookie cutter or small drinking glass and place on greased cookie sheet. Prick surface with fork to keep dough from blistering and to keep the surface flat. Bake at 375 degrees for 8-10 minutes or until pale golden in color (not brown).

To make Chocolate Shortbread, process sugar and chocolate in a food processor, using steel blade, until well blended and very fine. Add butter and continue to process until mixture is creamy. Add flour all at once and process until batter is smooth and forms a ball.

Pat mixture into a 9 x 13-inch cake pan and bake at 300 degrees for 35-40 minutes or until center is firm. Cool and cut into squares but do not remove from pan until shortbread has cooled completely.

35-40 cookies

Butterfly Pinwheels

Linda Davis

1¹/₂	cups all-purpose flour
1	cup butter, chilled
¹/₂	cup sour cream
1	teaspoon grated lemon zest
10	tablespoons sugar

Place flour in bowl and cut in butter with pastry blender (or use food processor). Stir in sour cream and lemon zest until well blended. Wrap in waxed paper and refrigerate at least two hours. Cut into 4 pieces. Work with 1 piece at a time, keeping other pieces refrigerated until ready to use.

Sprinkle 2 tablespoons sugar on working surface. Coat all sides of dough with sugar. Roll dough out on sugar into a 5 x 12-inch rectangle. Roll up, jellyroll fashion, from each side toward center. (It will look like a scroll.) Wrap well in waxed paper and chill again. Repeat procedure with remaining dough.

Cut each roll into ¹/₂-inch slices and dip each side in sugar. Place on foil-lined baking sheet 2 inches apart. Bake at 375 degrees for 15 minutes. Turn over with a spatula and bake 5 minutes more. Remove to rack and cool.

40 cookies

Raspberry Chocolate Tea Cake

Linda Davis

6	ounces semi-sweet chocolate, melted and cooled
¹/₂	cup unsalted butter, room temperature
²/₃	cup sugar
3	eggs
¹/₂	cup sifted cake flour
	Raspberry jam
	Confectioners sugar

Whisk together chocolate and butter. Add sugar and then beat in eggs, one at a time. Blend in flour until just mixed. Pour into a buttered 9-inch cake pan that has been lined with waxed or parchment paper and buttered again. Bake at 350 degrees for 20-25 minutes. The cake will rise slightly, then sink in the center. Cool cake in the pan. This is a dense and moist cake.

Invert onto serving plate and remove parchment paper. Chill one hour and spread top with raspberry jam; sprinkle with confectioners sugar. Serve on a cut glass or china cake stand; surround cake with fresh flowers interspersed with fresh raspberries.

8-10 servings

Blueberry Cake with Lemon Filling

Linda Davis

3 eggs

1 1/2 cups sugar

1 1/2 cups sifted cake flour

2 teaspoons baking powder

1 1/2 cups heavy cream

2 teaspoons vanilla

1/4 teaspoon salt

1 cup ground walnuts

1 cup fresh or frozen blueberries

Lemon Filling

1/2 cup butter, room temperature

2 cups confectioners sugar

1 tablespoon lemon juice

1/2 teaspoon vanilla

2 egg yolks

Butter three 8-inch layer pans, line with waxed paper and butter again. In large bowl, beat eggs until thickened. Beat in sugar, 2 tablespoons at a time, until mixture is light and fluffy. Sift flour and baking powder together. Reserve. Beat cream, vanilla and salt in a chilled bowl to stiff peaks. Fold whipped cream into egg mixture, alternating with flour mixture and nuts.

Divide batter among pans. Sprinkle each layer with 1/3 cup blueberries. Bake at 350 degrees for 30 to 35 minutes. Cool 5 minutes on racks; remove from pans and cool.

Prepare Lemon Filling by beating butter, sugar, lemon juice and vanilla until light and fluffy. Beat in yolks, one at a time, until well combined.

Invert 1 cake layer on serving plate. Spread with half the lemon filling; add a second layer and spread with remaining filling. Top with last layer and sprinkle top of cake with confectioners sugar. Garnish with fresh blueberries and lemon leaves.

12 servings

White Chocolate Sauce

Linda Davis

1 cup heavy cream

9 ounces Tobler Narcisse (or a white chocolate coating)

1/2 cup Grand Marnier or kahlua

Scald cream and remove from heat. Cut white chocolate into bits and add to the cream. Process briefly in the food processor until smooth. Add liqueur.

Freezes well.

For a matchless dessert, form a puddle of White Chocolate Sauce on each dessert plate. Add a smaller puddle of *Raspberry Sauce* and a slice of *Chocolate Truffle Cake.* Garnish with fresh raspberries.

Jumbo Double Chocolate Chip Cookies

Jumbo cookies with a warm country look. Wrap individually in plastic wrap and gingham to tuck in your picnic basket.

Linda Davis

For each batch, use the following ingredients. You will need 2 batches.

1/2	cup flour
1/2	teaspoon baking soda
1/2	cup whole wheat flour
1/2	cup butter, room temperature
3/4	cup sugar
1	egg
1	teaspoon vanilla
6	ounces semi-sweet chocolate chips
1/2	cup chopped nuts (optional)
2	ounces unsweetened chocolate for second batch

Sift flour and baking soda. Add whole wheat flour. In separate bowl, beat butter, sugar, egg and vanilla until fluffy. Gradually stir in flour mixture to blend. Add chips and nuts.

Make second batch, using same recipe but adding 2 ounces melted unsweetened chocolate to the butter mixture.

To assemble: For each cookie, drop a rounded tablespoon of each dough side by side on a greased cookie sheet. Spread dough to form a large 2-toned cookie. Space 5-6 inches apart on cookie sheet.

Bake at 375 degrees for 12 minutes or until golden. Transfer to wire rack to cool.

2 dozen

Sautéed Cucumbers with Blue Cheese and Cream

Laura Bluhm

4	cucumbers, peeled
3	tablespoons butter
	Bunch fresh dill
2	ounces blue cheese
1/4	cup heavy cream
	Salt and pepper to taste

Cut cucumbers in half lengthwise and scoop out seeds. Slice each half once again lengthwise, then crosswise into 2-inch sticks. Turn edges with a knife so they are rounded. ("Turning" a vegetable is a French technique used to make vegetables look like young, spring vegetables.)

Boil cucumbers in salted water about 4 minutes or until almost tender; drain. (Cucumbers can be boiled 6 hours ahead, covered and refrigerated.) In a saucepan, melt butter and add dill, blue cheese, cream, salt and pepper. Stir over medium heat until bubbly and well mixed. Add cucumbers, tossing gently until heated through. Do not overcook or cucumbers will be bitter.

4-6 servings

Country Terrine

Laura Bluhm

¹/₂	pound sliced bacon
1	onion, chopped
1	tablespoon butter
¹/₂	cup heavy cream
¹/₂	pound chicken livers
1	pound ground pork
¹/₂	pound ground veal
2	cloves garlic, crushed
¹/₄	teaspoon allspice
	Pinch of ground cloves
	Pinch of nutmeg
2	eggs, beaten
2	tablespoons brandy
	Salt and pepper
¹/₂	cup pistachios (optional)
¹/₂	pound ham, cut in strips
1	bay leaf
1	branch thyme
¹/₃	cup flour, mixed with 2-3 tablespoons water to form a paste

Use a 2-quart terrine or casserole with a tight-fitting lid. Line with bacon so that it hangs over the edges.

Sauté onion in butter until soft. In a saucepan, bring cream to a boil and add chicken livers; poach for 10-15 seconds and then remove from heat. Strain. Reserve, separately, both the cream and livers.

In a large bowl, mix sautéed onion, pork, veal, garlic, allspice, cloves, nutmeg, eggs, reserved cream, brandy and plenty of salt and pepper. Mixture should taste quite spicy, since the terrine is served cold and flavors are therefore diminished. Add pistachios, if desired.

Spread one-third of the meat mixture in the bacon-lined terrine and press down with wet fingers. Add a layer of ham strips and reserved chicken livers. Top with remaining meat mixture. Place bay leaf and thyme on top and bring bacon up and over the top. Cover with the lid and seal the gap between the mold and the lid with prepared paste.

Set terrine in a water bath and bake at 350 degrees for 1¹/₂ hours. Regulate heat to keep water in pan simmering. Cool terrine and then refrigerate. Terrine is best if made 3 days before serving to allow flavors to mellow. It can also be frozen for 3 months.

To serve, unmold terrine and remove as much of the bacon as possible. Cut into slices and serve with cornichons and French bread.

8-10 servings

Sole with Scallop Mousse and Buerre Blanc Sauce

Laura Bluhm

1/2	pound fresh scallops
1	tablespoon Cognac
1	tablespoon sweet port
	Salt and pepper to taste
1	egg
1/2	cup sour cream
1/4	cup heavy cream or 3/4 cup *Crème Fraîche*
8	fresh sole fillets
	Julienne of leeks and carrots
1	bottle clam broth
1/2	cup white wine

Buerre Blanc Sauce

2	shallots, minced
1/4	cup white wine
1/2	cup cold butter, cut into pieces

In a food processor, process scallops with Cognac, port, salt and pepper until smooth. With machine running, add egg and process until mixture resembles mayonnaise. Transfer to another bowl. Mix sour cream and cream together and, with a spatula, fold into the scallop mixture. Cover and refrigerate until ready to assemble.

Butter a baking dish and arrange 4 of the sole fillets on the bottom. Spread each fillet with scallop mousse, using it all if possible. Top with another fillet, trying to match sizes. Garnish with leeks and carrots and salt lightly.

Bring clam broth and wine to a boil and pour over fish. Cover with parchment paper and bake for 15-20 minutes at 400 degrees. Remove from oven and serve immediately with Buerre Blanc Sauce.

To make Buerre Blanc Sauce, combine shallots and white wine in a saucepan and cook until liquid is reduced to about 2 tablespoons. Over medium heat, whisk in one piece of butter at a time, stirring until melted. Serve immediately.

4 servings

Iced Fruit Soufflé

Laura Bluhm

1	pint strawberries (or any berry of your choice)
3/4	cup confectioners sugar, divided
1 1/2	cups heavy cream, divided
1/2	cup sugar
1/2	cup water
2	egg whites, beaten until stiff
	Almonds, *Candied Violets* or fresh berries for garnish

Wash and stem berries; drain well. In a blender or food processor, purée strawberries with 1/2 cup confectioners sugar. Refrigerate. Whip 1 cup cream and refrigerate.

In a heavy saucepan, dissolve sugar in water and bring to a boil. Boil till the soft ball stage (235 degrees). Remove from heat. Gradually pour hot sugar mixture into beaten egg whites, beating constantly. Continue beating until mixture is completely stiff and cool. Fold in berry purée and whipped cream.

Spoon mixture into 4 glasses or ramekins; smooth the top. Freeze until firm, at least 2 hours. (Can freeze, tightly covered, for 2 weeks.)

Whip 1/2 cup cream with 1/4 cup confectioners sugar. Fill a pastry bag with whipped cream and, using a medium star tip, pipe each soufflé with a rosette. Garnish with an almond, *Candied Violet* or whole small berry. (Let soufflés soften 1-2 hours in the refrigerator if they have been frozen more than 24 hours.)

4 servings

Grilled Mako (Shark)

Judith Cooke

1/4	cup sweet vermouth
2	tablespoons soy sauce
1	teaspoon Worcestershire sauce
2	cloves garlic, minced
	Freshly ground black pepper
4	fresh shark steaks, 1 inch thick (5-6 ounces each)

Combine vermouth, soy sauce, Worcestershire, garlic and pepper. Marinate the steaks 4-6 hours. Grill over hot coals very briefly, 5-7 minutes, basting with the marinade. Do not overcook!

4 servings

Serve with a braised rice with toasted almonds and steamed avocado. (To steam avocado, peel and slice vertically; cut into large chunks. Steam 2-3 minutes in bamboo steamer. Lightly salt and top with lemon juice.)

Boned Trout Stuffed with Pine Nuts, Currants and Rice

Judith Cooke

4	boned trout
1½	cups chopped onion
4	tablespoons best-quality olive oil
½	cup uncooked rice
2¼	cups chicken broth, divided
2	ounces pine nuts
2	tablespoons oil
⅓	cup black currants
	Juice of 2 lemons
	Salt and white pepper
	Avgolemono Sauce
2	egg yolks
2	tablespoons lemon juice
½	cup chicken broth

Sauté onion about 5 minutes in oil. Add the rice and cook over high heat until opaque, about 2-3 minutes. Add 1¼ cups chicken broth, cover and cook over low heat for 15 minutes or until liquid is absorbed. Brown pine nuts in oil. Mix with the currants. Add nuts and currants to the rice mixture. Season with lemon juice, salt and pepper.

Stuff each trout with ⅓-½ cup of rice mixture. Wrap each stuffed trout on a length of cheesecloth and lay in a buttered baking dish. Add ¾-1 cup chicken broth, moistening the cheesecloth. Bake at 450 degrees, 10 minutes per inch of thickness. When done, lift fish onto plate and unwrap. Serve with Avgolemono Sauce.

4 servings

To make Avgolemono Sauce, whisk egg yolks until thick in a pan. Beat in lemon juice. Set over a pan of hot water. Whisk; then whisk in chicken broth until lightly thickened.

Baked Baby Sea Bass with Champagne Sauce

Judith Cooke

Small sea bass are generally available only in the spring. Other whole fish can be substituted. Avoid strong fish such as salmon or mackerel.

	Baby sea bass, 2-3 pounds, scales removed
10	6-inch long fennel branches
2	large bay leaves
1	large onion, thinly sliced
1	cup champagne
2	tablespoons butter
	Cooking liquid from bass
6	tablespoons cold butter

Butter a baking dish large enough to hold the whole fish and place fish in it. Tuck 5 branches of fennel in cavity of the fish and five branches underneath. Place bay leaves and onion slices over the fish. (Can be prepared in advance to this point.) Pour champagne to a depth of ¼ inch. Cover fish loosely with parchment. Bake at 400 degrees, 10 minutes per inch (fish measured at the thickest point) plus 5 minutes.

Ten minutes before fish is done, pour cooking juices into a saucepan. Bring juices to a boil over high heat and reduce liquid by half to two-thirds. Cut butter into pieces and whisk into hot liquid, bit by bit, as for hollandaise. Serve over fish. Sauce can be held for 15-20 minutes off the heat.

El Cid Sangria

Pam Gradinger

For each drink:

1	ounce frozen concentrated limeade
1	ounce vodka
	Crushed ice
	Red wine

Combine limeade, vodka and ice in a tall, slender glass. Rest a spoon against the inside edge of the glass and carefully pour wine over the spoon into the glass until glass is filled. You should have two distinct layers, one green and one red. Serve with a straw.

Jicama, Orange and Pecan Salad with Cumin Dressing

Pam Gradinger

	Butter lettuce
	Orange slices
	Red onion rings
	Sautéed pecans
	Slivered jicama
	Juice of 1/2 fresh lime (squeezed over jicama)

Cumin Dressing

1 1/2	cups vegetable oil
1/2	cup vinegar
1	teaspoon salt
	Cracked pepper
1/4	teaspoon cumin

Make salad dressing by combining ingredients and mixing well. Toss with salad ingredients.

Black Bean Soup

Pam Gradinger

1	pound black beans, soaked in water for 30 minutes
1/4	cup chopped salt pork or fatty ham
1	onion, chopped
1	clove garlic, minced
5	cups chicken broth
	Salt and pepper to taste
	Sour cream
	Corn tortilla strips

Drain beans. Cover again with water and cook 1-2 hours or until tender. Purée in food processor.

Cook salt pork, onion and garlic together. Drain fat. Stir in beans and add chicken broth. Season with salt and pepper. Simmer.

Serve with a dollop of sour cream and corn tortillas, cut into thin strips with scissors and sautéed briefly in butter.

8 servings

Duck Salad with Avocados and Oranges

Julie Kirk

2	ducks, approximately 4¹/₂ pounds each, roasted
	Freshly ground pepper
2	large avocados, peeled, halved and cut into lengthwise slices
	Juice of 1¹/₂ lemons
4	navel oranges, peeled, cut horizontally into ¹/₄-inch slices
2	scallions, cut in diagonal rings

Salad Dressing

¹/₂	cup fresh orange juice
¹/₂	cup dry sherry
	Juice of ¹/₂ lemon
¹/₂	teaspoon grated orange zest
¹/₄	teaspoon grated lemon zest
	Pinch of salt
1	large clove garlic
1	egg yolk
¹/₂	cup best-quality olive oil
¹/₂	cup half and half

Remove skin and cut meat from bones. Sliver meat into pieces about 2 inches long and ³/₄ inch wide. Transfer duck meat to a large bowl and sprinkle with freshly ground black pepper.

Prepare Salad Dressing by combining orange juice, sherry, lemon juice, orange zest, lemon zest and salt in a small saucepan. Bring mixture to a boil and reduce to 3 tablespoons. Cool to lukewarm.

In a food processor, combine garlic, cooled citrus mixture and egg yolk; pulse until well combined. With machine running, add olive oil in a slow, steady stream. Dressing will thicken to a light mayonnaise. Add cream and pulse just to combine.

To serve, place avocado slices in lemon juice and toss lightly to coat. (Citrus juice retards discoloration.)

Arrange avocado slices, pinwheel fashion with tapered ends toward the center, around outer edge of a round platter. Place orange slices between each avocado slice.

Pour half the dressing over the duck and toss lightly. Spoon duck meat into center of the platter and sprinkle with sliced scallions and a good sprinkling of fresh cracked pepper. Accompany salad with remaining dressing.

6 servings

Duck and dressing may be prepared 24 hours in advance.

Grilled Lamb Noisettes and Sauce

Libby Pence

8 7-ounce lamb noisettes (boneless sirloin from the top side)

Worcestershire sauce

Accent

Garlic powder

Sauce

1 tablespoon Dijon mustard

1 tablespoon prepared mustard

2 tablespoons brown sugar

1 clove garlic, crushed

1 teaspoon soy sauce

2 tablespoons lemon juice

2 tablespoons oil

1 tablespoon Worcestershire sauce

1/2 teaspoon salt

Cracked pepper

Trim excess fat from noisettes and reserve fat. Shape lamb by inserting short (3-4 inches) metal or wooden skewers through the meat. Sprinkle both sides with Worcestershire, Accent and garlic powder; refrigerate.

Prepare Sauce by combining ingredients. Refrigerate. May be made 5-6 days before using.

Two or 3 hours before serving, brush lamb with sauce. In a heavy skillet, render the fat from the reserved trimmings and add 1-2 tablespoons fat to the remaining sauce.

When ready to grill lamb, heat skillet until hot, but not smoking. Sauté noisettes about 4 minutes on one side and 3 minutes on the other (for very pink lamb). Remove from skillet to warm plates, salt lightly and pour a little of the remaining warm sauce over each noisette. Garnish with watercress or fresh mint and serve.

Noisettes are delicious grilled over charcoal. Depending on distance from the grill and heat of the fire, it usually takes more time; try 7 minutes on one side and 4 on the other.

8 servings

Butter Lettuce with Balsamic Vinaigrette

Libby Pence

Butter lettuce

Balsamic Vinaigrette

1/4 cup balsamic vinegar

1 teaspoon fresh lemon juice

3/4 cup oil (combine virgin olive oil, salad oil, walnut oil, French peanut oil — any combination)

1/2 teaspoon Dijon mustard

Salt and pepper to taste

Combine vinaigrette ingredients and refrigerate. Bring to room temperature before tossing with butter lettuce. Fresh chives, parsley or garlic may be added.

Dressing may be made several days in advance and refrigerated.

1 cup

Note: Balsamic vinegar can be found in specialty food stores.

Sautéed Green Beans and Jicama

by Pence

1½	pounds fresh green beans
⅓	cup chopped onion
½	cup butter
	Worcestershire sauce, soy sauce, Knorr's seasoning
	Salt and pepper to taste
1 cup slivered jicama

Steam or blanch beans and refresh in cold water. Drain and refrigerate. When ready to serve, sauté onion in butter 2-3 minutes. Add seasonings and beans. Sauté until hot, but do not overcook. Correct seasonings. Toss with the jicama and serve.

The beans should be bright green in color and crisp.

8 servings

Orange-Lemon Tart

by Pence

Pastry

1½	cups all-purpose flour
¼	cup chilled butter
¼	cup vegetable shortening or lard
½	teaspoon salt
¼	cup cold water (or lemon or orange juice combined with water)

Filling

⅓	cup fresh lemon juice
⅓	cup fresh orange juice
	Grated zest of 4 lemons and 1 orange
½	cup sugar
6	tablespoons butter
	Dash of salt
5	large eggs, beaten
¼	teaspoon vanilla

Blend flour, butter, shortening and salt together with a pastry cutter until mixture is crumbly. Add cold liquid and mix quickly with a fork. Form into a ball and chill 1-2 hours. Roll out on a lightly floured board and press into a 10-11-inch tart pan. Trim off excess pastry and pinch edges. Prick bottom with a fork. Line bottom with waxed paper or parchment paper and cover with dried beans to prevent shrinkage. Bake on the bottom shelf of a 425-degree oven for 10 minutes. Remove from the oven. Discard beans and paper.

Prepare Filling by combining lemon juice, orange juice, grated zest, sugar, butter and salt in a double boiler. Heat until warm. Add eggs and cook until custard coats a spoon. Add vanilla and remove from the heat. Pour into tart shell. Bake at 350 degrees for about 30 minutes or until filling is set.

When tart has cooled, sprinkle with sugar and place under broiler until sugar carmelizes. Watch very carefully so it does not burn.

Serve room temperature or warm. Decorate with lemon and orange slices, if desired. Serve on a plate with a green ivy leaf and a dollop of sweetened whipped cream.

8-10 servings

Cowboy Coffee Cake

Mary Don Beachy
Kristie Wolferman

. . . whose recipes were chosen with young chefs in mind.

2¹/₂	cups flour
2	cups brown sugar
¹/₂	teaspoon salt
2	teaspoons baking powder
1	teaspoon cinnamon
¹/₂	teaspoon nutmeg
²/₃	cup shortening
¹/₂	teaspoon baking soda
1	cup buttermilk or sour milk
2	eggs, well beaten
¹/₂	cup finely chopped nuts (optional)

In mixing bowl, combine flour, sugar, salt, baking powder, cinnamon and nutmeg. Cut in shortening with pastry blender until mixture resembles fine crumbs. Set ¹/₂ cup mixture aside for topping. Note: Mixture may be stored in a glass jar. When ready to use, remove ¹/₂ cup crumbs for topping and proceed with recipe.

Dissolve baking soda in buttermilk. Add buttermilk and eggs to flour mixture and blend well. Pour batter into two greased 8 or 9-inch round cake pans. Sprinkle with reserved crumbs. If desired, sprinkle with nuts. Bake in preheated 350-degree oven for 15-20 minutes.

Navajo Fried Bread

Mary Don Beachy
Kristie Wolferman

The original Navajo fried bread was made with cornmeal, but during the 1800's it was made with white flour. The bread serves as a "plate" to hold lettuce, peppers, tomatoes and Monterey Jack cheese, or it can be eaten with honey as a sweet bread.

2	cups all-purpose flour
2	teaspoons baking powder
2	teaspoons coarse salt
1	tablespoon shortening
³/₄	cup lukewarm water
1	cup shortening for frying

In mixing bowl, combine flour, baking powder and salt. Cut in shortening with a pastry blender (or with the tips of your fingers) until mixture resembles cornmeal. Slowly add water, stirring with a fork, using just enough water to hold dough together. Knead dough gently for about 3 minutes.

Cover dough with a towel and let rest 10-15 minutes. Divide dough into 6 round balls and let rest. Pour fat into a skillet until it is ¹/₄-¹/₂ inch deep and heat to 380 degrees. Roll each ball of dough on a floured surface into a 6 or 7-inch round. Make a 3-inch cut with a sharp knife in the center of the circle, making a crease.

Fry each round in fat for about one minute per side or until golden brown. Transfer bread to paper towels to drain, using a slotted spatula. Fry next round of bread. Make sure fat does not smoke but stays hot enough to fry the bread. Add shortening as needed.

Casserole Swedish Rye

Mary Don Beachy
Christie Wolferman

3¹/₂-4	cups all-purpose flour
1¹/₂	cups rye flour
¹/₃	cup firmly packed dark brown sugar
2	teaspoons salt
1	teaspoon caraway seeds
2	packages dry yeast
1	cup milk
1	cup water
2	tablespoons butter

Combine flours and set aside. In a large bowl, thoroughly mix 1¹/₂ cups flour mixture, sugar, salt, caraway seeds and undissolved yeast.

Combine milk, water and butter in saucepan. Heat over low heat until liquids are very warm (120-130 degrees F.). Butter does not need to melt.

Gradually add liquid mixture to flour-sugar mixture and beat 2 minutes on medium speed, scraping bowl occasionally. Add ³/₄ cup reserved flour mixture. Beat at high speed for 2 minutes, scraping bowl occasionally. Stir in enough additional flour mixture to make a stiff dough. (If necessary, use additional white flour to obtain desired consistency.) Cover; let rise in warm place, free from draft, until doubled in bulk, about 40 minutes. Stir down dough. Cover; let rise again until doubled in bulk, about 20 minutes. Stir down; turn into a well-greased 1¹/₂-quart casserole.

Bake at 400 degrees about 40 minutes or until done. Remove from casserole and cool on wire rack.

1 loaf

Irish Soda Bread

Mary Don Beachy
Christie Wolferman

3	cups all-purpose flour
¹/₃	cup sugar
1	tablespoon baking powder
1	teaspoon salt
1	teaspoon baking soda
1	egg
2	cups buttermilk
¹/₄	cup butter, melted

Combine flour, sugar, baking powder, salt and soda. Mix egg and buttermilk together; add to flour mixture and stir until batter is moistened. Stir in butter. Pour into a greased 9 x 5 x 3-inch loaf pan. Bake at 325 degrees for 65-75 minutes. Do not underbake. Cool on rack. Wrap and store 8 hours before slicing.

1 loaf

Note: If buttermilk is not available, use 2 teaspoons vinegar to enough milk to fill a 2-cup measure.

Testing Chairmen:

Mary Jane Young Barnes   Brunch

Polly Palmer Brunkhardt   Meat

Candy Wells Clevenger   Desserts

Jennifer Hanna Coen   Breads

Courtney Risner Earnest   Soups

Becky Keyte Johnson   Desserts

Mary Lynn Hendricks Lawler   Salads

Linda Schaerrer Owen   Poultry & Game

Jo Stewart Riley   Pasta & Pizza

JoAnn Hughes Sullivan   Foods for Giving

Mary Jo Jensen Truog   Appetizers

Susan Rosse Truog   Vegetables

Gail Gotzian Weinberg   Fish & Seafood

Editorial:

Mary Locke Cashman

Marilyn Rockwell Driscoll

Barbara Frasher Harmon

Nancy Egy Jacobs

Julie Turtle Kirk

Anne Owen Leifer

Barbara Lundell Moriarty

Polly Blackburn Wolbach

Presentation Committee:

Courtney Risner Earnest

Julie Turtle Kirk

Merikay Boucher Lott

Kathleen Mueller Moore

JoAnn Hughes Sullivan

Marilyn Sisk Wollard

Design Committee:

Jane Miller Deaver

Dianne Turner Deckert

Teri Vecchione Fulton

Merikay Boucher Lott

Suzann Smith McElvain

Cathy Brown Roelke

Joan Schulzke Shields

Mina Olander Steen

JoAnn Hughes Sullivan

Marketing Advisors:

Nancy Egy Jacobs

Carolyn Kunz Patterson

Nancy Hodgson Ruzicka

Sales Chairman:

Caroline Hampton McKnight

The Junior League of Kansas City,
Missouri, would like to thank those
whose diligence and expertise have
made this book possible:

The Testing Committee

whose thoroughness and commitment of
time, money and talents have assured the
quality of this book:

Kathryn Hanson Adams
Jan McFarland Allen
Jenny Weber Arms
Donna Perkins Baltis
Mary Jane Young Barnes
Ada Lewi Beal
Janet Cerny Beall
Edith Sargent Beck
Amy Bumgarner Beck
Sharon Rogers Bell
Judy Kay Myers Bellemere
Vicky Reick Berg
Jan Schoeneman Bergeson
Daphne Donnell Bitters
Carol Growdon Bliss
Jim Snook Bowen
Jane Virden Brent
Connie Spelts Brouillette
Polly Palmer Brunkhardt
Sally Gorton Buffum
Cynthia Fuller Burcham
Betty Reaves Burner
Martha Hall Callaway
Doreen Collins Carbaugh
Nancy Bodwell Carnes
May Conrad Carpenter
Susan Virden Carpenter
Eugenia Francis Cartmell
Mary Locke McCraw Cashman
Julie Boutross Clarkson
Candy Wells Clevenger
Jan Whittier Closser
Jennifer Hanna Coen
Martha Freeman Collet
Jane Huwaldt Cook
Jill Johnson Coughlin
Mary Doolittle Crowther
Helen Piller Davis
Joanne Turner Deckert
Tommye Bryan Dodd
    Pauline Fox Dolan
Courtney Risner Earnest
Mary Metzler Eberle
Jill Hasburgh Embry
Julie Campbell Esrey
Susan Schoenfeld Fate
Susan Zack Fillmore
Sharon Powell Frazier
Margaret Ann Kurt Freeman
Peggy Massman Freeman
Kathryn Garrett Gates
Barbara Jackson Gattermeir
Virginia Melzarek Gibbons
Betty Hauck Goolsbee
Josephine Pickard Gordon
Nancy Risk Green
Helen Underwood Groner
Marlene Barrett Hall

Jean Challinor Hall
Margaret Weatherly Hall
Stephanie Brown Harper
Jean Elmburg Helmers
D'Ann Reed Hickok
Paget Gates Higgins
Linda Moore Hoffman
Dianne Selders Hogerty
Kathleen Strayer Honan
Lora B. Buckingham Hopkins
Mary Reiff Hunkeler
Trula Guiou Hunt
Cathy Turner Hunter
Martha Nelson Immenschuh
Paula Jennings Johnson
Rebecca Keyte Johnson
Lynnsay Williams Jones
Giff Brooks Kassebaum
Janet Kelley
Jean Titus Kiene
Susan Hunter Kircher
Diana Shand Kline
Connie Smith Koester
Carolyn Steele Kroh
Mary Leigh Reardon Krull
Lois Dubach Lacy
Audrey Hansen Langworthy
Mary Lynn Hendricks Lawler
Vicky Brigham Leonard
Georgia Quatman Lynch
Joanna Mitchell MacLaughlin
Marilyn Poehler McConnell
Virginia B. McCoy
Judy Gray McEachen
Suzann Smith McElvain
Jaye Eddie McGuire
Marli Yeo McInnes
Carole Popham McKnight
Mary Helliker McPherson
Nancy Webster Menihan
Betty Branson Merritt
Barbara Buesking Milledge
Patricia Murphy Miller
Jo Meyer Missildine
Karen Huhn Monsees
Kathleen Mueller Moore
Sue Ann Roberts Northcraft
Daly Jordan O'Brien
Jean Jefferson Oglethorpe
Jane Fulton Olsen
Sharon Wood Orr
Linda Schaerrer Owen
Elisabeth Kiene Pace
Carolyn Kunz Patterson
Marie Habbegger Pawsat
Elizabeth Thwaite Pendleton
Donna Pascoe Pohl
Ann Van Dyk Poindexter
Christine Barrows Preston
Cathy Dunn Remley
Jo Stewart Riley

Margaret Joe Helmers Sams
Elizabeth Jones Schellhorn
Millicent Cross Scrivan
Martha Jo Guenin Seifert
Patricia Piller Shelton
Genie Durden Shoffey
Melissa Newby Shores
Mary Judith Lane Sowden
Susan Small Spaulding
Sharon Petersen Stratemeier
Jo Ann Hughes Sullivan
Mary Jo Jensen Truog
Susan Rosse Truog
Susanne Sharpe Tyler
Susan Sayles Waldeck
Judi Golden Walker
Elaine Terrell Wassermann
Patricia Wilbanks Watters
Margie Farmer Weber
Gail Gotzian Weinberg
Anne Turner Wells
Leslie Spurck Whitaker
Jill Anderson Winn
Polly Blackburn Wolbach
Marilyn Fish Wollard
Gay Bagby Woosley
Helen Foster Wooster
Eulalie Bartlett Zimmer

Other Junior League Members

who supported the project by contributing recipes and valuable assistance:

Patricia Thomas Allain
Rebecca Sayles Baker
Cynthia Drips Ballard
Lizbeth Henson Barelli
Brenda Anne Barton
Joan Westmen Battey
Linda Flynn Becker
Lucy Kennard Bell
DeDe Johnson Benham
Janice Yukon Benjamin
Sara Dickerson Bernard
Robin Rivers Berner
June Schlanker Berry
Susan Ellis Berry
Susan Lightfoot Biggs
Kay Bisagno Bleakley
Doris Rucks Bliss
Laura White Bluhm
Prudence Hearst Brito
Jane Egender Bruening
Suzanne Agnew Buffum
Jill Stewart Bunting
Christine Irwin Bush
Barbara Butler
Alice MacCorkle Carrott
Patricia Broeg Clouser
Catherine Devereux Corey
Karen Winfrey Craft
Jane Reusser Davis
Linda Zey Davis
Louise Swigart Davis
Nancy Lindbloom Davis
Jill Deramus Dean
Pamela Miller Deramus
Suzanne Moore Dierks
Mary Kelley Dobbins
Ann Thornberry Dodderidge
Marilyn Rockwell Driscoll
Linda Waters Dro
Regi Taylor Early
Margaret Lynn Fitzgerald
Susan Henson Flury
Melissa A. Biggs Folger
Candace Lee Fowler
Alice Young Frost
Teri Vecchione Fulton
Kathy Gannon
Diane Dougall Gee
Christina Tanner German
DeSaix Evans Gernes
Charlotte Johnson Gibson
Lynne Dodson Gilbert
Janie Hedrick Grant
Virginia Ward Graves
Jennifer Hurst Gunter
Janice Bellemere Hamill
Mary Ann Wiles Hamilton
Diana Rhines Hanslip
Kathleen Hage Hardin
Elizabeth Westbrooke Haw

Nancy Nordstrom Heiser
Jeannette Heller
Virginia Houston Helmstetter
Julie Wilks Hendricks
Connie Frantz Hesler
Karen Hubbard Hibbard
Elizabeth Bryant Hobart
Judith Kay Hoffman
Sharon Katz Hoffman
Nancy Hogan
Ann Rome Hogueland
Beverly Burrus Holsman
Nancy Ewing Houston
Dee Halsey Hughes
Vera Radford Hughes
Judy Henry Hunt
Kathleen Israel
Nancy Egy Jacobs
Diane Beaver Johnson
Joy Laws Jones
Sandy Nye Jones
Susan Weiss Kasle
Barbara Reichmann Kemp
Susan White Kingsbury
Joann Hurwitt Kinney
Julie Turtle Kirk
Judi Spicer Knight
Beth Buchanan Koenig
Sara McGuire Kombrink
Caroline Bliss Langknecht
Helen Jones Lea
Cynthia O'Brien Leffel
Sharon Grant LeMoine
Lisa Leonard
Peggy Leslie
Susan Marie Linden
Ann Foster Lombardi
Barbro Andersson Lucas
Virginia Atkins Lynd
Daisy Park MacDonald
Jane MacGee
Linda Warwick Manco
LaDonna Anderson Marietti
Joan Knight Marsh
Jody Hanes Maughan
Suzanne Morgan Maughan
Gayle Maurin
Janice Harvey McCollum
Cherie McCracken
Laura Michele Berger McDermand
Pat McClure McDonald
Marilyn Muehlbach McGilley
Caroline Hampton McKnight
Louise Hohman McNeive
Betsy Pitman Merriman
Nancy Senter Meyerdirk
Corliss Chandler Miller
Holly Boxer Miller
Mary Mitchell Minturn
Linda Grimshaw Moore
Cathy Smith Moseley
Ann Richmond Musser

Becky Bradley Newcomer
Margaret Waters Newlin
Martha Dodge Nichols
Ruth Edwards Nicholson
Linda Fries Nixon
Rebecca Culpepper O'Connor
Jody Gegan Olson
Mary Beck Palmer
Patricia Rattle Parsons
Linda Katz Patterson
Elizabeth (Libby) Pence
Marilyn McDonald Peterson
Marian Willits Petrie
Julie Evans Pfeiffer
Nancy Alexander Pinnell
Sally Hardy Pollock
Cynthia Ullom Porter
Margi Dasta Posten
Andrea Gray Presson
Carol Haworth Price
Martha Gaston Priest
Ann Townley Reaves
Ann Buck Renne
Patricia Uhlmann Rich
Susan Cregan Richardson
Cathy Brown Roelke
Helen McCulloch Rogers
Susan Cowden Rowan
Nancy Hodgson Ruzicka
Nancy McKinley Sandoval
Katherine Prescott Scarritt
Melinda Mueller Scovell
Joan Schulzke Shields
Carolyn Schwartz Steinwart
Norma Umlauf Stevens
Judy Peterson Stokes
Mary Cabot Lull Sweeney
Jeanne Tinsley Tapp
Emma Louise McLaughlin Theis
Sue Haskins Tholen
Sharon Hellinger Townsend
Sylvia Kelso Tucker
Jill Jenkins Turner
Sydney Ann Whitehead Uthoff
Andrea Ash Varney
Kimberly Wakeford
Madaline Reeder Walter
Eleanor Radford Walters
Alison Wiedeman Ward
Olive Hickman Warwick
Margaret Reardon Whitaker
Julie Peters White
Margaret Ann Welch Whittier
Jane Kellogg Willey
Katherine Kennedy Williams
Leslie Hand Williams
Nancy Tobin Williams
Ellen Lopinsky Wolf
Melanie Woodson
Patricia Hixson Wright
Barbara Gross Zitron

Junior League Friends

who shared recipes and advice:

Dee Dee Adams
Dorothy Arneson
Tom Barelli
Mary Don Beachy
Virginia Benner
Donna Blackwood
Richard P. Bruening
Paul R. Bruening
Bill Cardwell
Judith Drake Cooke
Robin Copas
Marti Crockett
Craig Davis
Shirley Doering
Colleen Douglas
Barb Dyas
John Elliott
Louise Enyart
Linda Evans
James L. Fries
Jane Fowler
Irene Glennon
Mica Gilson
Pam Grudinger
Mary Gubser
Annemarie Hunter
Jennie's Restaurant
Marsha Katz
Robert S. Kelley
Myrtle Kemp
William Kircher
Al Lea
Mary Jane Liepold
Amy McInturff
John McMeel
Marianne Odom
John Oliver
Pam Orton
The Prospect of Westport
John Ralston
Don Shanks
Art Siemering
Frances Sifers
Karen Sloan
Jane Stewart
John Swanay
Richard Twyman
Bonnie Winston
Kristie Wolferman
Millie Wyckoff
Barbara Zagnoni

The Junior League of Kansas City, Missouri wishes to express its appreciation to all the local cooking school instructors whose classes helped to inspire many of the recipes found in this collection.

Photo Credits

Andre's
Mrs. William Boose
Carthage Marble Corporation
Cummings Corner Antiques
The Fiddly Fig
Function Junction
James F. Göhl
Jennie's Restaurant
Halls
Mrs. Paul Henson
Just Herbs
Constance Leiter, Inc.
Mrs. George McClelland
Mrs. Lawrence Starr
Tiffany & Company
Robert D. Trapp

Production Credits

Walsworth Press, Inc.
 Lopez Graphics

Gazlay Graphics